The politics of feeling in Brexit Britain

Manchester University Press

The politics of feeling in Brexit Britain

Stories from the Mass Observation Project

Jonathan Moss, Emily Robinson
and Jake Watts

Manchester University Press

Copyright © Jonathan Moss, Emily Robinson and Jake Watts 2024

The right of Jonathan Moss, Emily Robinson and Jake Watts to be identified as the authors of this work has been asserted in accordance with the Copyright, Designs and Patents Act 1988.

Excerpts reproduced with permission of Curtis Brown, London on behalf of the Trustees of the Mass Observation Archive © The Trustees of the Mass Observation Archive.

Published by Manchester University Press
Oxford Road, Manchester M13 9PL
www.manchesteruniversitypress.co.uk

British Library Cataloguing-in-Publication Data
A catalogue record for this book is available from the British Library

ISBN 978 1 5261 5250 3 hardback
ISBN 978 1 5261 5251 0 paperback

First published 2024

The publisher has no responsibility for the persistence or accuracy of URLs for any external or third-party internet websites referred to in this book, and does not guarantee that any content on such websites is, or will remain, accurate or appropriate.

Typeset
by Cheshire Typesetting Ltd, Cuddington, Cheshire

For Wilbur and Sadie

Contents

Acknowledgements	viii
Introduction: using an 'archive of feeling' to understand Brexit Britain	1
Part I Beyond 'heads vs hearts': personal feelings in political life	**33**
1 Voting decisions	37
2 Judgements and stereotypes	67
Part II Stories of excessive emotions: political feelings in personal life	**105**
3 Moods	109
4 Relationships	138
Conclusion	175
Notes	189
Bibliography	229
Index	247

Acknowledgements

This book could not have been written without the Mass Observation Project. We would like to thank archivists Kirsty Pattrick and Jessica Scantlebury for their help, guidance, and encouragement; the anonymous writers, who so generously shared their thoughts and feelings about the referendum and its aftermath; Curtis Brown on behalf of the Trustees of the Mass Observation Archive for permission to quote from their responses, and Rachel Thorne for helping us through that process. We would also like to acknowledge the work of Liz McDonnell, who commissioned the first two directives on which this research is based and led us to this project in the first place.

We have benefited enormously from the thoughtful engagement, critique, and support of the colleagues with whom we have shared earlier versions of this work. This includes audiences, and fellow panellists, at the Modern British Studies conference at the University of Birmingham, the North American Conference on British Studies (twice), and the annual conferences of the Political Studies Association, the Council for European Studies, and the Social History Society. We are very grateful for the opportunities we have been given to present to small workshops and seminars: the

Acknowledgements

University of Edinburgh's Political History Research Group, the Institute for Historical Research's Modern Britain reading group, 'Dilemmas of Brexit: Reimagining Political Traditions' at the University of California, Berkeley, and the Politics Research in Progress seminar at the University of Sussex.

We would particularly like to thank Ellen Boucher and James Vernon for inviting us to join a workshop on Affect and Subjectivity in Postwar British History at the University of California, Berkeley, in the spring of 2022. This came at a time when we were just picking up the pieces of a project that had been shattered by the pandemic. The intellectual generosity, insight, and rigour of the scholars we spent those few sunny days with were a much-needed spur to finishing (and hopefully improving!) the book. Thank you: Jordanna Bailkin, Laura Beers, Ellen Boucher, Stephen Brooke, Claire Langhamer, Hilary Marland, Marc Matera, Radhika Natarajan, Kennetta Hammond Perry, Tehila Sasson, Camilla Schofield, Florence Sutcliffe-Braithwaite, Natalie Thomlinson, James Vernon.

We have also found encouragement closer to home. Thank you to the Directors of the Sussex European Institute, Neil Dooley and Aleksandra Lewicki, who supported a workshop on Emotion, Brexit, and European Politics in September 2022. We are particularly grateful to everyone who attended and engaged so thoughtfully with the theme and with our draft text: Sabina Avdagic, Robert Barrington, Stephen Coleman, Neil Dooley, Rosalind Eyben, Nicolai Gellwitzki, Ben Highmore, Anne-Marie Houde, Francis McGowan, Alistair Reid, Paul Taggart, Sofia Vasilopoulou, Monika Verbalyte. Again, this came at a pivotal moment in the writing and gave us many suggestions for improvement, to which we hope we have done justice. In the summer of 2018

Acknowledgements

we were fortunate to have the research assistance of Sam Gower, supported by the Sussex Junior Research Associate Scheme. We would like to acknowledge his enthusiastic and rigorous work.

At Manchester University Press, we would like to thank Tom Dark, who was incredibly supportive of the project and extremely patient when our plans were repeatedly derailed, Shannon Kneis, who steered us through the final stages of writing, and David Appleyard for managing the production process. We owe particular thanks to Rachel Goodyear, for her careful and thoughtful editing, and Zoe Ross for her index. We are grateful also to the anonymous peer reviewer, who pushed us to think much more clearly about what the book really was and who it was for.

Throughout the writing process, each of us has incurred debts to friends and colleagues who let us talk, moan, and think about the book with them. A non-exhaustive list includes Marianela Barrios Aquino, Hester Barron, Nick Clarke, Neil Dooley, Cathy Elliott, James Hampshire, Will Jennings, Laura Kounine, Claire Langhamer, Catalina Meija Moreno, Chris Moores, Gerry Stoker, Florence Sutcliffe-Braithwaite, Paul Taggart, Michal Weisze. Emily would also like to thank the students in her Politics of Feeling class for their energy, insight, and imagination in tackling these themes, and Jonathan appreciated the enthusiasm and critical engagement of the students in his Anti-politics module.

This book has taken longer than we hoped to complete, and the three of us have experienced a lot of feelings along the way: from the Brexit exhaustion we name in the book to the pandemic anxiety and fatigue, which delayed its completion. Our feelings about the academic system within which the text was written have been particularly complicated. While we have drawn solidarity, energy, and inspiration

Acknowledgements

from each other and from those around us, we have also been forced to repeatedly withdraw our labour – both temporarily, through recurrent periods of industrial action, and permanently in the case of Jake, who moved on to more fulfilling ventures during the period of writing. In doing so, we have been made intensely aware of the way that feelings (love, care, responsibility, resilience) are mobilised in the workplace.

Thank you to those who have lived through this with us – and who avoided throwing the slogan 'Get Brexit Done' at us: Jenny, Jon, Ryan, and all our parents. We dedicate the text to Wilbur, who was born into the weeks immediately after the referendum, and Sadie, who arrived just as we completed our first full draft. Our final thank you is to each other. If this has not always been a labour of love, it has certainly been one of companionship, patience, kindness, and good humour.

March 2023

Introduction: using an 'archive of feeling' to understand Brexit Britain

During the Brexit debates, questions about the nation's political future were continually framed in terms of feelings. The referendum was seen as a conflict between reason and resentment, fear and hope, heads and hearts. The Leave vote was widely interpreted (by both its supporters and detractors) as the triumph of passion over rationality. Its aftermath was marked by intense concern about the feelings generated on both sides and their consequences for British political culture. The capacity of this question to tear through personal relations and to provoke emotional encounters between strangers became as much a part of the debate on Brexit as the political and economic issues it raised. Yet at the same time, the mobilisation of feelings was presented as the solution to very real economic and diplomatic problems. If only people were more optimistic, less anxious, they were told, everything would be okay.[1]

The ideas that the Brexit vote both ushered in an unusually emotional moment in national life and that it was caused by an excess of unrestrained emotion have become commonplace.[2] Analysts have tried to diagnose it as part of a collective pathology, and to set it within a broader political and cultural frame which suggests we are living through an *Age of Anger* in which *Feeling Took Over the World*.[3] This growing reliance on feeling is generally understood to have negative consequences for the health of democracy. As well as being associated with nativist attitudes and support for populist parties, the strengthening of emotional attachments to group identities reduces opportunities for collaboration and compromise and increases intolerance and political cynicism.[4] Feelings of anger, fear, nostalgia, and resentment are understood to be particularly powerful and disruptive for established democratic norms. Indeed, supporters of Brexit, as well as Donald Trump and nationalist parties across Europe, are often perceived to be drawing upon these negative feelings in place of expert knowledge.[5]

Yet, analyses like these have also been implicated in themselves *creating* the conditions for this supposed explosion of populist emotion – in opposition to the norms of rational liberalism. As the psychotherapist Philippa Perry put it in the *Guardian* two days after the referendum: 'We are pretending to be computers. But we are not computers. Reason by itself will not work, because we are first and foremost creatures of feeling.'[6] The clash between the contradictory ideas that political division has been caused by *privileging* feelings and by *suppressing* them is at the heart of this book. We show that both have seeped into popular consciousness – and have left an irreconcilable problem. This was not inevitable. As Perry herself noted in a radio documentary two years later, the way we imagine the relationship between feeling and reason is culturally and historically contingent.[7] The historian Thomas Dixon, for instance, has argued that the present moment is only an 'age of anger' because political discourse increasingly *focuses on* anger, but it does so in ways that too often take

Introduction

use of the word 'anger' at face value, as if it referred to a universal and stable experience rather than being linked to its particular cultural context.[8] Dixon's own research offers an important corrective to the idea that the present moment is uniquely emotional and also reminds us that the very category of 'emotion' is itself a historical and political construct.[9]

While Perry's injunction 'to start acknowledging our own and other people's feelings' was addressed to both camps, her own position as a Remain voter meant that her column naturally emphasised the need to listen to Leavers: 'If we had slowed everything down, listened to fears, found a way of framing them, and taken action to include people who feel like an older child being pushed aside, would Europe even have been the issue?'[10] We will return to these themes throughout the book, in particular the representation of the Leave vote as a case of misdirected feelings and the application of psychotherapeutic solutions to political problems. But the idea that the feelings of Leave voters needed particular attention, and that Remain voters had been most guilty of 'over-rationalising', was a common theme in Brexit commentary. Unsurprisingly, academics (and especially political scientists) were seen to be particularly at fault. As the artist (and Philippa Perry's husband) Grayson Perry put it in an address to the Political Science Association's 2016 annual conference:

> the one thing that all the experts need to [improve] is their emotional literacy because what the liberal academic elite has done is let us down because they are not emotionally literate enough to understand what 52% of the electorate was thinking – or feeling, should I say [when they voted to leave the EU]. There is a whole world out there that we need to have more empathy with even if we don't like the results of what those kinds of feelings bring about.[11]

Since the EU referendum, we have seen a cultural turn to examining and prioritising the emotions Grayson Perry identifies here – not least through his own documentaries.[12] This has helped to reinforce the twin beliefs that feeling is somehow more authentic than thinking and that the two are necessarily opposed. Yet, as his linguistic slip shows, such a distinction is harder to maintain than we might like.

In this book, we try to satisfy Grayson Perry's plea for a more emotionally literate approach to political studies, but to do so without privileging certain feelings over others, or losing sight of their political context or consequences. Like Thomas Dixon, we start from the position that this is not a case of people simply *feeling more*; it is about the weight such feelings bear in public discourse and how this affects the way people experience their own feelings and those of others. Neither is it straightforwardly about why Britain's membership of the European Union generated such passionate responses on both sides. It is about how those feelings came to dominate political debate and the *feelings about feelings* that they generated in turn. We depart here from dominant approaches in political studies which have either used psychological methods to measure how distinct emotions affected voters' decision-making processes or inferred their 'feelings' from their demographic characteristics and geographical locations.[13] Such approaches have reinforced the idea of a binary distinction between emotion and reason, and ignored important work in both the history of emotions and other areas of the social sciences – most notably human geography and sociology – which has historicised and complicated such assumptions.[14]

Political studies of Brexit are also notably empty of the voices of 'ordinary people', in marked contrast to the detailed ethnographic work undertaken by colleagues

Introduction

in other disciplines.[15] We have therefore turned to the Mass Observation Project, which collected around 550 anonymised discursive responses to three questionnaires ('directives') on Brexit, conducted during the referendum as well as one and three years afterwards. What stands out from these accounts is the extent to which respondents, of all political positions, tried to make sense of the role that feelings could and should play in political life. Respondents were intensely aware of the emotional resonances of different political positions, and many described how in the absence of 'dispassionate information' they relied on weighing the political currency of their own feelings and those of others.

While this indicates the overlapping ways that cognitive and emotional factors were brought into play, it also suggests that a cultural belief in the ideal distinction between the intellect and the emotions persists, despite having long been discredited within the academy and (more significantly) despite respondents' inability to maintain such distinctions in their own lives. This material, therefore, offers a unique window into popular views about existing and emerging ideas about the politics of feeling, during a period in which they seemed to be in flux. Our close analysis of this material both lends a new perspective on everyday experiences of the EU referendum and its aftermath, and makes a significant contribution to the politics of feeling within political studies.

Rather than tracing specific emotions themselves, we explore how the *idea* of 'emotion' functioned during the Brexit debates and how voters of all political persuasions weighed, deployed, disavowed, and rejected it as a source of moral and political legitimacy. We show, for instance, how the tropes of the angry Brexiteer and rational/grieving

Remainer were mobilised in media commentary, academic analysis, and parliamentary debate, and how they have been both internalised and resisted by people themselves. We look at the intrusion of politics into everyday life and the effects this had in encouraging some people to express their feelings in ways they would not normally do, while others felt a responsibility to suppress theirs. Above all, we uncover how people experienced the EU referendum as an event marked by an excess of emotion, and the common understandings about the place of feeling in political life that they drew on in narrating this.

This introductory chapter outlines our approach to understanding feelings and their place in political life. First, it sets out our conceptual approach. Next, it introduces the Mass Observation Project and its particular value in recording (and shaping) the interaction between feeling and thinking in how people understand their experiences of politics. The final part of the chapter outlines the structure and the arguments of the book, and its contribution to studying both the specific narratives about the emotional politics of Brexit and the politics of feeling more broadly.

The politics of feeling

Feelings and politics have an awkward relationship. As Ute Frevert and Kerstin Maria Pahl point out, 'Ideally, as many have claimed, politics should work without emotion or at least keep emotions at bay. At the same time, few have doubted the importance of emotional ties between rulers and ruled.'[16] The idea that politics has become increasingly emotional rests on a simplistic yet disproven reason–passion dichotomy, by which feelings are seen as impulsive, disruptive, and irrational forces that impede political judgement.

Introduction

The normative assumption that politics should be based on dispassionate deliberation was encoded into the very foundations of its institutions – as was the (gendered, classed, and racialised) fear of the potentially corrosive effects of emotion on the emerging mass democracy.[17] Such judgements continue to structure political debate, as attested by the prominence of negative feelings – such as anger, fear, and anxiety – in conventional understandings of far-right populism in Europe, Trump in the United States, and of course Brexit in the UK.[18] Yet, the popular idea that Brexit resulted from an increasingly – and worryingly – emotional politics disregards the place of feeling in Britain's different political traditions, as well as a significant body of literature within political theory and science showing that emotion is (and always has been) an intrinsic part of political life.[19]

Feelings in Britain's political traditions

The relationship between feelings, reason, and expertise has been constructed very differently across political traditions. Most obviously, Conservative thinkers have long characterised 'rationalism in politics' as an artificial and disembodied (though culturally dominant) tendency to overlook the human, emotional element in social life.[20] Yet, they have also been cautious about the potential of mass politics to unleash destructive and irrational emotions, and about the capacity of self-expression to lead to social collapse.[21] The Conservative understanding of emotion is social rather than individual. Experience may be preferred to expertise, but the former is located within the bounds of an imagined 'common sense', seen to be not only shared, stable, and inherited but reinforced by a strong sense of national identity and political authority. Conservative philosopher Roger Scruton denounced what he called the 'cult of "authenticity"' and insisted that 'self-identity' should be found within the national community, rather than in opposition to it. For Scruton, true 'authenticity' was located in 'custom, tradition and common culture'.[22] We will see in chapter 2 how such arguments worked to shore up existing social and racial hierarchies but also how the 'right to feel' challenged established forms of cultural and political authority.

It is perhaps surprising to find that a concern for customs, traditions, and common culture also runs through left-wing thought. The various traditions of Marxism, Fabianism, and ethical socialism grew out of a shared ethic of 'humanitarianism and fellowship'.[23] And although this has often been lost behind more technocratic politics, the need to recover what Tony Crosland called the 'moral-cultural-emotional appeal of the William Morris tradition' has been a recurrent refrain in Labour politics.[24] Moreover, left-wing thinkers (in a mirror image of Scruton) worried throughout the post-war period that individualism was eroding traditional emotional ties to place, community, and class.[25] Yet, recent scholarship has emphasised that post-war social change in fact encouraged new modes of emotional community, whether through expanding the scope of workplace solidarity or grounding personal relationships on affection rather than obligation.[26] The recovery of these practices could be read as an implicit challenge to attempts to create an explicitly socially conservative and nostalgic form of affective left politics.[27]

This concern to set out a left politics of emotion stems from a long-standing perception that socialism (and particularly social democracy) has been both too puritanical and mechanistically rational.[28] It is not necessarily that the left have ignored emotions but that they have seen them to be something that can be cultivated and harnessed for

Introduction

the greater good.[29] The concern with higher and lower emotional states can be traced from Marxian concepts of alienation, through post-war attempts to shape the developing welfare state according to psychological theories, and the cultural politics of the New Left.[30] It also infuses the liberal tradition, with its emphasis on self-flourishing.[31] More recently, we might think of New Labour's hate crime legislation as an attempt to regulate the expression of particular kinds of emotion. While this all stems from a desire to cultivate a more humane society, it has been interpreted by social conservatives (across the political spectrum) as artificial attempts to impose rationality upon what they perceive to be straightforward 'human nature'.

This points to one of the core contradictions of the emotional culture of late twentieth-century Britain. While, as the historian Claire Langhamer has noted, 'dominant emotional styles shifted from those rooted in self-discipline to those that celebrated self-expression', this was associated with wider 'permissive' changes, often seen to have been imposed from above by a liberal elite, out of step with the assumed conservative instincts of the country.[32] As we will explore further in chapters 1 and 2, this has created a tension in the way that feelings are conceived in political and popular discourse. For cultural conservatives, they signify both the authentic (often implicitly nativist) instincts of 'ordinary' people *and* the disintegration of a national culture of restraint; on the other side of the same coin, for progressives, the politics of feeling are simultaneously liberating and coercive. This late twentieth-century ambivalence went hand in hand, as Langhamer reminds us, with the 'burdens' of emotional capitalism. Feelings were increasingly seen as something to be managed, as part of a constant project of self-improvement, in ways that tempered the emancipatory potential of self-actualisation.³³ Most recently, this has manifested in the trend for mindfulness, which suggests that feelings should be acknowledged, examined, then set aside.³⁴ Such ideas implicitly counter dominant cultural narratives that imagine emotions to be expressions of the true self and further reinforce deep-seated understandings of unregulated passion as a destructive force in public life.

We can see how the relationship between feelings, reason, and expertise has been constructed very differently across political traditions. Far from reflecting unchanging physiological reality, feelings and emotions are rooted in changing understandings of human nature. And there is a politics to this.

Feelings and political studies

Feelings and emotions are crucial to explaining why and how citizens engage with politics, given that the likely impact of one vote is minimal and the costs of participation are likely to exceed the benefits.³⁵ Emotional attachments to political parties and group identity are the missing ingredient in such collective action problems. Yet, political studies have also struggled with how to reconcile the emotional aspects of liberal democratic politics with its rational norms. The onset of widescale survey research in public opinion from the 1940s produced unprecedented amounts of data and information about voters' knowledge and attitudes in western democracies. Debates within political science initially focused on questions about voters' competence.³⁶ Studies suggested the majority of voters were ill-informed, 'innocent' of ideology, and lacked knowledge of government institutions and policy issues.³⁷ These debates pivoted

Introduction

around an implicit distinction between the respective influence of reason and emotion on decision-making. Competent voters were expected to be well-informed and to develop their opinions through fact-based deliberation, while incompetent voters were expected to be ill-informed and to base their opinions on pre-existing emotional judgements.

From the 1980s, this dichotomy was challenged by the development of affective intelligence theory, which aimed to incorporate new insights from neuroscience and psychology into understandings of political behaviour. The theory was developed by George Marcus, Michael MacKuen, and Russell Neuman, who argued that all political judgement and decision-making was driven by preconscious emotional responses occurring below the surface of awareness.[38] These studies adopted what could be described as a naturalist conception of emotion derived from the evolutionary and phenomenological theories of Charles Darwin and William James.[39] They understood emotions as a form of embodied expertise, or innate universal objects that reside within individuals. Affective intelligence theory built on a theory of human cognition known as the 'dual process model', which suggests people hold two distinct decision-making systems: the dispositional and surveillance systems. The dispositional system refers to the intuitive, preconscious responses that guide individuals' habitual behaviour. The surveillance system, by contrast, involves conscious deliberation and informs decision-making when individuals find themselves in novel, threatening, or unfamiliar situations. This approach to political decision-making dissolved the reason/emotion dichotomy by suggesting that emotions are an inescapable aspect of all forms of human behaviour – including political judgement. Emotional reactions to people, groups, and events will always precede conscious reasoning and shape how individuals interpret and engage with different sources of information.

A range of research has since gone on to use experimental methods to empirically demonstrate how each appraisal system operates in practice. Voters who profess to experience anxiety are more likely to engage in information-seeking behaviour. Angry voters are less likely to be influenced by new sources of information and tend to rely upon pre-existing attitudes. Likewise, hope and enthusiasm are associated with higher levels of interest and participation in political campaigns.[40] Various studies highlight the role of emotion specifically in shaping attitudes towards the EU and European integration. For instance, Sofia Vasilopoulou and Marcus Wagner found that voters who reported feeling angry with the EU were less receptive to cost–benefit considerations, less nuanced in their opinions about integration, and – unsurprisingly – more likely to want to leave the EU than those who reported feeling anxious.[41] Monika Verbalyte and Christian von Scheve have drawn similar conclusions from Eurobarometer data, which shows a correlation between negative emotions and Euroscepticism.[42]

The main point for our study is that, contrary to popular narratives that framed the Brexit debate in terms of reason versus emotion, the now well-established field of affective intelligence theory rejects 'dystopic images of ill-informed and irrational publics, as well as more utopian aspirations for full-time rational citizens'.[43] Instead, it paints a more complex and dynamic picture where citizens move from steadfast partisan decisions to deliberative convictions in different contexts. Yet within these accounts, there is a tendency to treat the individual as the unit of analysis and emotion as a set of fixed physiological and cognitive processes, which operate largely outside the realm of personal

Introduction

control or social influence. Emotion thus becomes an additional independent variable which can be measured and added into existing models. Such positivist treatments of emotion are curiously out of line not only with work on the history, philosophy, and social theory of emotions but also with recent psychological thinking, all of which understand emotions to be socially created and culturally specific.[44] Moreover, even the very category of 'emotion', and its place in public and political life, should be understood as culturally, historically, and ideologically contingent.[45]

In this book, we approach feelings as socially embedded and subjectively experienced. This distinguishes our contribution from existing political studies of emotion and Brexit which have generally approached feelings experimentally or through the lens of affect theory in a way that emphasises their cognitive, strategic, instrumental, or nonintentional dimensions.[46] This is not to deny that feelings are experienced and expressed by real people with mental and physical consequences in the real world. Rather it is to highlight the cultural resources, scripts, and storylines individuals share with each other as they seek to understand and communicate their feelings with others. We have chosen to use the deliberately nebulous term 'feelings' because it allows us to go beyond tracing specific named emotions (fear, hope, anger, love) and to capture the wider ways in which 'feeling' featured in the debates and experiences of Brexit. This includes, for instance, respondents' articulations of the role that a more nebulous sense of 'feeling' might play in forming their political thought (e.g. 'gut feelings' or 'instincts') or the way they narrate their encounters with political 'moods' or 'atmospheres'.

To summarise, whilst many pundits, and indeed some scholars, continue to share the idea that feelings are unpredictable and unruly reactions that have no place in political decision-making process, we have shown how these normative assumptions disregard the place of feeling in Britain's political traditions, as well as a significant body of literature within the social and political sciences that demonstrates how emotion is an unavoidable and essential aspect of how individuals form political judgements. This literature has primarily been concerned with trying to empirically measure and demonstrate how specific, named emotions influence political behaviour and decision-making. While such studies may be able to explain why certain individuals are more prone to certain voting decisions or how particular groups of emotions can motivate political action, they tell us little about what that means to the individuals concerned, whether they perceive their own decision-making as emotional, or how that sits with their views on the political legitimacy of feelings more widely. Our book aims to address these questions. We ask how people understood the role of feelings within their own decision-making processes and what that can tell us about the politics of feeling in Brexit Britain. We seek to establish this from looking at the place of feeling in individual narratives about Brexit found in the Mass Observation Project.

Mass Observation: an 'archive of feeling'

Mass Observation (MO) is a social research organisation, which deployed a variety of methods to obtain information about everyday life in Britain between 1937 and 1955. MO restarted in 1981 and has continued ever since to issue 'directives' containing open-ended sets of questions to a panel of around 1,000 volunteer writers every three or four months. Numerous historians and social scientists

Introduction

have demonstrated that MO materials can be used as evidence of popular understandings of various aspects of everyday life in Britain including race, social class, and formal politics.[47]

Mass Observation was created in the aftermath of the Abdication Crisis of 1937, by a group of left-liberal thinkers who set out to create an 'anthropology of ourselves', designed to infuse policy-making with an understanding of 'the politics of everyday life'.[48] It was, from its inception, concerned with recording and understanding public feelings, and it was to play an influential role in shaping the norms of democratic culture.[49] The founders of Mass Observation wanted to use the directive responses to access ordinary people's private thoughts and to capture individual beliefs 'at the stage before they crystalised into definite organised institutions'.[50] James Hinton has identified how these aims preceded Raymond Williams' desire to identify and understand 'structures of feeling', which he defined in a very similar fashion as the 'preliminary level of awareness' that shapes developing attitudes before they institutionalise as established norms.[51]

Claire Langhamer has shown how MO's attention to the feelings of 'ordinary people' was inscribed into the political culture of post-war reconstruction. She pays particular attention to its practice of asking Observers how they *felt* about social and political events, rather than what they *thought*, and places this within the context of an emerging 'right to feel', which developed alongside other rights discourses and soon became central to political and cultural life:

> in the decades after 1945 emotion came to matter a great deal within public as well as private worlds, as dominant emotional styles shifted from those rooted in self-discipline

to those that celebrated self-expression. We see evidence for this shift in the changing self-representations of politicians and within an everyday political culture which increasingly used feeling to unify the nation and to exclude others from it. We see it too in the field of journalism and in a growing obsession with taking the 'mood' of the nation. It is also apparent in the pervasiveness of psychological ways of thinking within the developing welfare state, as well as in the permissive legislation of the 1960s in which the right to feel and to act on one's feelings gained a measure of legal sanction. Even the economy was not immune to the advance of feeling. A turn towards 'emotional capitalism' harnessed emotional labour, imposed emotional burdens and claimed to valorise emotional intelligence.[52]

The shift from a political culture of restraint to one of self-expression (epitomised in the 'Diana moment' of 1997) is a familiar story. While politicians have long cast their enemies and outsiders as overly emotional, it is only relatively recently that they have been expected to display their own emotions as a marker of personal authenticity.[53] What Langhamer's work points to is a corresponding assumption that emotion confers political legitimacy. The use of what she terms 'feelings-evidence' became an increasingly legitimate form of social knowledge over the decades after 1945.

Langhamer's argument connects to the way that social theorists have identified a growing focus on intimacy and selfhood as a key characteristic of late modernity, though they have differed in their judgements about this process. An insightful article by Gabriele Linke contrasts Richard Sennett's complaint that, since the nineteenth century, 'tyrannies of intimacy' have brought about the 'fall' of the rational public sphere, with Lauren Berlant's more optimistic reading of the development of 'intimate publics', underpinned by complex affective relations, over the same period.

Introduction

Attention to everyday life and to ordinary people's thoughts and feelings was itself a key influence in shaping the norms of post-war democratic culture.[54] Both agree that twentieth-century American society was fundamentally shaped by the recognition of the emotions and personal experiences of ordinary citizens; similar currents in British history are the context in which MO was formed. This is why it represents an ideal source for understanding how ideas about emotion circulated through British society.

In 2016, 2017, and 2019, MO collected around 550 anonymous reflections on the EU referendum and Brexit, creating a uniquely rich resource. These discursive accounts provide evidence of how people interpreted the referendum campaign, the EU, and their own subjective responses to both. They also highlight the cultural understandings of both the political issues at stake and the feelings of the campaign that were in circulation. In line with MO's standard approach, the Brexit directives were framed in emotional terms, asking about 'hopes' and 'fears' twice and 'feelings' six times. It is, therefore, not surprising to find that – as we will see throughout this book – Observers responded in these terms.

Responses to MO provide us with evidence of what Alison Pugh describes as 'meta-feelings' – or feelings about feelings.[55] In the words of Stephen Coleman, 'when people talk about their feelings, they are not simply reporting real time visceral responses to a given situation, but they are trying to make sense of the distance between how a situation made them feel at the time and how they believed they ought to feel'.[56] Looking at meta-feelings helps us 'situate emotions culturally giving a sense for how safe or free or proud (or ashamed or horrified) someone might be to claim a particular feeling, and thus to act upon it'.[57] In practice, our study focuses on the stories people told about Brexit and the words through which they expressed their feelings. In this sense, we have adopted a pluralist approach to emotion advocated by psychologist of emotion Lisa Feldman Barrett and historian of emotion Thomas Dixon. They challenge theories of 'basic emotions', espoused by psychologist Paul Ekman, that treat emotions such as anger or sadness as transhistorical singular entities. Instead of universal hard-wired instincts, they consider emotions as psychological constructions 'where language, education and situated personal experience shape "core affect" in different culturally specific forms'.[58] Reading responses to Mass Observation allows us to identify how different people drew upon their own feelings and evaluated the feelings of others as they described their experiences of Brexit. So rather than looking at evidence of instinctive reactions or affect, we are really looking at the position of emotion in shared stories circulating in British society at the time of the referendum. This allows us to observe the interaction between individual and collective feeling.

Our focus on stories is inspired by the methodological approach of historians working with oral history and other sources of personal testimony. After reading British soldiers' letters from the First World War, Michael Roper stressed the importance of focusing on subjectivity as a means of investigating the emotional significance of events and practices.[59] The aim is less to establish a more 'authentic' version of past events than to identify the different cultural resources individuals draw upon to compose the stories they tell about those events. The concept of 'composure' is essential to understanding how individuals narrate their experiences. It is now widely understood that people relate the stories they tell about themselves to popular and public

Introduction

narratives. In the words of Penny Summerfield, the oral historian must examine not only 'the voice that speaks for itself, but also the voices that speak to it'.[60] This involves thinking about popular and public narratives, as well as the influence of personal knowledge constructed from interaction with family, friends, and workmates.[61] A focus on individual testimony and personal stories enables the researcher to see 'the assimilation of cultural codes as a matter of negotiation involving an active subject'.[62] James Hinton advocates a similar approach to understanding the past in his analysis of Mass Observation diaries from the Second World War. He also emphasises the point that examining individual stories is not necessarily to offer more 'authentic' accounts of events but to 'locate individuals in their social context, and to understand how, in constructing their own selfhoods, they contributed to larger patterns of continuity and change'.[63] Focusing on stories provides a window on to how individuals don't just passively internalise public narratives and discourse but actively engage with such discourses to make sense of their own experiences.

Another advantage of focusing on individual life-writing is that we get a deeper insight into writers' internalised dispositions than we might expect to glean from focus group or interview data. Whilst talk from a focus group is generated in public, writing for Mass Observation is completed anonymously in private. This context affords writers greater space for reflection.[64] People may express ideas they would be reluctant to share in public or in one-to-one interviews. As Stephen Coleman has recently pointed out, emotional regulation shapes all aspects of self-presentation but has specific implications for how people talk about politics. He suggests this is because political disagreements generally have less to do with what is explicitly said out loud and more to do with one's assumptions about the values and intentions framing an individual's viewpoint. He suggests this phenomenon is rarely acknowledged but universally felt. It leads individuals to consider a series of questions before they decide to talk about politics, which include:

> Is this the right moment to speak? Could my words reveal more about what is on my mind than I want to share? Could the unruly tone of my voice or movement of my body undermine the constrained propriety of my utterance? Might my speech be smothered by my feelings? (And who is to say that it should not be?)[65]

We also need to recognise how these 'meta-feelings' or feeling rules have uneven effects throughout society. People used to being heard and who believe their voices count are plausibly more likely to express their political feelings than others who have not been socialised in this way and so may perceive their own feelings as too 'raw, vulgar, fickle and unmanageable' to be articulated in public.[66] Coleman identifies these – what could be described as – feeling rules circulating in Britain from his own interview research carried out around the time of the EU referendum. Our use of MO helps us gain a better sense of how individuals engaged, accepted or rejected, and – in so doing – actively constructed these feeling rules at the time.

The anonymous and private nature of writing for Mass Observation helps access not only the responses of individuals without social constraints but also their reflections on those constraints themselves. The sources are full of reported encounters, and the silences as well as the conversations they engendered. Observers frequently recounted biting their tongues or saying something they did not mean, as well as their thoughts about the words of others. Some also addressed the researcher directly, inviting or defying their judgement. Yet it would be misguided to assume MO provides a window on to pure individual disposition. Talking or writing about politics is a social interaction that compels individuals to position themselves within the 'cultural atmosphere' in which they speak. Ben Highmore explains that reading the 'social mood' involves recognising how public events, trends, and emotions are interrelated.[67] Lauren Berlant suggests people find themselves riding 'the wave of collectively recycled affective knowledge' as the collective moods they are caught up in provide an affective lens through which they interpret their experience.[68] It is in this sense that our book prioritises the space between individual and collective feelings. We have focused on the writing of individuals about the feelings they associated with Brexit. We have not read their views as representative of general or particular social groups. Instead, we have analysed the material for evidence of the cultural world inhabited by the writers and the resources they used to construct understandings, form judgements and expectations, and interpret their experiences.

The most common criticism about Mass Observation surrounds its representativeness. Respondents to MO are, by definition, more practised in expressing themselves in such terms than the 'average' person and more likely to be dutiful, engaged, reflexive, and critical.[69] It also must be emphasised that MO is not representative of the population. Respondents are disproportionately white, and older women from the south-east of England are over-represented in the panel, as are people of the Left. In the case of Brexit, this cuts two ways. The left-liberal bias means that we would expect to find more Remainers in the panel, but its age and ethnic profile would tend towards Leavers. These would be significant disadvantages if we were using these accounts to explain the referendum result. Unlike other analysts, however, we are not interested in measuring how specific feelings affected individuals' decision-making. Rather than reading the responses as representative of certain demographic categories, then, we follow Clarke et al. in using the responses to establish the common understandings, expectations, feelings, and judgements circulating at the time of the referendum.[70] These accounts provide windows on to the cultural resources and everyday episteme individuals use to make sense of the world and their place within it, resources which circulated within families, workplaces, and friendship groups throughout the UK.

A final aspect of our methodology worth commenting on here concerns the role of affect within the writing process itself. A social scientist interested in measuring the impact of specific emotions on certain behaviours might argue that focusing on retrospective writing of individuals about their feelings does not tell us very much about the specific emotions that guided their reactions or decision-making at the time. Instead, the act of writing in itself represents a form of conscious and deliberative reflection – where the individual actively rationalises and imposes order on their feelings as they seek to justify and explain their past behaviour. We do not see this as a weakness of our methodology but as a strength. Their writings for MO make clear how individuals interacted with broader ideas and cultural resources circulating in society. They provide evidence of the meta-feelings and feeling rules in operation at the time of the EU referendum.

Introduction

How can the politics of feeling help us understand Brexit Britain?

The 2016 EU referendum has generated a large amount of scholarship that has either aimed to explain Brexit or identify the consequences of Brexit. History and emotion occupy a prominent position in explanations for why the Leave campaign won in 2016. Historical explanations have emphasised Britain's 'awkward relationship' with Europe, which has long been understood as a cultural phenomenon – a product of Britain's search to define itself in the aftermath of Empire when Britain initially decided not to join the European Coal and Steel Community and EEC.[71] Survey evidence from Eurobarometer indicates that British opposition towards the EU was deeper and more long-standing than other member states'.[72] Alongside this, the British print media and political class have also been shown to be uniquely Eurosceptic by comparison with their counterparts elsewhere in Europe.[73] Evidence of the UK's long-term ambivalence and opposition to Europe within public opinion, the media, and the political class contributes to social identity theory-based explanations for Brexit as well. Such explanations highlight a long-term lack of European identity within Britain, which according to multiple studies was a key factor distinguishing Leave and Remain voters in 2016.[74]

History and emotion also underpin social-political explanations for the referendum result. Perhaps the most accepted account of the Leave vote focuses on broader sociopolitical changes in Britain since the 1970s. New social divisions developed in response to globalisation, deindustrialisation, and education expansion have been understood to have eroded established links between political parties and the electorate and produced new political identities that were 'activated' by the referendum.[75] Feelings are crucial to these explanations that have been put forward by most political scientists. So, for Sara Hobolt, 'the *sentiments* that led to this outcome ... reflect a divide between those who *feel* left behind by the forces of globalisation and mass immigration and those who welcome such developments' (emphases added).[76] Goodwin and Heath agree: 'Brexit was delivered by the "left behind"' who they define as 'social groups that are united by a *general sense* of insecurity, pessimism and marginalisation, who do not *feel* as though elites share their values, represent their interests and genuinely *empathise* with their intense *angst*' (emphases added).[77]

Feelings of being 'left behind', having 'lost control', or 'imperial nostalgia' occupy a prominent position in these long-term explanations for the Leave vote.[78] But emotion is also important to more immediate explanations focused on the campaign itself. Another factor explaining the Leave vote was a lack of political trust and the rise in anti-establishment sentiment. During and after the referendum, commentators have argued that the Leave campaign actively misled the public and relied on lies, misinformation, and populist rhetoric. These arguments build on earlier work regarding Britain's long-term anomalously Eurosceptic media that primed and legitimised a campaign based on 'strategies of fear, resentment and empowerment'.[79] Glencross argues that 'Nothing was inevitable about the Brexit vote: the campaign mattered profoundly' and that the Remain campaign was undermined by its focus purely on economics at the expense of positive arguments about integration or identity issues.[80] Others have argued that the lack of an emphatically pro-EU, social democratic political leader outside of Scotland during the campaign undermined Remain, with David Cameron leading a divided Conservative Party and the

Introduction

historically Eurosceptic Jeremy Corbyn leading Labour.[81] It is clear to see how such explanations implicitly draw upon a distinction between reason and emotion.

The book is not about the causes of the Leave vote. What we can say is that feelings are often implicitly cited as being important without being understood on their own terms – or, rather, in the terms of those experiencing them. In this sense, our book makes an empirical contribution to understandings of Brexit by analysing new evidence of the affective experiences of 'ordinary' people writing for MO. But our focus on feelings is also relevant to the growing literature on the consequences of Brexit. Sara Hobolt et al. argue that affective polarisation is occurring.[82] People have become emotionally attached to Leave and Remain positions in a similar fashion to partisan identities in the USA. This affects their political identities, how they differentiate themselves from alternative groups, and, perhaps most importantly, their evaluative biases, perceptions of the world, and decision-making processes. Quoting Christopher Achen and Larry Bartels, they suggest that 'people use their partisanship to construct "objective facts"'.[83] Leavers are less willing to listen to Remainers and vice versa, while both groups are likely to interpret information on the basis of their emotional attachment to each identity. While there is widespread academic agreement on the existence of polarisation, the extent to which this was produced, rather than simply revealed or 'activated', by the referendum process is contested – as is the potential longevity of this political division.

The results of the 2019 General Election and 2021 local elections were interpreted as further evidence that Brexit continues to divide the British electorate.[84] They testified to a fragmentation of political allegiance, with the number of people identifying with their side of the Brexit vote significantly exceeding the number who strongly identify with a political party. Robert Ford has described this as a continuation of a long-term reversal of old class divides centred around education, with the Conservatives gaining support from former UKIP voters and increasing their support in wards where voters have few formal qualifications. The 2021 by-election results indicated that COVID-19 did not disrupt the hold of Leave and Remain identities on British politics.[85]

Yet, there is a danger of reifying divisions through the kind of survey research that is structured around them. As Jon Lawrence points out, we should be wary of mistaking responses to pollsters' trigger questions on crime, LGBT rights, or immigration as fixed markers of identity.[86] It is also important to consider questions about not just negative detachment from the opposing side but also positive attachment to one's own side. Sociologist Katherine Davies argues that popular narratives that emphasise the divisive nature of Brexit do not fully account for how people talk about politics in their everyday lives. Using qualitative interview material, she shows how talk about Brexit is context-dependent and shaped by existing relationships and knowledge of companions' pre-existing political beliefs. Rather than dividing families, Davies argues, Brexit actually reveals the stickiness of family relationships and the desire to stay together despite division.[87] Our book takes these attempts to assess the true complexity of responses to Brexit still further. By exploring how Mass Observers managed and described the emotional fallout from Brexit in their own words, we are able to see not only how it impacted their own sense of identity but also its presence in the everyday situations in which such identities are developed and performed.

Introduction

About the book

The book is broken into two parts, each of which explores one of the prominent public narratives about the politics of Brexit Britain. The first of these narratives is that the referendum campaign and its aftermath can best be understood as a clash between 'heads' and 'hearts', and that the result was part of a newly emotional form of politics where personal feelings intruded into political life. In the first section of the book (chapters 1 and 2), we explore how people made sense of this idea in their everyday lives. In chapter 1, we focus on the role of feelings in voting decisions. Rather than treating it as a straightforward causal factor (e.g. anger led to Leave votes), we look at the ways that people consciously drew on their feelings as a form of evidence, alongside (and intertwined with) reason. It is notable that, while the EU referendum was frequently framed as a choice between 'heads' and 'hearts' in media discourse, Mass Observers rarely articulated such a distinction; indeed, only one put it in those precise terms. Instead, they turned to an altogether messier organ: the gut. References to 'gut feeling' and 'gut instinct' came up time and time again. Rather than pitting the wistfulness of 'heart' against the cold rationality of 'head', Mass Observers described something different. Having digested as much information (and disinformation) as they could stomach, they had to make the call on what felt right.

One of the notable features of both public debate and scholarship on the EU referendum is the extent to which Leave and Remain have been taken to represent fixed positions and to carry (increasingly antagonistic) cultural and political identities. Our sources complicate this story, showing that many voters made their decision late in the process, based upon agonised attempts to get to grips with the issue at hand. They also complicate the contradictory assumption embedded in the head/heart distinction that Leave and Remain voters thought and felt in similar terms but chose to privilege these differently. Instead, we show that they displayed similar attitudes to the (il)legitimacy of feeling as a source of political judgement but that this led them in divergent directions.

In chapter 2, we move on to look at the stereotypes that emerged as people judged the feelings of others and made sense of new political divisions surfacing in the aftermath of the referendum. We explore how certain kinds of feelings, held by particular types of people, came to acquire a greater political weight than others. Although, as we have seen, many Mass Observers turned to their feelings as a way of transcending the grubby world of politics and media bias, they were often deeply suspicious of the emotions of others, who they felt should have been more 'rational'. This tendency was reinforced by the widespread mobilisation of the tropes of the rational Remainer and the passionate Brexiteer. Although they did not reflect how feelings were actually deployed (in fact, both sides emphasised their own rationality and condemned their opponents' feelings as unruly and disruptive to political norms), we show the power of these stereotypes in shaping voters' understandings of their own feelings and of those around them. This reinforced two not-quite-contradictory ideas: first, that feelings were a dangerous and base impulse, and second, that the only 'true' emotional response was that associated with a deeply racialised, classed, and anglicised construction of 'ordinariness' and of 'the mood of the country'. The first part of the book, then, aims to complicate the popular narratives that suggest Brexit represented a new form of 'post-truth' politics – where feelings trump facts – and instead

Introduction

draws attention to multiple, overlapping, and sometimes competing discourses surrounding the role of feelings in political life.

In part II, we turn to another popular narrative about the feelings of Brexit, which is that they were excessive. The period of the referendum campaign and its aftermath was experienced as a peculiarly emotional time, in which feelings carried both greater power and greater danger than usual. It seemed that just as feelings were shaping political decisions and attitudes, so politics was intruding into the most intimate areas of affective life and personal relationships. Chapter 3 explores the way that the emotions of Brexit were experienced at an individual and collective level as a particular public 'mood' or 'atmosphere'. The Mass Observation accounts indicate that this was an intense experience for many. They also indicate a wide spectrum of feelings, from 'elation' to 'distress', as well as more ambivalent experiences of revulsion, boredom, and fatigue. We reflect on how voters made sense of these affective experiences, interpreting them not only through their pre-existing political frameworks but also through dominant cultural discourses about emotion and mental health, most notably anxiety.

In the final chapter of the book, we turn to how feelings were managed and negotiated (and the concerns around how they should be negotiated) in intimate relationships. One of the distinguishing features of discourse on Brexit – from the mass media to Mass Observation – is the extent to which it was seen to pervade everyday life, impacting relationships with friends, family members, neighbours, and colleagues. In this chapter, we follow the emotions of Brexit into these intimate realms, examining how Observers navigated tensions and divisions in their daily lives. We find them drawing on – and rewriting – various sets of 'feeling rules'. Media depictions reinforced the idea that Brexit was a matter for intimate exchange as much as public deliberation, but also contributed to the sense that feelings on the topic were dangerous and volatile – a concern voiced in parliamentary debate too. Although the EU referendum was presented as a chance for public debate, it actually closed it down. Individuals felt drained by the heightened public and private discourse, and frightened by the emotions it had unleashed, in themselves and in others. And while popular culture recommended therapeutic talk and prioritised bridging divides, most of our Observers avoided this, even at the cost of personal relationships. Some also began to feel they had a moral obligation to cut ties with those whose bigotry they had previously been able to tolerate.

Why this matters

The EU referendum and its aftermath were experienced as a time of heightened emotions, which reshaped the public realm and also pervaded the most intimate spaces. While our analysis demonstrates that the tropes of the rational Remainer and passionate Brexiteer are unable to capture the complex interrelations of feeling and thinking across the political spectrum, it also highlights their cultural power and political consequences.

We argue that this scenario must be understood in historical terms. On the one hand, we might think of historical characterisations of 'the mob', linked to fears about democracy and demagoguery. On the other, we might consider the attention to the emotions of 'ordinary people', which grew out of the social democratic models of the mid-twentieth century before being leveraged by the 'emotional capitalism' of the twenty-first.

Introduction

We want to suggest that Brexit highlighted a clash between feeling rules, whereby cultural norms *both* valorise individual feelings *and also* maintain the belief that they are separate from, and inferior to, reason. The referendum grew out of, and amplified, these tendencies. It was born of public distrust with representative government and took place amidst even higher levels of distrust with political institutions and sources of information. Being unable to rely on established structures for collective decision-making, voters turned to their own feelings as a source of seemingly apolitical political knowledge. But they did this while simultaneously rejecting (and fearing) the feelings of others.

Although emotion was produced socially, in the interactions between people and communities, it was primarily *understood to be* personal and individual. Feelings were simultaneously taken to be markers of political authenticity and steadfastness *and also* a dangerously irrational and selfish element in public life. We argue that this situation has produced a particularly toxic sense of a divide, not only between irreconcilable views but between emotional responses which have come to seem unbridgeable because of the way they are understood to be fixed reflections of our authentic selves.

Our analysis emphasises that this divide was produced by the experience of the referendum itself, with many voters making their decision late in the process and regretting the lack of adequate and impartial information. Yet, while this divide may have been contingent, it has been reinforced by the political debate since 2016, in which Leave or Remain has become the clearest political cleavage in Britain. While individuals are finding ways to bridge these new divisions in their daily lives, too often this means avoiding talk of politics altogether.

Part I

Beyond 'heads vs hearts': personal feelings in political life

2016 was the year that definitively launched the era of 'Post-Truth'.
Matthew D'Ancona, *Post-Truth: The New War on Truth and How to Fight Back* (London: Penguin, 2017)

[I'm] trying to avoid news coverage about the EU ... it doesn't help and just descends into calling the other side liars, fear-mongering and/or racism. I have started to believe I would be better off trying to psychically intuit whether we would be better off in or out than polluting my brain with this.
M4859, F, 40, software engineer, Devon, Remain, 2016

The starting point for this book was to interrogate the popular narrative that the referendum campaign and its aftermath can best be understood as a clash between 'heads' and 'hearts', and that the result was part of a newly emotional form of politics. In the next two chapters, we want to explore how these narratives shaped individuals' experiences of these events.

First, we look at how people understood the place of feelings within their own voting decisions. We show that, although the EU referendum was frequently framed as a choice between 'heads' and 'hearts' in popular commentary,

Mass Observers rarely articulated such a distinction. Instead, both Leave and Remain supporters justified their decision-making in terms of 'gut feeling'. In the context of an unhelpful and confusing campaign, gut feelings about Brexit were represented as an apolitical, morally neutral source of knowledge, which depended upon the seemingly natural authority of feeling and the authenticity of individual experience. We show that this turn to 'feelings-evidence' has a history, rooted in the increasing legitimacy of 'ordinariness' as a form of political expertise in post-war Britain but also influenced by long-standing Conservative, and newer neoliberal, privileging of individual experience over collective ideology.

In chapter 2, we shift our focus to how people understood the feelings of others as they made sense of new political divisions emerging in the aftermath of the referendum. We show how stereotypes of the unthinking Leave voter and patronising Remainer circulated, creating their own emotional economy, and how voters on both sides of the referendum defined themselves both through and in defiance of such scripts and the 'feeling rules' they entailed. In contrast to popular assumptions that Brexit represented a new form of 'post-truth' politics – where feelings trump facts – we draw attention to multiple, overlapping, and sometimes competing discourses surrounding the role of feelings in political life. We show how Mass Observers on both sides of the debate drew explicitly on critiques of 'post-truth' politics. They justified their own positions by asserting their rationality and denigrated those of others by deeming them too emotional. But this was not simply a case of dismissing feelings as improper to political life. We also see the racialised and classed deployment of civility and empathy, as 'feeling rules' long associated with political legitimacy.

Beyond 'heads vs hearts'

Taken together, these two chapters complicate the dominant narratives that understand Brexit as the consequence of an age of heightened emotion, where feelings have increasingly shaped political decision-making. Far from the clash between reason and passion presented in elite (liberal) discourses surrounding the referendum, instead we see a complex landscape, marked by contestation over the authority of different *types* of feelings. By historicising discourses surrounding the politics of feeling circulating 'from below', we contribute a more nuanced account of how feelings have come to be understood as a form of expertise in everyday life, and of the operations of power which determine whose feelings count. Further to this, we question dominant understandings of the referendum as a passionate rejection of neoliberal rationality, by showing how deeply neoliberal logics and sentiments (including rational self-interest) shaped Leave voters' self-understanding.

Throughout all of this, we argue, the problem is not that politics is emotional, but that (against the evidence of our lived experience) we expect it not to be. Even as our political culture valorises feelings as authentic reflections of our inner selves, it simultaneously reinforces the perception that they are separate from, and inferior to, reason. Political opinions therefore not only seem to encapsulate who we *are*, rather than what we *think*, but also highlight our personal failures to transcend this situation. At the same time, the lingering faith that there are 'right' answers raises the stakes of engaging in debate.

1
Voting decisions

During the referendum campaign, a repeated refrain circulated in news reports that voters would have to choose between their heads and their hearts. While their hearts resounded with a passionate desire to leave the EU, their heads were concerned about the economic impact of such a decision.[1] This binary choice between the patriotic feelings of the heart and the rational economic interests of the head was shared in stories about voters and smaller business owners, particularly in regional and national newspapers.[2] The well-known executive and Conservative peer Karren Brady, who also served as the government's Small Business Ambassador, wrote in her column for the *Sun*:

> I don't need to tell you it's not a simple decision to make. And I'm sure you, like most people, have a battle going on between your head and your heart. Certainly, I'm feeling a struggle. My heart is saying, 'I love my country, I want to protect it. We don't want anyone telling us what to do and we'd be OK on our own.' My mind, though, is telling me to overrule my heart. Sure, being part of the EU is far from perfect. I'm under no illusion. But there simply isn't a convincing enough argument to leave it either. To take the plunge and leave is a step so riddled with uncertainty that only chaos, confusion and economic catastrophe can result.[3]

Beyond 'heads vs hearts'

This trope was shared by political commentators who emphasised the important role feelings would play in shaping the referendum outcome and suggested that the Leave campaign was winning this battle for voters' hearts. The director of UK in a Changing Europe, Anand Menon, wrote in *The Times*: 'Ultimately, how much control you want your country to exercise over its own destiny is a matter for the heart as much as the head. For some people, the feeling of reasserting control would outweigh some of the economic pain resulting from Brexit. To what extent this is the case is one of the central issues that will determine the outcome of the vote.'[4] Simon Jenkins wrote in the *Guardian* about voters making their decision on the basis of gut instinct, and Gavin Hewitt explained for the BBC that, while the Remain campaign warned against wrecking the economy, 'The appeal of the Leave campaign is to the heart, to the gut. It resonates with those who feel alienated from politics, who feel powerless in the face of global forces like migration.'[5]

The unspoken assumption here was that there was a single 'rational' course of action and that the only conceivable political passion was for a patriotic (and nativist) reassertion of sovereignty. Neither rational arguments to leave the European Union nor internationalist sentiments were countenanced. The Leave campaign was perceived to be winning the battle for people's hearts by appealing to voters' patriotism and love for their country, their anger against out-of-touch bureaucrats and elites, and their resentment towards immigration, while simultaneously undermining the Remain campaign's appeal to voters' rational economic interests and anxieties, by attacking the credibility of experts and the establishment.

These arguments were picked up and shared by politicians and campaigners themselves. Nigel Farage explained during the campaign: 'People who've made up their minds on our side of the argument, it's almost like a conversion. Once you've decided, you believe it strongly, you tell your friends and family, and you're more likely to go out and vote'; in contrast, he suggested that Remain supporters 'might not be bothered to go down to the polling station and vote, because there's no passion'.[6] On the Remain side, David Miliband warned campaigners not to 'cede passion or patriotism to the other side' and to continue to fight to stay in the EU.[7] The former prime minister Sir John Major similarly identified 'the underlying mantra of the "out" campaign is – and I use their words – "I want my country back." It is an emotional appeal but a bogus one. If emotion triumphs over reality, we will lose power, prestige, security and some of our future economic well-being.'[8]

After the surprise referendum result, commentators worried that campaigners and voters had abandoned rationality in favour of passion. As John Curtice put it:

> Brexit has stirred up a degree of political passion of which, in the wake of the long-term decline in the strength of party identification, voters had long since seemed incapable. Perhaps the decline in party identification has always been more a consequence of a growing inability of parties to secure the affection, loyalty and commitment of voters than, as widely assumed, the emergence of a more rational, sceptical electorate that was no longer willing to invest emotionally in a political party or cause.[9]

In a context of 24-hour news cycles and social media, experts warned that instant reaction was taking precedence over considered judgement.[10] Citizens were thinking fast when they should be thinking slow.[11] People were trusting their feelings instead of evidence and facts. These narratives circulated in mass media reports, intensifying the perception that this was an unprecedented 'Age of Emotion'.[12] This was the context in which Oxford Dictionaries declared 'post-truth' to be its international word of 2016, defining it as 'circumstances in which objective facts are less influential in shaping public opinion than appeals to emotion and personal belief'.[13]

Yet, as we saw in the Introduction, to suggest politics has become more emotional is simplistic, ahistorical, and disregards a significant body of research in both political science and the history of emotions. In this chapter, we also show that it runs against the way that citizens understood their own voting decisions. By examining the stories they told about the referendum, we show that, rather than balancing the competing demands of 'head and heart', both Leave and Remain supporters justified their decision-making in terms of 'gut feeling'. Gut feelings about Brexit were represented as an apolitical, morally neutral source of knowledge, which depended upon the seemingly natural authority of feeling and the authenticity of individual experience. We argue that these narratives about feelings obtained greater weight within the specific context of the referendum, due to the unhelpful campaigns and lack of clear information. Yet we also highlight that these narratives reflect longer-term trends, including the decline in political parties functioning as useful heuristics and the valorisation of 'ordinariness' as a form of political expertise.

Heads vs hearts?

The 'heads and hearts' trope repeated in elite discourse surrounding Brexit highlights the presence of two competing narratives – or what could be described as 'feeling rules' – shaping popular understandings of political decision-making. On the one hand, the trope was used normatively to undermine the Leave campaign by casting them as being emotional *instead of* rational. This reflected the long-standing (if misleading) assumption that western political thought privileges reason over emotion in political decision-making, which we examine further in chapter 2. The Leave campaign was therefore seen to contravene the feeling rule that political decision-making should be based on reason, rationality, and objectivity. On the other hand, the perceived failure of the Remain campaign's appeal to reason and cost–benefit calculation helped to reinforce a second feeling rule, which suggested that politicians had ignored voters' feelings for too long and should now rectify this by appealing to their passions – imagined almost exclusively in terms of patriotism.

Despite the prevalence of this trope among commentators, Mass Observers rarely articulated a distinction between 'head' and 'heart'. Indeed, only one respondent framed their decision in those precise terms: 'My head says we should stay in, whilst my heart calls for me to come out.'[14] A handful of Leave voters described placing questions of personal and collective identity, the need for control, and expressions of resentment above material or political considerations. One explicitly said that he had voted 'Regardless of the economic issues', adding that he 'would rather be a poor little Englander than a poor and oppressed vassal of the EU'.[15] Another explained that she 'came to resent the feeling that we no longer had the power or the ability to live our own lives and determine our own future, without interference or direction from "Europe"'.[16] In her view, this 'loss of sovereignty … easily outweighed all pro-Europe arguments'.[17] A retired community worker from Sheffield who ended up abstaining was the only other respondent who distinguished their 'head' from their 'heart':

Beyond 'heads vs hearts'

> I intend to vote in the forthcoming European Union Referendum. But despite my efforts to discover the pros and cons of remaining or leaving – I still lack conclusive evidence one way or the other ... I am following news of the referendum via all forms of the media – newspapers, radio, television – and the internet. But the more I read, see and hear – the more confused I become ... But I shall vote – and I shall be voting with my heart as my head remains confused.[18]

Other respondents shared this Observer's dissatisfying search for conclusive evidence, which we discuss below. The key point here is that most voters did not attempt to separate their feelings (for either Leave or Remain) into those that came from the 'head' and the 'heart'. 'Feeling' was deployed in ways that encompassed both organs and combined them into a form of political intuition. It was also used in ways that challenged the automatic association between passion and patriotism. Many Remain voters invoked a 'feeling' of political unity with the EU. As one put it: 'a lot of people are just saying if you don't know, vote with your heart. My heart says remain; I think the future is about more unity and less borders, more global citizenship and less nationalism'.[19] While this was an argument from the 'heart', it was explicitly also underpinned by political 'think[ing]'. Other Observers who made similar points were more reluctant to acknowledge the interaction of feeling and thinking, presenting their political reasoning as purely a matter of 'feeling':

> I had heard various people on the TV and radio giving their points of view and how it would affect them and I just had this feeling that I would be happier to remain than to leave. I felt if we were just on our own how could we get any help from anyone?[20]

A 35-year-old self-employed writer from Renfrewshire admitted she did not have great knowledge of the workings of the EU but noted that 'it feels better to be part of something; contributing to something bigger, than peering in from the outside'.[21]

A similar dynamic can be seen in the way Leave supporters described their feelings about sovereignty. A 26-year-old administrative assistant explained that it made her 'feel uncomfortable that people in their millions are governed and controlled by a force we have no say over', while a 53-year-old locksmith 'felt it's wrong to pay someone in Brussels to tell me what I can and can't do'.[22] Likewise, an engineering works manager from Wiltshire described that he wanted 'to regain what I felt was a sense of destiny, rather than being forced to accept the resolve of unelected people in Europe'.[23] A retired banker from West Sussex resented

> the increasing way in which the EU was imposing its laws upon us. I wanted us to regain our sovereignty and take control of our own laws. Our forebears fought wars to prevent German domination of Europe, but this now seems to be happening surreptitiously ... the feeling has strengthened bearing in mind the way in which we are being treated by the EU leaders.[24]

These are arguments grounded in what the historian Claire Langhamer calls 'feelings-evidence', whereby (as we will see below) the personal intuition and experience of 'ordinary' people have become an increasingly legitimate form of political knowledge. Just like the post-war Mass Observers whose responses Langhamer examined, the Brexit respondents were also 'seeking to relate their feelings to evidence; indeed often using their feelings *as* evidence'.[25] In the words of an artist, also from West Sussex: 'I voted to remain but a not very well thought out remain. It just seemed so obvious to remain that I didn't really think in terms of pluses and minuses.'[26]

Their stories – whether about losing sovereignty or benefiting from actively participating in European decision-making – clearly reflect prominent discourses shared by both the campaigns and the media. Yet the MO respondents presented these arguments as a form of embodied intuition. Contrary to popular belief, they did not think in terms of choosing between their heads and hearts but employed their feelings in ways that encompassed both emotion and reason. Their testimony reveals that voters rarely made an unambiguous distinction between facts and feelings; instead, the two combined in a form of intuition that was implicitly (and sometimes explicitly) informed by information and media discourses that had soaked into their consciousness. This is only surprising from the relatively recent psychological perspective that separates emotions from rational and moral judgements, rather than more nuanced pre-Victorian notions of 'affections' and 'moral sentiments'.[27] Yet, our findings also highlight a dissonance between Observers' experiences of and beliefs about feelings.

Gut feelings

We were struck by how many Observers reported relying on their 'gut feelings' or 'gut instincts'. Again, this had been present in media commentary on the campaign (and, as we saw above, was occasionally used as a synonym for 'heart'[28]).[29] It is also consonant with academic understandings of emotions as simultaneously corporeal and mental.[30] As described in the Introduction, the 'dual process' decision theory identifies two distinct yet complementary types of thinking that guide human action. System 1 is a form of instinctive fast thinking guided by emotion-related associations. System 2 is a form of deliberative slow thinking guided by reason and logic. Cognitive psychologists and neuroscientists have emphasised how the two systems are intertwined: decision-making becomes embodied as reciprocal communication between the affective and sensorimotor neural regions, blurring the boundaries between perception, action, and cognition.[31] When it comes to decision-making, ultimately, how we feel in the moment will shape how we deliberate.[32]

If decision-making is an embodied experience, 'gut feeling' is the vernacular concept that captures this sensation – and has been described by the psychologist Gerd Gigerenzer as 'the intelligence of the unconscious'.[33] We can see the language of 'gut feeling' in a range of professional discourses. Business leaders are frequently encouraged to use their head (logic), heart (emotions), and gut (intuitions) to make more effective decisions.[34] Likewise, in the NHS, midwives use a BRAIN acronym, which asks expectant parents to consider the benefits, risks, alternatives, instinctive reactions, and implications of not acting when making decisions during and after labour.[35] In political science, Eric Groenendyk describes gut feelings as shortcuts that shape political attitudes and preferences often below the level of conscious awareness. He suggests gut feelings are frequently drawn upon by voters in contexts where the 'head' might feel confused or conflicted over a specific candidate or issue, or where the 'heart' may lack any strong feeling of attachment to a party, candidate, or issue. Thus, gut feelings reconcile this distinction between head and heart and help conflicted or ambivalent voters make political decisions.[36] So, although decision-making has traditionally been viewed as a rational process where reason calculates the best way to achieve a goal, contemporary discourses focus on the role of intuition. Reason and emotion are therefore no longer pitted against one another but understood to work in tandem to guide individuals' decision-making.

If expert opinion is increasingly focused on the role of gut feelings in decision-making, we need to ask where these ideas come from. How do they fit into the broader systems of knowledge that have made the contemporary political moment? And how do they intersect with (and contribute to) popular understandings of the relationship between knowing, thinking, and feeling? If political scientists are increasingly likely to weigh voters' gut feelings as a factor in their decision-making, how do voters themselves see this process? What moral, political, and social judgements does it entail? And how is the recourse to gut feeling judged itself in turn?

In the rest of this chapter, we show that gut feelings were represented by both Leave and Remain supporters as a form of embodied expertise. We historicise these vernacular claims, suggesting they build on conservative discourses that stress the natural authority of feeling in response to the unknowable, which was accentuated by the specific task of voting in the referendum. The recourse to 'gut feeling' as a form of expertise also fits with longer-term trends that have seen the categories of 'ordinariness' and personal authenticity privileged, whilst the social and political have been denigrated.

Feelings-evidence

The recourse to 'gut feeling' was particularly prevalent among Remain voters and tended to align with the arguments for political unity made on the basis of a more general 'feeling', which we examined above. For instance, a pharmacist from Solihull explained that she had 'no real knowledge of whether Britain is better off in Europe' but had a 'gut feeling that we should not be alone'.[37] Similarly, a waitress and student from Cheshire described how 'my gut reaction is that we should stay in the EU, I feel that we work better together and we as a nation have a responsibility not just to look after number one'.[38] A 43-year-old charity funding development worker from Derbyshire, whose 'gut instinct' was similarly that the UK should stay, explained that this was partly a matter of wanting to 'vote the opposite' to Leave campaigners like Nigel Farage and Boris Johnson, who were 'like throwbacks to the 1950s in their attitudes and values. They feed my gut instinct'.[39] A community health worker conceded that 'The EU, like most – if not all – big political organisations, is corrupt and full of red tape and it isn't perfect. But my gut feeling is that it's better to be a part of something and to try to influence changes from within than to sit outside of it.'[40] Likewise, this air traffic services assistant from Southampton pointed out:

> I can honestly say I do not mind which decision is made. My gut feeling is to remain. My children's opinions matter as it is their world which we are deciding on. Either way, make it work. In these weeks leading up to the referendum I don't think my opinion has changed drastically since I began thinking about it and made up my mind. I have grown increasingly despairing of the lies and misinformation, and more baffled and disengaged with the process as it appears most people have.[41]

As we have already suggested, the gut feeling trope was far more prevalent than that of balancing head and heart, and was often attributed to having insufficient information to make a purely cognitive decision. A 50-year-old administrator from Birmingham outlined the problem:

> I find it difficult to write about this topic. There is so much conflicting information coming from politicians and the media that I find it hard to know what to think ... I voted to remain in the European Union last June. It was not a particularly issue-driven decision; rather it was my first gut reaction ... Although I have typically felt more British than European, I am interested in many different aspects of European culture, and also conscious of (and embarrassed by) the UK's reputation for xenophobia and isolationism.[42]

Despite noting his inability to think about the issues, this response could also be read as an attempt to set aside his personal identity in favour of wider moral and political concerns. The interaction between consciousness and embarrassment also indicates the complex mix of cognition and emotion in play. This relationship also operated in the other direction. A 36-year-old scriptwriter from Bury who 'thought A LOT about it and was obsessed with the news coverage', explained that she 'thought about why did I vote to Remain' and concluded that 'It was always my gut instinct ... I liked being part of the EU, part of something bigger. I liked being in the EU queue at the airport and feeling we were connected.'[43] While this Observer cannot be dismissed as unthinking or uninformed, her drive to understand was clearly informed and supported by her intuition.

While we encountered the recourse to 'gut feeling' more frequently among the responses of Remain voters, it was also used by Leavers. A carer from Sunderland explained: 'I believe people do have a civic duty to vote though, so I will do so anyway even if I have to trust my gut instinct – it's probably what 90% of the people voting will be doing anyway, if they're honest.'[44] An online jewellery retailer from Salisbury explained her vote on the basis of an overwhelming sense of 'a million reasons, all of them personal.

They can't be generalised' and suggested this was understandable because 'Referendums are by their nature reductive, boiling down a complex thing to be put to the electorate ... Of course people are having a gut reaction to such a blunt question.'[45] One 69-year-old retired nursery teacher repeatedly and helplessly suggested that she had no option but to rely on 'gut feeling' in the face of a deluge of contradictory information:

> after the initial arguments I was fairly drawn to the idea of Brexit but determined to keep an open mind. Since then I watched and read until I have reached saturation point. Is anything clearer than it was? Of course not ... apparently there are 'facts' to consider but amazingly these can be totally different depending on which camp you belong to. Everything else is conjecture. Nobody can actually predict the outcomes. So how do we decide? Gut feeling probably... [original ellipses] Will we all be Muslim citizens in two generations if we remain in? Will we be blown up or raped in the streets by foreigners if we stay in? So many questions and no solid answers. What can we rely on? Our vision of the country we hold dear? Common sense? Gut feeling?[46]

Her account of the questions and arguments she was weighing speaks of a highly emotive public debate, as well as a disturbing web of prior assumptions and associations. The way this Observer responded to information overload by creating her own form of expertise, drawn from her 'feelings-evidence', is particularly explicit.[47] Her linking of a 'vision of the country we hold dear', 'Common sense', and 'Gut feeling' in opposition to threats from imagined 'foreigners', and particularly Muslims, illustrates Sara Ahmed's point about the way the 'reading of others as hateful' is able to 'produce' or to 'animate an imagined ordinary subject, to bring that fantasy to life, precisely by constituting the ordinary as in crisis, and the ordinary person as the *real victim'*.[48] We will examine the racialised logics at work in this account – and others like it – in chapter 2. For now, let us stick with the repeated turn to 'gut feeling'.

Embodied expertise

We need to ask what the recourse to 'gut feeling' was doing as a form of argument. It could, for instance, be read as a performance of political modesty, disavowing specialist knowledge. This was particularly resonant when Observers recorded their doubts about the ability of 'ordinary' people to make such an important decision. In the absence of 'correct' answers, gut feeling was represented as an apolitical, morally neutral source of knowledge, which could not be disputed:

> Forget making judgements about the future, so much about Europe as it is today is unknown that voters are likely to decide on the basis of crude gut instinct, probably acquired from the increasing number of dubious sources.[49]

> I have no knowledge of the pros and cons, not having exhaustively studied the merits of the matter but, like most people in this country am dependent entirely on the propaganda showered upon us by the various activists. So, I shall decide on my own feelings, whether supposedly intelligent or not.[50]

Some wrote of their embarrassment at their lack of knowledge:

> I am ashamed to confess that I know virtually nothing about this subject other than how vitally important it is. I intend to vote because I feel that I should. I will vote to remain in the EU. This is my gut feeling & it is only based upon my thinking that all the nations should be helping one another & sticking together. I imagine that the key issues are focussed around trade on an international basis. I know a lot of literature has been posted to me but I have not taken the time to

read it. I know that I should do. ... I do not watch the news & I rarely read the paper so the only news [I] really know of is just the brief headlines on the radio. Therefore any news coverage will not affect this brief & pathetic response. Sorry![51]

In other cases, it is difficult to know whether the recourse to gut feelings was defiant or apologetic. One 42-year-old National Health Service manager wrote simply: 'Don't care. Will vote, but it's an uninformed instinctive thing rather than a careful and rational choice' but then sent an updated response after the result explaining that she was 'an IN voter' who could 'see only benefits to membership of the EU' and that 'nothing the Remain camp said (or insinuated) changed my mind'.[52] It is not clear whether this was a typing error or a declaration of independence from influence of any kind. She was not alone in asserting that 'No politician of whatever persuasion will make me change my mind'.[53] A care worker from Sunderland expressed similar sentiments when he wrote admiringly: 'What shocked me most about the referendum is that so many people actually had the guts to vote to leave rather than stick with what they know.'[54] Such statements can be read as claims to personal authenticity, pitched against politicians, the media, and other voters. This aligns with Langhamer's point that emotional claims can be used as a tool for subversion and resistance – especially when feelings and perceived cultural expectations are in conflict. Expertise becomes embodied within the individual because the veracity of feeling is difficult to dispute.[55]

The embodiment of expertise raises questions about vernacular understandings of how (and, indeed, where) decision-making is located in the body. Movement between gut feeling and gut instinct in the preceding quotes of this section implies that these are relatively fluid and unstable categories. In Linda Åhäll's words, sensation is important precisely because it leaves individuals 'with an impression that is not clear or distinct'.[56] This indistinct – yet unshakeably bodily – sensation that something is not right is arguably what makes feelings so powerful in shaping intersubjective relations and judgements. But this ambiguous sense of 'embodied expertise' also needs to be historicised. How people interpret their feelings and draw upon them to narrate and explain their political decision-making is shaped by the norms and values of the specific context in which they find themselves.[57] We argue that MO respondents' recourse to their gut instincts should be understood within the twin contexts of long-standing conservative discourses emphasising the natural authority of feeling – in which sensation takes priority over reason – and of neoliberal subjectivity, which stresses individual morality over social and political intervention.

Historicising the turn to gut feelings

The treatment of feeling as a privileged way of knowing is deeply rooted in Conservative thought. Throughout the twentieth century, Conservative thinkers, politicians, and activists expressed scepticism about the abstractions of reason and emphasised instead the extent to which their politics derived from innate feelings and dispositions, which were presented as natural and unpolitical. Rather than a doctrinal position, Toryism was believed to be 'only a special kind of way of being British'.[58] Yet, while personal experience and sensation were privileged over reason or collective political claims, this was not about individual authenticity so much as belief in a shared cultural and racial inheritance, which might be transmitted through sights, sounds, tastes, and smells. Indeed, the increasing political legitimacy of *individual* feeling and self-expression in the post-war years, which we noted earlier, posed an existential challenge to this mode of politics. Common sense, after all, depended upon a *common* set of values and interests, which could be intuited precisely because it was embedded in social and political hierarchies.[59]

On first sight, Conservatism's privileging of intuition appears to conflict with neoliberalism's celebration of the invisible hand of the market. Yet, while neoliberalism is often seen as a rational system, based on atomised individuals pursuing a calculated idea of self-interest – '*homo economicus*' in Foucault's terminology[60] – recent studies have emphasised that its original formulations relied on the belief that societies are held together by organically evolved and inherited customs and morals.[61] The socially conservative and economically liberal strands of Thatcherism were not, then, as contradictory as they might appear. Moreover, despite their emphasis on intuition over reason, the feeling rules associated with both were explicitly *un*emotional, building on a Conservative tradition that valorised self-control and emotional restraint as national characteristics.[62]

Yet, neoliberalism as a governing project emerged in societies already shaped by social democratic and social liberal notions of the inherent worth, value, and rights of the individual and by the radical turn to individual consciousness during the 1960s. The shift from a 'culture of restraint' to a 'new, more emotionally charged, "culture of sensation"' was already embedded.[63] Indeed, it was a new vernacular sense of anti-deferential popular individualism that arguably allowed Thatcherism to take root.[64] It has even been suggested that the latter 'worked with the grain of the 1960s' – picking up the anti-authoritarian and anti-establishment impulses of the counterculture with its 'rhetoric of self-determinism, classlessness and meritocracy'.[65] Even movements which explicitly pitted the 'common sense' of an imagined 'silent majority' against the supposed indulgence of individual self-expression drew their political authority from individual feelings, transforming '"private" sensibilities' into 'new public, political forces'.[66] The rhetoric of these movements was often deeply physical, drawing on the body and embodied feelings in order to reinforce the 'naturalness' of conservative moral traditions.[67]

The recourse to gut feeling in vernacular understandings of decision-making performs a similar function to the assertion of 'ordinariness', as a denial of being 'political'. Claire Langhamer (drawing on the work of Catherine Neveu and John Clarke) has traced the development of the category of 'ordinary citizen', which obtained power from its association with an independent, detached, apolitical individual, whose beliefs were seen to be less biased, and more genuine or 'authentic', than those of individuals representing specific group, collective, or corporate interests.[68] We can see this dynamic particularly clearly in studies of working-class women's industrial activism in post-war Britain, in which oral history interviewees frequently denied the political nature of their participation and challenged perceptions they were doing anything extraordinary or suspect by asserting their ordinariness.[69] While there are specific, gendered reasons why these women might want to privilege their role as 'ordinary' women, wives, and mothers over their political activism, we can also see similar dynamics at work in other contexts, including Nina Eliasoph's study of local volunteers and activists in the United States.[70] In a context of rising anti-political sentiment, individuals are reluctant to identify as political out of fear it implies they are motivated by ulterior, ideological forces. But this in turn fuels the perception that politics is itself neither an 'ordinary' activity nor pursued in the interests of 'ordinary people'.

Many critiques of contemporary politics have noted the evacuation of the territory of both ordinariness and emotion by mainstream (neo)liberal politics, claiming that this leaves both areas open to co-option by populists.[71] Yet, our sources tell a different story. We see repeated pleas for dispassionate debate and uncontested facts – even for clear sources of authority, and for the removal of the responsibility for this decision from 'ordinary' people like themselves. But while Observers explicitly reacted against the disconcerting sense that political and epistemic authority had collapsed, in navigating this situation they drew on the very same feeling rules that had created it. They asserted the authority of their feelings in order to show that they were authentic, independent, and autonomous and that they had not been hoodwinked by a specific campaign or ideology, while simultaneously insisting that it should be possible to make a 'purely rational' decision.

An unhelpful campaign

So far, we have shown that both Leave and Remain supporters emphasised the importance of 'gut feelings' when deciding how to vote in the 2016 EU referendum and traced this back to the valorisation of ordinariness and strengthened authority of feeling in post-war British political culture. In the rest of this chapter, we show how this common narrative about feelings was also a clear response to more short-term uncertainty about Brexit in a context of political distrust.[72]

Beyond 'heads vs hearts'

Respondents to Mass Observation were particularly angry about the referendum campaign, which they saw as confusing, unhelpful, and unreliable. A library manager from Norwich reported: 'The campaign has been dirty and scaremongering with personalities having too much air/print time and experts like economists silenced.'[73] A retired civil servant from South Tyneside was 'very disappointed with the tenor and substance of the referendum campaign' and went on to explain: 'what's most depressed me has been the utter parochialism of the debate'.[74] Other respondents expressed their disappointment more intensely. An electronics engineer from Southport was 'completely disgusted' by both David Cameron and George Osborne, who had 'done nothing but tell lies and used scare tactics in the worse possible way. I find them both abhorrent for the way they have behaved during this campaign.'[75] A student from East London reflected: 'This debate will go down in history. Not just because of the result but because of the nature of the debate. It was fought often quite disgracefully and blindly. On both sides politicians lied to the general public.'[76] A Scottish teacher wrote in her diary weeks before polling day: 'I've lost the will to live. I am sending in this Directive now, not later. Sick, sick of politicians and their claims and counter claims.'[77] This complaint about claims and counterclaims was widely shared; a student from Southampton summarised the challenge facing voters:

> I think one of the main problems with the EU Referendum and campaigners on both sides is that they have clouded the issue by resorting to almost propaganda claims and fearmongering. ... Who is to be believed? So many different news channels say different things that it is hard to know what to believe and whether we will be better off one way

or the other. It is quite sad that news channels are being so biased, pushing forward their agendas ... It is for this reason that I am unsure which side I want to vote for.[78]

The tone of debate caused some Mass Observers to switch off and withdraw. A self-employed respondent from Newcastle described herself as 'bored of the entire "debate". It is another opportunity for ministers to argue. I am actively avoiding the media coverage and therefore bow out of this part of the activity.'[79] This administrator from Birmingham felt the same: 'As with the last general election, the constant reiteration of each side's accusations and counteraccusations (many of them hypothetical) have had a numbing effect on me.'[80] A communication support worker from London explained: 'The referendum has dominated the news for the past week or two and a lot of the coverage is about the two sides criticising each other ... I'm finding it extremely boring.'[81] And a software engineer in Devon wrote about how he was 'trying to avoid news coverage about the EU' and suggested, 'It doesn't help and just descends into calling the other side liars, fearmongering and/or racism. I have started to believe I would be better off trying to psychically intuit whether we would be better off in or out than polluting my brain with this.'[82] Despite its slight sarcasm, this response encapsulates how many respondents understood their decision-making process during the referendum campaign – they wanted to base their decision on an evaluation of the costs and benefits of EU membership, but that information was not forthcoming.

Disappointment with the nature of the campaign was widely shared by both Leave and Remain supporters from different backgrounds across the country. As we will see in chapter 3, many people felt bored by the campaign and switched off. Here we want to focus on the implications of respondents' experience of the campaign for how they understood their decision-making. A common complaint was nobody knew what would happen if Britain left or remained in the EU. A community health worker in her forties from the East Midlands was disappointed that 'neither side can categorically and truthfully say what will happen'.[83] The problem was put clearly by a student in his twenties from north-west England: 'It is impossible to have facts about the future. There can only be speculation.'[84] A nurse from Southport complained: 'It's very confusing as we are being fed conflicting information everyday [sic]. I really don't know which way I will vote.'[85] In the words of this carer from the north-east: 'It would be nice to find reliable and unbiased sources of data about the subject so that I could make an educated guess.'[86] A retired civil servant who was also from the north-east complained that 'there's no completely disinterested and impartial person, institution, or corpus of knowledge out there to whom appeals for advice and accurate information on the merits and drawbacks of EU membership can be directed'.[87]

The absence of clear information left many Mass Observers feeling ill-informed and uncertain about how to vote. This raises some questions about the dominant narrative that the referendum was a result of polarisation. Polarisation requires positive 'in-group' attachments alongside detachment from those with opposing views. On the contrary, Mass Observers' uncertainty and confusion indicate a lack of strongly held Leave or Remain identities during the campaign. For example, a waitress from Cheshire wrote: 'Will definitely vote though at the moment I am not sure ... that I am informed enough.'[88] A student in his twenties from north-west England wrote:

Voting decisions

'I just don't know what to think.'[89] A civil servant from Bath agreed: 'I expect I will vote to stay in, but to be honest I don't think I really know all the implications of either option..., I'm afraid that both sides have put up convincing arguments, and as such this hasn't helped me make up my mind.'[90] A writer in North Ayrshire expressed similar levels of uncertainty: 'I will vote in the EU referendum, and I'm pretty sure I'll vote to stay in, although I'm not certain yet.'[91]

Some respondents expressed the idea that 'ordinary people' like themselves should not have been asked to make this decision. There were Remain supporters who saw the referendum as a means of solving a problem within the Conservative Party: 'Cameron should never have initiated the referendum, but wanted to squash Ukip', explained a retired teacher in Exeter.[92] An IT manager in Cambridge agreed: 'I'm not sure that, political aspirations aside from the Conservative party, there is need for a referendum.'[93] A project manager from Brighton reported: 'There is a lot of anger amongst the people I speak with. Anger that the referendum happened in the first place (it was completely unnecessary, a way of Cameron solving an internal squabble in his party...)', and went on to ask, 'should we have been given a referendum on such a complex and nuanced issue? How can you capture all of that in a yes/no answer? We elect politicians to make difficult decisions for us.'[94] Disappointment about the outcome clearly drove many of these responses. But we also see wider doubts about the electorate's *ability* to make this judgement. A caseworker asked: 'Why are we having this referendum?' before answering their own question: 'solely because Cameron could not manage the Tory party. The general public are not educated enough to make this decision. What are they basing their ideas on, myths and hysteria in the right-wing media?'[95] A retired teacher from Birmingham felt the same:

> There should not be a referendum. We have been presented with convincing arguments by thoughtful people on both sides so how can <u>we</u> know what to vote? The government should never have sent out a one-sided leaflet; they should have given us pros and cons. It is ridiculous to accept a simple majority in favour of Brexit; such an important change should require a large majority.[96]

A community health worker from Nottingham shared similar concerns: 'I don't want to have to be involved in making such a monumental decision' and went on to suggest: 'the politics of this issue are very intricate and I'm finding it difficult to get a clear understanding of it all. Politicians are paid and elected to make these decisions. I know they don't always get it right, but it should be their job to sort these things out, not ordinary people.'[97] A civil servant from Bath agreed: 'I am really annoyed that the Conservatives have left such an important decision to the electorate. I really do believe that the public are stupid enough to be swayed by the media, and I see the government as abdicating its responsibility to govern .... The general feeling amongst everyone I've spoken to is one of disenchantment and cynicism.'[98]

We have shown that Mass Observers' recourse to gut feeling built on established (and historically specific) modes of justifying political decision-making that privilege embodied expertise and the natural authority of feeling. But we have also seen that feelings took on even greater legitimacy in the specific context of the campaign itself. People wanted to make informed decisions based on impartial information about 'what would happen' if Britain left or remained in the EU. Such information was not forthcoming from the campaign itself, which left them feeling confused and uncertain. Many doubted their own and the wider public's ability to make this decision. Within this context, Mass Observers became increasingly conscious of the role of instinct in their decision-making. This team leader from an insurance company in Bristol highlighted the link between uncertainty and his reliance on instinct: 'rather than being educated about both sides of the argument, I feel – as usual in the run up to an election – I have been hit by a barrage of scare mongering and vague guesses about the future. Consequently I still don't feel knowledgeable about such a major decision. What I do know is that my instinct is to be part of Europe rather than pulling up the drawbridge.'[99]

Post-truth and the decline of valence politics

Since the referendum in 2016, a range of popular books have been published declaring that we are now living in an age of 'post-truth' politics.[100] The guiding idea here is that political actors promote misinformation and fake news, whilst voters make decisions on the basis of feelings instead of facts. Populist and anti-elite movements are seen to have achieved success by rejecting basic principles of reason and spreading mistrust of authoritative 'experts'. Political scientists like Colin Hay and Cyril Benoît have suggested in a more moderated form that we are witnessing the decline of valence politics, whereby people no longer base their decision-making on a cost–benefit analysis of a specific issue.[101] For Hay, the Leave campaign's victory in 2016 is largely explained by its approach to Brexit as a positional issue – defined as 'a question of raw, almost visceral, political preference'; in contrast, the Remain campaign approached Brexit as a valence issue – defined as a 'dry almost technical question of determining the policies by which uncontroversial shared ends can be achieved'.[102]

These analyses are underpinned by assumptions similar to the 'head and heart' rhetoric we examined above. They understand Brexit as a rejection of established depoliticised forms of governance, whereby voters made rational judgements of politicians' competence in handling issues perceived to constitute the public good, and politicians placed positional issues in the hands of independent 'experts'. In contrast, they argue, Leave supporters sought to 'take back control' not only from the EU but also from expert governance. Hay supports this assertion with evidence from the 2016 British Election Study showing that 80 per cent of those who agreed with the proposition 'I'd rather put my trust in the wisdom of ordinary people than the opinion of experts' voted for Brexit.[103]

The idea that Brexit represents the rejection of rational expertise is premised on an interpretation of British political history centred around the decline of the mass party and the increasing individualisation of voters' behaviour. Various literatures on 'cognitive mobilisation', the decline of deference, and the rise of anti-political sentiment point towards an electorate that is less likely to defer to elite authority, trust politicians, or identify with political parties than in the immediate post-war period, which is sometimes understood as a 'golden age' of mass parties.[104] These narratives all share the assumption that voters hold (and have always held) inconsistent and ill-informed views about politics but that in the past this mattered less because they were willing to be guided by the political establishment.

In a recent development of this argument, Jonathan Hopkin and Ben Rosamond quote a 1954 critique of voters:

Voting decisions

> For many voters political preferences may better be considered analogous to cultural tastes...Both seem to be matters of sentiment and disposition rather than 'reasoned preferences'. While both are responsive to changed conditions and unusual stimuli, they are relatively invulnerable to direct argumentation and vulnerable to indirect social influences. Both are characterized more by faith than by conviction and by wishful expectation rather than careful prediction of consequences.[105]

And yet, as they note, at this time political parties and trade unions were trusted to produce policy proposals that represented the broader collective interests of different social groups. In their words, 'the classic "mass party" had not only a robust organisational apparatus to root it deep in the fabric of society, but also a set of ideological beliefs that could serve as a heuristic for voters in evaluating the likely consequence of different policy choices'. The subsequent decline in political trust and party identification means parties no longer fulfil this role, and so 'voters are left to make judgements about complex matters they understand poorly, under unreasonable time constraints, with no discernible consequences for error'. They suggest it is therefore unsurprising that 'voters' political views are likely to be suffused with bullshit'.[106] What they mean by this is voters are likely to draw on narratives which, rather than being outright falsehoods, are misrepresentations indifferent to the truth and which proceed without concern for the veracity of the claim in question.

Hopkin and Rosamond's main argument is that this phenomenon pre-dates Brexit and is not confined to anti-elitist populist actors and their supporters. They demonstrate this through the widespread yet misguided belief, promoted by mainstream centre-left and centre-right parties, that the 2008 financial crisis was caused by loose fiscal policy and excessive spending which was used to justify austerity. The key point here is not that people have become more emotional or susceptible to bullshit than they were in the 1950s but that the hollowing out of democracy and decline of ideologically coherent parties have left a void filled by opportunistic political actors who perform the function of legitimating democratic government and communicating with citizens, without parties' intellectual and political substance.

The idea that we are living in an age of post-truth politics implies voters are wilfully choosing to make decisions on the basis of their feelings instead of facts in a new way. Hopkin and Rosamond's work shows that this claim is ahistorical, and the evidence found in Mass Observation supports their argument.[107] But the personal testimony considered in this chapter also shows that, even during the Brexit referendum, people did not actively choose to rely on their feelings in place of making a cost–benefit calculation. Mass Observers *wanted* their decision-making to be informed by facts from trusted sources but found themselves overwhelmed by competing claims which they were unable to filter. They were (rightly) sceptical about the campaign messages and keen to show that they would not be taken in by them. Instead, they turned to their feelings and instincts – sometimes defiantly, often reluctantly, and mostly from a position of uncertainty. These ways of making decisions are not necessarily new, but they were intensified in the context of a referendum campaign marked by the absence of elite cues and trusted political actors who could provide a heuristic to enable voters to negotiate this uncertainty more comfortably.

Conclusion

In this chapter, we have moved away from elite discourse and looked at the place of feelings in how people narrated and explained their own decision-making about Brexit. We showed that they did not distinguish between head and heart, as media narratives suggested, but instead drew upon their feelings as a form of embodied expertise.

The prominence of the two tropes of 'gut feeling' and the 'unhelpful campaign' in Mass Observers' stories about their Brexit votes points to the existence of multiple understandings of the role of feelings in political decision-making. The widespread dismay with the campaign shows that, despite narratives to the contrary, people want to see themselves as rational decision makers, ideally drawing on impartial knowledge and facts but also able to demonstrate scepticism and wariness of misinformation. That 'gut feeling' emerged as a substitute source of supposedly apolitical knowledge is more surprising. We showed that this turn to 'feelings-evidence' has a historical and political context, growing out of both conservative and neoliberal discourses that valorise ordinariness, common sense, and the natural authority of feeling, whilst simultaneously denigrating the social and political sphere. But we also suggested that these discourses gained heightened prominence amidst the specific context of the referendum and the uncertainty and unknowability it engendered.

Yet, despite this ambiguity surrounding the place of feeling in decision-making, we will see in the next chapter how the idea that voters could be divided into intuitive and rational categories on the basis of their voting decisions was deeply influential at a vernacular level as well as in media narratives. It shaped how voters understood their

Beyond 'heads vs hearts'

own position within the electorate – and how they judged the behaviour of others. These distinctions were not only deeply politicised and racialised but they also complicate popular understandings of the place of neoliberal sensibilities in the referendum campaign.

2
Judgements and stereotypes

In the previous chapter, we examined the idea that the referendum reflected a division between those who voted with their 'head' and those who were led by their 'heart'. Although we showed that this did not reflect the way that voters thought about their own decision-making processes, we suggested that this narrative did influence the way they judged those of others. In this chapter, we take that analysis further, examining how stereotypes of the unthinking Leave voter and patronising Remainer circulated, creating their own emotional economies; and showing how actors on both sides of the referendum defined themselves both through and in defiance of such scripts. Crucially, we argue that this should be understood not as the opposition between reason and passion but as a contest between the competing legitimacy of different sets of 'feeling rules'.

We also saw in chapter 1 how gut feelings were drawn upon as apolitical, neutral sources of knowledge to justify and explain Mass Observers' decision-making. But 'gut feelings' are obviously not neutral. As Ann Laura Stoler reminds us '"gut feelings" in psychology and cognitive science may be considered intuitive. But ... for those designated as racial others or precariously perched on racial divides, these gut feelings are a perilous beast, armed with discriminatory ammunition.'[1] Feelings are, then, not just a form of knowledge or expertise but measures of worth and value; and we use judgements about the feelings of other people as evidence of their character. Such judgements not only reflect but work to construct hierarchies of power by producing normative ideas about whose feelings count; whose feelings are legitimate or justified; whose feelings are irrational and selfish; whose feelings are subordinate to whom. In this chapter, we explore these questions further as our attention shifts away from how people understood the role of feelings in their own decision-making towards how they evaluated the feelings of others.

One of the (many) reasons the referendum was considered transformative is because it produced – or uncovered – key divisions which have continued to structure British politics in the period since 2016. In the immediate aftermath of the referendum, people were far more likely to report feeling a strong attachment to Remain or Leave than to a political party.[2] These emotional attachments were found to colour voters' interpretations of the Brexit process and policy outcomes more generally.[3] Maria Sobolewska and Rob Ford argue that the referendum provided labels for a latent political division between 'identity liberals' and 'identity conservatives' which had been present in British society since the 1960s.[4] They define identity conservatives as bound by an ethnocentric worldview that involves attachment to native in-groups and hostility to out-groups, while identity liberals oppose ethnocentrism as immoral and against their commitment to anti-prejudice norms. We are concerned less with the nature, veracity, or causes of these divisions than with how they were felt, experienced, and reproduced by individuals. We highlight the stereotypes surrounding

Judgements and stereotypes

Leave and Remain identities that were used to understand these emerging divisions.

In public discourse on the EU referendum, Leave was invariably cast as the emotional choice and Remain the rational one. It is not difficult to see where this distinction came from. It is, for instance, possible to read the whole European project as an attempt to overcome the dangers of emotional politics (particularly nationalism). Moreover, popular Euroscepticism has tended to characterise the EU as both coldly bureaucratic and disdainful of national particularity – despite its work in protecting regional food cultures and traditions. This has rubbed up against a romantic sense of British/English exceptionalism.[5] It also picks up on long-standing themes within Britain's political traditions, with Leave representing 'commonsense', 'authentic' conservative patriotism (and, to a lesser extent, romantic socialism) in the face of calculated rationality and 'sensible' centrism – whether liberal, social democratic, or conservative.[6] Yet, this is a very partial view of the complex attitudes towards political emotions within the various political traditions involved (as outlined in the Introduction). It is also a reductive characterisation of the long-standing debate over Britain's membership of the European Community, which has in fact been far more richly patterned on both sides.[7] Besides there being an unemotional 'technicist/modernist' strand to British Euroscepticism, the European project was rooted not only in passionate idealism but even in discourses of romantic love.[8] The accounts of Mass Observers show that something of this variegation survives in public feelings about the EU.

In chapter 1, we complicated the divisions between Leave and Remain voters, showing that, in the build-up to and immediate aftermath of the referendum, voters' descriptions of their decision-making revealed widespread uncertainty rather than clear articulations of distinct identities. This is important because polarisation requires not only a negative detachment from those with opposing views but also a positive attachment to one's own side. We also noted deep public unease and anxiety over the idea that the nation was dividing into polarised factions. In this chapter, we look in more depth at how Observers imagined these factions – how they described, labelled, and stereotyped those who had voted differently from themselves. In particular, we show how these divisions were articulated through a discourse of *feelings*, which imagined them simultaneously as dangerous and irrational; authentic and unanswerable; civilised and empathetic. Far from a clash between reason and passion, then, instead we see contestation over the authority of different *types* of feelings, and the 'feeling rules' through which they were expressed. In doing so, we challenge the idea that the Leave vote represented a backlash against a coldly rational neoliberal sensibility and draw attention to the political implications of such arguments.

The (il)legitimacy of feelings

The correct management of feelings has been one of the cornerstones of liberal modernity. Historians have shown how the global order of imperialism was founded on notions of 'civility', not only associated with the Scottish Enlightenment but reaching back further into the Jacobean period.[9] And while the emergence of discourses of sympathy, and later empathy, has been credited with enabling the conception of universal human rights,[10] it has also been shown to have underpinned imperialist narratives of racial difference, in which some were deemed more capable of refined feeling than others.[11] At the same time, the opposition between passion and reason was built on the gendered and racialised privileging of rational discourse as the preserve of white men.[12]

Within the political science literature, such work has been taken up to demonstrate how the bounds of contemporary political discourse continue to be policed in terms of linguistic norms of polite, rational conversation. Attention here has shifted from the policing of gendered and racialised emotional styles to the supposed silencing of working-class voices. Stephen Coleman, for instance, shows how eighteenth-century notions of civil discourse underpinned the adoption of a liberal democratic model that values all voices during elections but is underpinned by structural inequality and cultural hierarchies.[13] In Coleman's words, 'No longer disenfranchised, the vulgar and dispossessed are less likely to be silenced than ignored, ridiculed or classified as "chavs", "white trash", "the angry left-behind" or mere noise.'[14] Such interpretations have been particularly important to discussions of populism, with scholars in the tradition of Ernesto Laclau and Chantal Mouffe demonstrating how accusations of emotionality have been applied unevenly, with the effect of deeming certain kinds of political argument to be outside the bounds of civic discourse.[15] They note that even naming certain kinds of politics as 'emotional' is itself a way of suppressing them; and that, while this may now be used against populists, it is the same manoeuvre that has long been used to silence women, people of colour, and working-class politics.[16]

As pointed out by Stephen Coleman, disadvantaged social groups are excluded not just from getting what they need but also from interpreting what they need discursively. Discursive exclusion occurs as individuals dismiss a person's right to wellbeing and a person's moral accountability where 'they are considered incapable of speaking or answering for their own actions.' As we will see below, such interpretations have been applied to Leave voters. Yet, one of the ironies is that this group was far from silenced. Their concerns, feelings, and needs dominated public debate – albeit to the repeated refrain that this was an overdue correction. As we will see in this chapter, while the 'passionate' stereotype did work to undermine Leave voters' perceived ability to participate in democratic politics, it also served to legitimate their claims as something that required an urgent and sympathetic response.

It is important to note that class here is a racial category: invariably imagined as white.[17] And that, as Sadiya Akram has recently argued, not only was the British parliamentary system's privileging of 'reason' imbued with racialised logic from the start, but this has been simultaneously ignored and reproduced by political science.[18] The urgency with which the supposed 'silencing' of the 'white working class' has been addressed has been notably absent for those racialised as non-white. We might also observe how, during the Brexit campaign, strong emotion became gendered as masculine. While some of our sources depict Remain-supporting female politicians as 'screeching' and 'frothing',[19] the dominant image of the passionate Brexiteer was undeniably a white male – at its most extreme in the classed caricature of a red-faced angry man, described derogatorily as 'gammon' on social media.[20] This must of course be understood within the wider context of women's exclusion from public debate,[21] but it also had the effect of inverting the historical ways in which excess emotion and calm rationality have been gendered and racialised. Taken together, these reversals seem intimately connected with the way that the politics of victimhood have been appropriated by British nationalists and white supremacists.[22]

The idea that the Leave campaign successfully manipulated and appealed to public anger with the status quo has become an axiom in British politics. Much ink has been sacrificed to the topic of the 'left behind' and we are not interested in adding to it further, other than highlighting that this is a racialised affective category which ignores the actual composition of the British working class. It doesn't account for urbanised, multi-racial, migrant, and young working-class people and focuses solely on the feelings of an imagined homogeneous category of older white working-class men.[23] As Aurelien Mondon argues, it is an elite construction that works to legitimise reactionary anti-immigration politics, while simultaneously absolving liberal democratic institutions of responsibility for them, under the claim that they are simply enacting the will of 'the people'.[24] Rather than further adding to this (now well-established) critique of 'the left behind' as an analytical category, then, we focus on the 'throw' of this idea – how it circulated among Mass Observers and structured the response of both Leave and Remain voters to the referendum result.

Narratives of neoliberalism

As we saw in chapter 1, the Leave vote was presented by mainstream commentators as a backlash against neoliberal values. The nation was seen to be divided between cosmopolitan social liberals voting with their heads and communitarian social conservatives driven by their hearts. The former were at home in a globalising world and had benefited from a neoliberal culture, with its individualised imperative to continual self-improvement. They were competent, rational voters. The latter, the narrative ran, had been economically, culturally, and socially excluded. With little left to lose, political sentiment trumped perceived economic imperatives. They gave in to uninformed or irrational feeling and wilfully voted against their own interests in revulsion against neoliberal hegemony and thirty years of depoliticisation.[25]

As we will see below, this narrative has been enormously influential. And yet, if we approach it through the lens of individual subjectivity, it quickly begins to crumble. First of all, we might note that the two camps did not perceive themselves in this way. Remainers were as likely to emphasise their emotional investments in the topic, and Leavers (if anything) more likely to emphasise the logic of their position. Neither does this distinction hold true when we look at how people characterised those who had voted differently from themselves. Both sides accused the other of being emotional; neither was willing to relinquish the territory of rationality themselves. And yet, we do see significant differences in *how* feelings were conceived on both sides.

This brings us to the second point, which is that politically the Leave vote was far more closely aligned with actually existing neoliberalism in Britain. Its advocates may not have been judged to be its 'winners', but they tended to identify with both its logics and its sentiments – emphasising self-reliance, anti-welfarism, anti-bureaucracy, law and order, and racialised patriotism. They described leaving the EU as an escape from a dependency culture, both domestically and internationally. This was a position that lent itself to a *critique* of the increasing prominence of feelings in public life, seen as a symptom of cultural degeneration. In contrast, strong Remain identifiers tended to emphasise notions of collectivity, strong-statism, pacifism, internationalism, and (crucially!) empathy and fellow feeling. Many explicitly described EU membership as a bulwark against the worst effects of neoliberalism and praised its defence of workers' rights.

These contradictions show that both Brexit and a focus on everyday discourses surrounding feelings have implications for understandings of neoliberal subjectivity. In line with Ellen Boucher's analysis, they indicate the presence of multiple and overlapping sensibilities in place of a dominant structure of feeling guided by entrepreneurialism, self-reliance, and competition.[26] Debates provoked by Brexit and national populism more broadly highlight a complication in equating the neoliberal subject with the rational, calculative subject. Janet Newman suggests Brexit represents a departure from dispassionate registers of technocracy, which have been replaced by a politics of rage.[27] Similarly, Wendy Brown notes that we are now seeing subjectivities 'fashioned by neoliberal reason and its effects' but:

> far from the calculating, entrepreneurial, moral, and disciplined being imagined by Hayek and his intellectual kin, this one is angry, amoral, and impetuous, spurred by unavowed humiliation and thirst for revenge ... It does not need to be addressed by policy producing its concrete betterment because it seeks mainly psychic anointment of its wounds ... it is fuelled mainly by rancor and unavowed nihilistic despair. It cannot be appealed to by reason, facts, or sustained argument because it does not want to know, and it is unmotivated by consistency or depth in its values or by belief in truth.[28]

Neoliberalism was supposed to produce *homo economicus* – self-interested individuals guided by entrepreneurialism, self-discipline, and market values who 'respond systematically to modifications in the variables of the environment'.[29]

But the structural effects of actually existing neoliberalism instead produced new political communities not formed around objective interests or geography, but as affective publics through shared sentiment.[30] Yet, this shared sentiment often took the form of explicit hostility to cultures of self-expression or the recognition of identity, which were read as unreasonable and selfish demands, particularly when they came from marginalised communities.[31] Camilla Schofield has forcefully argued that the specific politics of UKIP can be traced to the 'crisis of white supremacy' that accompanied the end of Empire and the emergence of 'a reactionary discourse' that 'rejected any liberal "guilt complex"'.[32]

We can see evidence of such attitudes in two recent Mass Observation directives. In 2019, some respondents dismissed an inquiry about 'personal identity' as indicative of a tendency towards 'too much self-analysis, by half! Not an appropriate subject, in my view.'[33] Others explicitly condemned it as stemming from 'the whines of coloureds and Muslims that they are being "offended" by our customs and laws'.[34] The following year, this latter respondent (a retired nurse) recorded that her 'heart was filled with despair' to receive a directive on Black Lives Matter, on account of being 'fed up to the teeth [sic] hearing about BLM'. She also noted that 'The Mass Obs [sic] team should not worry about a lack of ethnically diverse participants – most of them cannot speak English properly.'[35] While these are narratives about race, culture, and nationhood, it is striking how often they are framed as transgressing emotional codes: introspection, whining, over-sensitivity. A retired teacher in Leicester dismissed the protests as 'hyped by those with a chip on their shoulder' and 'all part and parcel of the present trend to be insulted and offended at anything that is the opposite to your opinion ... We are nurturing a pramful of toddlers. God helps us all.' Yet her response was explicit in the way it revealed not only her prejudices ('Personally I find all the miscegenation distasteful') but also, with no trace of irony, her *own* insult and offence at not having them reflected in popular culture ('why have all the adverts on ITV got a proportion of black people?').[36]

Schofield traces such attitudes back through Powellism, and we will see later in this chapter that the genealogy she establishes has been explicitly embraced by at least some Leave supporters, as well as their apologists in the media. Yet, we should not assume that they are therefore confined to older generations. Alan Finlayson's recent research on the online alt-right shows how contemporary disdain for 'social justice warriors' is similarly underpinned by a sense that they are interfering in 'natural' hierarchies, and likewise coalesces around targets associated with a particular version of the neoliberal state: from bureaucrats and 'experts' to feminism and multiculturalism.[37]

In the rest of this chapter, we take a closer look at the multiple and competing stories Leave and Remain supporters shared about each other as they attempted to make sense of the divisions and identities thrown up by the referendum. We also highlight how these stories worked to reinforce the idea that the nation was dividing into two distinct imagined communities, with their own political norms and feeling rules.

'The ignoramus masses'

The staging of Brexit as a damaging mistake stems from the idea that it was fundamentally irrational. In line with the dominant media narrative, Remain supporters frequently portrayed Leave voters as irrational, uneducated, and motivated by negative emotions of fear and prejudice; they also expressed anger that they had made the 'wrong' decision based on the 'wrong' sources of information. Leave supporters were imagined to lack the necessary resources – cognitive, educational, socio-economic – to make a reasonable decision. These form the basis of three dominant stereotypes through which Remain voters described their opponents – and against which they defined themselves.

The first stereotype was that Leave voters were irrational. In the words of a 36-year-old teacher: 'As a nation we seem to be rejecting reason and logic and facts to feed our own sense of injustice.'[38] An air traffic services assistant from Southampton suggested the referendum result represented 'a stark warning against letting unthinking emotions or uninformed opinion get the better of our voting sensibilities',[39] and this administrator from Birmingham drew upon a similar binary: 'If I was to generalise, I might say that the people who voted to remain did so for pragmatic reasons whereas those who wanted to leave based their decisions on fantasy.'[40] A 50-year-old 'creative' put it starkly: 'Brexit supporters were and are irrational.'[41] Conversely, a 'correct' vote could be used as a proxy for assessing the rationality of others. One woman noted that shared support for Remain had cemented her friendships and even 'made me see my in-laws in a more favourable light as ... knowing that they had voted remain made me see them as rational and considerate at least for some aspects in life!'[42] Remain supporters thus reinforced the dominant (though discredited) idea of emotion as a base impulse, which can overwhelm the higher functioning of reason.

The second stereotype Remain supporters shared about Leave supporters was that they were uneducated and ignorant. In the words of a retired landlord in Cambridge: 'the

Judgements and stereotypes

main determinant that I saw was an educated view versus an uneducated view'.[43] A teacher from Northwich suggested that 'A lot of ordinary people who voted for Brexit appear not to fully comprehend the reason for their choice, nor the effect it will have on the country ... comments like "making Britain great" and "take control of our country" showed what I can only describe as ignorance in relation to the impact Brexit will have.'[44] In this case, ignorance was linked to a lack of understanding of one's political interests. It discredited Leave supporters as competent (rational) voters.

Finally, we see the idea that Leave supporters were whipped up by negative feelings of fear, prejudice, and racism. In the build-up to the referendum, a pharmacist from Solihull wrote: 'I was disturbed by the proportion of Leave posts on Facebook that seemed full of anger, hatred and fear.'[45] The tabloid press, and particularly the *Daily Mail*, were held responsible by many respondents. A retired civil servant singled out an extended family member who was 'a grotty little racist goblin and he kept quoting horror stories and fake statistics from the Daily Mail',[46] while the 'creative' quoted above commented: 'Surprisingly, some of my more intelligent friends also supported Brexit. Mostly convinced by the drip drip reporting in the tabloid newspapers, that Turkey were about to join, that we were being overrun.'[47] A charity fundraiser summed up the views of many with her comment that 'This referendum is probably going to be decided by Daily Mail readers. How depressing.'[48]

Disinformation, irrationality, and inappropriate feelings are tied tightly together in these accounts. Yet, even as they criticised the emotional tenor of the Leave campaign, Remain supporters expressed their own views in strongly emotional terms. This was often deeply classed, anglicised, and aged (though, perhaps surprisingly, not gendered). In the build-up to the referendum, one woman wrote: 'I'm dreading the ignoramus masses (the sort who would vote to bring back hanging ...) voting with their little Englander brains and their clichés, immigration, take back control, border control, loadsa money to spend by opting out of the EU.'[49] And, in its aftermath, a woman in North Ayrshire commented: 'I am angry with the stupid English poor who chose to drag us all down with them.'[50] A charity worker from the East Midlands described looking at 'the common-sounding pensioners who were all around us, wondering angrily which of them had ruined my niece and nephew's futures by their xenophobia and lack of intellect'.[51] A mature student from North Yorkshire suggested: 'most of the people who voted to leave were of lower socioeconomic backgrounds with no critical thinking skills, of the older generation, and were heavily influenced by Rupert Murdoch's press and Nigel Farage's fascist politics'.[52]

As Gurminder Bhambra's work reminds us, such characterisations were inaccurate. Not only did they erase the experiences of working-class people of colour but they also disguised the extent to which the Brexit vote was driven by the propertied white middle classes of southern England.[53] Given this, we might think about why they stuck; why they seemed so particularly persuasive. What did these kinds of explanations offer to Remain supporters? Most obviously, they worked to shore up their self-perceptions as educated, liberal-minded, and mentally healthy people, able to navigate the perils of misinformation and prejudice:

> By the end of the campaign, I would describe myself as strongly remain. Not because I think the EU is the best thing ever and I endorse all its policies, but because I wanted to vote against the racist bullshit pedalled by the 'leave' campaign.

Judgements and stereotypes

It turns out that Gordon Brown was right, she was a 'Bigoted Old Woman' and there are some debates we just shouldn't have.[54]

I know I am sane and luckily all my friends and family are sane too. I also knew that a lot of people were angry or indifferent – those people did exactly what I expected them to.[55]

But this doesn't quite explain the significance of class in these accounts. The charity worker, whose anger at 'common-sounding pensioners' we saw above, sheds further light on this. She went on to comment: 'I don't have much time for people who blame immigration for their problems – if you are so shit at your job that a Polish teenager with a shaky grasp of English and no local knowledge can do it better than you, whose fault is that?'[56] This latter comment is telling. It hints at the way some Remain supporters used critiques of Leavers as a way of shoring up their own identities not only as educated, liberal, and progressive but also as *successful* participants in the neoliberal economy. This was particularly clear in the account of a 35-year-old self-employed writer, who noted that many of the Leavers she'd seen interviewed 'seemed to be retirees in the pub or housebound mothers with lots of children; not young, educated people striving for success and able to contribute to the economy'.[57] She acknowledged that this 'may be pandering to a stereotype', but not that this impression may have been deliberately created by the choice of interviewees.

The tying together of rationality, education, and economic success speaks to ideas of neoliberal subjectivity, examined above. And yet, we can also see that this is not quite the whole story. Remain identities were not built on a rejection of feelings in favour of rationality and self-interest. Instead, they depended upon a distinction between undesirable and desirable *types* of feelings in politics. If the former was reminiscent of nineteenth-century tirades against the irrational passions of the mob, the latter recalled the eighteenth-century concept of sensibility – whereby passion was seen to guide reason and to address social, political, and moral engagements.[58]

'Spoilt children'

Leave voters were intensely aware of the stereotypes just discussed. Some broadly accepted this interpretation and sought to distance themselves from other Leavers. One, for instance, noted that a 'politically savvy' friend had voted Remain on the basis of 'valid arguments' and '(admittedly boring) facts', in contrast to his own 'jingois[m]' and 'hope'. Yet, he also claimed to have 'voted based on the information (or misinformation) I had at the time, and not because of misplaced patriotism or ignorant racism, so my conscience is clear'.[59]

Others insisted that these characterisations were themselves the result of misinformation and prejudice. A retired FE lecturer in Chester was 'appalled' by 'the reaction of Remain voters', asking 'How dare they assume that those who voted for Brexit did so out of ignorance or because they are not educated?'[60] By 2019, her frustration had become only more intense, seeming to generate a physical response: 'It makes my blood boil when I hear the same old rubbish spouted by politicians or on the BBC that Brexiteers are old, uninformed and that they didn't understand what they were voting for in the 2016 referendum. I am not old, I am highly educated and I knew exactly what I was voting for.'[61]

We see here an insistence on political agency. As Stephen Coleman notes, political agency depends upon being heard, understood, and respected.[62] While Leave voices, opinions, and (crucially) feelings *did* prevail and *did* shape the political debate and its material outcome, this ran alongside a continuing sense of being ignored, misunderstood, and disrespected:

> Today every Brexit voter is officially a racist ... There was officially no other possible explanation of why they would vote Brexit except that they were racist or because they made a misplaced and now bitterly regretted protest vote and either way they should hang their heads in shame ... It's official the minority actually were right and Brexit supporters have an absolute cheek to imagine they know better than politicians, celebrity luvvies and rich elite about what is best for them or indeed what they actually want ...[63]

The frustration at being misrepresented was here overlaid with anger at those deemed to control public debate: the 'politicians, celebrity luvvies and rich elite'. This merged with a final type of response, which took the judgements of Remainers as evidence of a repressive political culture, in which 'The denial of the legitimate expression of concern on such issues certainly contributed to the build-up of pressure which has finally erupted in this referendum'.[64] We will return to the substance of this debate below.

What is particularly striking, though, is that, while Leavers described a political culture in which the expression of certain kinds of feelings was repressed, they rarely (if ever!) described Remain supporters as unemotional, cold, or rational. On the contrary, they painted a picture of excessive and unruly emotion hindering democratic processes. A retired teacher in Leicester complained that Remain voters 'have never accepted that they lost the referendum and have done everything legal and illegal to hinder the due process'.[65] An online retailer from Salisbury similarly complained she couldn't look at Twitter after the result due to 'all the bitterness', whilst the retired FE lecturer in Chester, who we heard from above, described them as 'bitter and disappointed'.[66] Indeed, a new cultural stereotype cast Remain supporters as 'spoilt children' used to getting their own way. One retired nursery teacher saw calls for a second referendum (appropriately, given her profession!) as 'temper tantrums' and imagined 'washing [Remainers'] mouths out with soap until they agreed to shut up'.[67] To a retired shop manager in Brentwood, the 'Remain brigade' were 'Just like spoilt children who didn't get their way … Thankfully the rightful winners (Brexit) remained calm'.[68]

Communal and mass emotion

Many voters who were undecided about which way to vote later came to identify with the decision they had made. The material examined above suggests that one of the ways they did this was by drawing distinct lines between acceptable and unacceptable feelings. Yet, this was not (as some narratives suggest) a case of reason vs passion. As we have seen, both sides cast the other as over-emotional and (in different ways) presented this as a threat to democratic politics. Not only does this reveal the extent to which popular perceptions of ideal public discourse centre on unattainable notions of rationality but it also suggests a tendency to judge the feelings of others as intrinsically 'unruly'.[69] And yet, both sides also made use of the expression of feelings to bind themselves to others – whether through grief or joy.

In their study of affective experience during the First World War, Todd H. Hall and Andrew A.G. Ross discuss the way that two popular tropes worked to legitimise, delegitimise, essentialise, or idealise particular forms of

Judgements and stereotypes

group identity.[70] While 'communal emotion' represented 'the pure, noble, or righteous sentiments that unify a community', 'mass emotion' represented 'the dangerous product of an irrational mob prone to panics, bursts of outrage, or other base impulses – susceptible to manipulation but also very volatile'.[71] We can see both sides of this in the Brexit discourse.

One of the emotional experiences of Brexit was a powerful sense that the nation was dividing. A single imagined community was becoming two, each with its own feeling rules. The differing responses to this process of division suggest that the norms of Remain mapped onto those previously assumed to be dominant within the nation. Remain voters expressed a disconcerting sense of no longer understanding those around them, of feeling newly and suddenly out of place. As a Museums and Heritage consultant put it: 'I don't recognise the people who voted for this in my own life. I live in North Tyneside. In my Local Authority 52% of people voted to leave and I don't know a single one of them.'[72] Similarly, a charity worker in Newcastle explained, 'I can't begin to grasp how they came to make the decisions they did. It is that gulf of understanding between me and the people around me that is the most frightening thing.'[73] In contrast, the experience of Leave voters was one of recognition, of finding themselves more at home than they had realised through the discovery that 'other people had thoughts like me!!'[74] As one 30-year-old online jewellery retailer put it, 'It's so gratifying and brilliant to see people who feel exactly as I do, so much pent-up anger at the Metropolitan elite who have controlled us for so long.'[75]

While there was a wilfulness, a deliberate unruliness, to this release of 'pent-up anger', it was also experienced as a 'communal emotion', in Todd and Hall's terms, in that it was seen to represent the authentic voice of ordinary people. This is why the presentation of Remain emotions in the aftermath of the referendum as unruly, childish, and excessive was important. It gave Leave identifiers an 'irrational mob' against which to define themselves. As Sara Ahmed suggests, 'unruly' emotions are used as a foil against which 'good emotions' can be cultivated.[76] Rather than a conflict between reason and passion, then, Brexit can be better understood as a clash between two types of 'good' feeling: 'civilised' vs 'authentic'. And, crucially, they were also each underpinned by different appeals to reason – whether imagined as the incontrovertible logic of progress or the suppressed 'truth' of national decline. In both cases, the path of reason was imagined to be obscured by the feelings of others: nostalgia and prejudice on one side; bleeding-heart sentiment on the other. However, Ahmed also offers us a way to avoid the binary that pits these two against each other: both are underpinned by a similar emotional logic, by which imagined 'others' (whether unintegrated immigrants or a racist white working class) are seen to demonstrate insufficient love for the modern multicultural nation.[77]

Bad feelings

One of the notable features of the Brexit debate was its whiteness. While it revolved around an often racialised discourse, it was overwhelmingly presented as a dispute between dissenting groups of white Britons. We have already mentioned Gurminder Bhambra's important intervention into this discourse.[78] Ben Rogaly's work on Peterborough also suggests how close engagement with individual testimony can complicate the assumed connections between ethnicity, nationality, identity, and political positions.[79] Our own sources are less able to contest these stories. Mass Observation does not record ethnicity, though its respondents are known to be overwhelmingly white.[80] What they can show, though, is how respondents imagined otherness and how, as Ana Y. Ramos-Zayas argues, whiteness becomes naturalised and reproduces itself in the everyday practices of neighbourhoods and communities, silently yet decisively excluding those who are not deemed to belong.[81] In the case of Brexit, white Europeans who had previously considered themselves indistinguishable from their British neighbours now found themselves similarly othered or, as Marianela Barrios Aquino puts it, they became 'migrantised'.[82]

For instance, we came across several stories of Observers suddenly realising – too late – that friends and colleagues now fell outside the national community and considering their feelings for the first time *after* the result:

> I had not truly appreciated until after the referendum the sheer number of people I know with connections to the continent ... All these groups are in limbo ...

> A friend of mind (originally from outside the UK and of a darker complexion) told me that they are scared today. ... That practically broke my heart.[83]

> After the result of the vote, I spoke to several colleagues who were all EU nationals ... I was aghast to discover the sense of rejection and hostility that they felt from the result. As I would never think of asking them to leave or treating them any differently ... I didn't anticipate the intense feelings that they experienced. It made me sad and I felt really short-sighted in my choice. It was not a pleasant feeling.[84]

These feelings of rejection and betrayal on the part of EU citizens are well attested in the literature.[85] It was clear that, for some Remain voters, connecting with European citizens – and migrants more generally – was an important expression of their own identity following the referendum. One woman described deliberately visiting John Lewis as her 'happy place' in the immediate aftermath and seeking an emotional exchange with a Polish shop assistant, 'blurting out "I hope you still feel welcome and safe!"' This didn't go quite as expected, however, when the woman laughed and 'said nothing would happen for ages, and besides her boyfriend had voted "out"'.[86] In interpreting this exchange, though, we should also be aware of the feeling rules governing the shop assistant's behaviour – both the emotional labour she was employed to carry out at work and the emotional work she may have been undertaking at home.[87]

Sudden attentiveness to the presence of (particularly Eastern) European migrants was common. A woman described walking her dogs 'in a daze' and being approached by 'An Eastern European man' who 'looked like he'd been sleeping rough in a park. I felt like apologising to him.'[88] A year later, a retired woman in Dorset wrote, 'when I come across people from other countries I try extra hard to be friendly & helpful to them' and another Remain voter in Cambridge noted that an 'upside' of the vote was that it 'has drawn us closer to our European acquaintances, who we spend much of our time apologising to'.[89] A library worker, who 'made a point of talking to my Dutch / Polish / Italian / French / German co workers [sic] to offer my support and say how sorry and ashamed I was of the result', also took part in a collective campaign to wear safety pins as 'a way of hopefully letting anyone from abroad know that they were "safe" and would meet no negative racism/attitude from me'.[90]

We can see how these narratives about 'bad feeling' worked to reinforce the respondents' views of themselves as 'good' people. It is a clear example of how 'antiracism becomes a matter of sustaining a positive white identity'

Judgements and stereotypes

whereby 'white subjects feel good by feeling good about "their" antiracism'. But, Ahmed suggests, this 'is what allows racism to remain the burden of racialised others' as bad feelings 'are projected onto the bodies of unhappy racist whites, which allows progressive whites to be happy with themselves in the face of continuing racism towards racialised others'.[91] Steve Garner's work shows how whiteness empowers individuals to construct their identities by positioning themselves in relation to other groups. They have the power to define the 'we' in vernacular discourse and to reduce complex stories to single narratives, and individuals to an undifferentiated group.[92] And, as Brexit reminds us, 'white' is a fluid category, defined as much by politics and culture as by skin tone.[93]

The 2017 directive asked Mass Observers whether they thought that 'prejudice is more prominent in UK society since the referendum'. It is noteworthy that respondents tended to depict prejudice as something that had become more visible, legible, or acceptable in the wake of Brexit, rather than something that was new in itself – this also reflects the experience of those targeted.[94] For instance, a Remain-voting artist in Bath declared, 'Prejudice has come out of the "woodwork"', whilst a 40-year-old software engineer observed: 'it is apparently now OK to come out and say that you don't like people who aren't the same as you'.[95] A community health worker from Nottingham explained, 'I knew there were ignorant racists living in the UK because I've had colleagues on the receiving end of racist comments, but it's sad to hear that the racists are being more prolific. (The following week we get an email from HR urging us to report racist incidents because there has been a racist attack on a member of staff directly referencing Brexit)'.[96] We will see in chapter 4 that many respondents felt newly aware that they had previously ignored racism and xenophobia in their everyday lives. Their obligation to confront these attitudes might be seen as an emerging feeling rule.

The responses of Leave voters are just as revealing. One revelled in a Britons-first defence of prejudice: 'Yes, prejudice is alive and kicking – thank God.'[97] More typical was the suggestion that this was being overplayed by the media. In the words of a retired FE lecturer in Chester, 'Prejudice has always been prominent in British society and there have always been racial slurs and attacks. They are now blamed on the referendum result but I think they would have occurred anyway.'[98] This is an example of the 'ideological creativity' which Eleni Andreouli, Katy Greenland, and Lia Figgou have identified in how prejudice figures in what they call the 'lay discourses' of Brexit.[99] This respondent positioned herself as both aware of and opposed to 'racial attacks and slurs', while also disavowing their connection to the Leave vote. As in Andreouli, Greenland, and Figgou's work, we also saw many attempts to project racism onto less civilised 'others' – both less enlightened whites and immigrants themselves. Both approaches are closely entwined in this account from a Leave voter:

> For some it was the question of immigration, but ... I do not mind who comes to this country, and never have minded, if (admittedly this is a big 'if') they are prepared to integrate properly, to become, first and foremost, British citizens, and to properly embrace British values and loyalty.[100]

In these accounts, 'bad feelings' about immigration are justified by the bad feelings, behaviour, and intentions of imagined others. As Garner identifies (drawing on David Sibley's work), 'space' is another category where the process of racialisation (and, we might add, migrantisation) becomes visible:[101]

Judgements and stereotypes

Most of the districts I knew and loved in London have changed beyond recognition. Foreign shops and restaurants are everywhere. Lots of the people no longer speak English! ... If I sound racist, believe me I'm not! But I do wish that immigrants who live here should embrace our ways of living, and not carry on in their own countries [sic] traditions.[102]

We do not want our country spoilt by foreign cultures – some areas – (West Yorks) – we hear of whole districts taken over by these people (in particular Romanians and Romano Gypsies) who throw rubbish into the streets because that is what they did back home and they have no conception of good behaviour or living decently.[103]

Over 48 years I have seen England change from a polite, courteous, hard working country where people could get treatment in local hospitals, there were schools for local children, and it was a lovely country to live in. Now we seem to have many undesirables that cannot be returned to their country of origin despite the fact they have committed serious crimes while living here. We have lost our own law of the land and have to bend over backwards instead of insisting the immigrants conform to our rules. We have immigrants who come to this country and have the benefits of employment, education and homes and despite this still try to create mayhem by bombing us and killing totally innocent people ... I know there are many good immigrants who do excellent jobs ... but I still feel we should be more careful who we let into our country and really secure our borders.[104]

In these examples, space is seen to have been invaded by others, whose behaviour is perceived as dangerous and threatening. Structural concerns about housing, education, and the NHS are listed in the previous quotation but are not framed in such terms. These responses allow us to see how white privilege operates in everyday discourse by empowering individuals to homogenise immigrants into an undifferentiated mass whose culture and behaviour are put at odds with 'ours'. It is also striking that – despite protestations to the contrary – this discourse was primarily conducted in racialised terms, which belied official attempts to dissociate concerns about EU free movement from older hostility to black and brown British citizens.

Legitimate concerns?

Qualifications, like the penultimate sentence in the final passage quoted above, worked to protect the writers' self-image as reasonable (perhaps, even, compassionate) people. And this was what allowed them to protest that they were being unfairly labelled as racist by an elite with little sense 'about what is best for them or indeed what they actually want'. These are the words of the retired nursery teacher in Coventry who, as we saw above, complained that in the eyes of 'politicians, celebrity luvvies and rich elite', 'every Brexit voter is officially a racist'. It is difficult to pick our way through these sources without vindicating this judgement – because they *do* contain deeply racist and xenophobic sentiments. As we saw in the previous chapter, this same woman also asked, 'Will we all be Muslim citizens in two generations if we remain in? Will we all be blown up or raped in the streets by foreigners if we stay in?' This came as part of a long list of questions including 'Will a plague of locusts descend on us if we leave?' so might be read as ironic. And yet, it was interspersed with more clearly heartfelt comments about 'the fear of being overwhelmed by uncontrollable immigration', followed by the observation that 'Politicians telling people it is only an imagined fear just engenders further resentment when they are experiencing first hand the detrimental effects on a daily basis'. She wrote of teacher friends 'literally drowning under the pressures of coping with up to thirty-two languages spoken in one school and dealing with such a diversity of culture and discipline issues'.[105]

For this Observer, as for many others, a political and economic critique of public service provision, the housing crisis, and economic insecurity were tightly bound up with immigration and a perceived attack on (in her words) 'traditional values'. These views were narrated in terms of political betrayal and cultural besiegement, which are familiar from Camilla Schofield's work on Powellism.[106] One elderly woman in Brentwood reported that her 'sister-in-law who has lived in London for 80 years, now tells me that "slums" are returning. Migrants are living in sheds and garages because of the housing shortage.' The fault here was not seen to be the housing market, but the immigrants themselves, who she presented as a drain on public services, particularly because they 'don't or won't speak English', before asking: 'What on earth is happening in London?? It is so over-crowded everywhere, and I liken it to a huge sponge that once is filled with water, it won't absorb anymore!!'[107] A retired teacher, who reported feeling 'completely overwhelmed and absolutely hate the proliferation of foreigners in my life', complained repeatedly about personal experiences of hospital waiting times and attributed this to 'the birthrate of immigrants, especially Muslims, who do not believe in birth control', which meant that 'It is difficult for the ordinary person to get to A&E and be treated [in] under 4 hours'.[108] 'Ordinariness' here was defined implicitly as white Britishness and explicitly in terms of a lifetime of work and National Insurance contributions.

These were the kinds of comments that fed the narrative that the Brexit vote – and even explicitly racist comments – were the result of 'legitimate concerns'. Feelings of insecurity, anger, and frustration prompted by NHS cuts and scarcity of affordable housing and school places were directed towards a deeply racialised image of 'immigrants' (which often bore little resemblance to actual EU migrants), instead of the economic and political programmes responsible.

Demonstrating empathy

The narrative of 'legitimate concerns' provided a further opportunity for Remain voters to demonstrate their good/bad feelings. Just as with apologies to (perceived) EU citizens, expressions of empathy towards Leave voters might be understood as one of the emerging feeling rules through which new divisions were both narrated and reproduced. A 76-year-old in Worcestershire felt 'sorry for the people who were lied to by the "leave" politicians and who believed the lies'; while an artist from West Sussex could 'completely understand if you're poor, unemployed, and not a lot of positives in your life you're going to look for the easiest target to blame, because the government certainly aren't going to help, as they caused all the problems in the first place'.[109] Likewise, a manager from Devon reported a conversation with her boss, which she paraphrased as: 'What breaks my heart is that the people who want to vote out are the very ones who'll suffer most if we leave. People who's [sic] pay and working conditions are only protected by the EU now we don't have unions. And all they can think about is voting to leave because they're scared of immigration.'[110]

These responses not only show the dominance of the 'left behind' narrative but also underline how Remain voters enabled themselves to sympathise with Leavers by interpreting their political choices as a form of self-deception: 'these people must be angry about something else', as a 52-year-old man in Birmingham put it. He went on, 'If you

Judgements and stereotypes

feel powerless in your own life ... it might be attractive to have something to focus your helplessness on'.[111] Indeed, we see here another set of 'bad feelings', rooted in awareness that, in the words of an archivist in Cardiff, 'polarisation might be down to geography and the economic climate of certain areas'.[112] An artist in Lincolnshire similarly noted the 'huge gap between the very wealthy and those struggling on benefits or the minimum wage' and concluded, 'It is not surprising that the Referendum was the chance to voice the anger felt by so many people.'[113]

Some Remain supporters reflected on their own failures. An artist from Bath mirrored Grayson Perry's concern about the left's emotional illiteracy, which we outlined in the Introduction, as she explained: 'people like myself who feel very European haven't given enough thought to the feelings of the leave voters; we just thought they were wrong'.[114] A company director in Brighton reported her 'Sadness – and if I'm honest, a bit of shame – that I didn't realise how many people were seriously hurting and suffering with the effects of globalisation and the problems of a low-wage economy'.[115] A project manager from West Yorkshire reflected on her own privilege: 'I want to live near middle class white people like me, so how could I say it was wrong for other people to want to belong with people like themselves?'[116] Similarly, a retired civil servant in the north-east reflected, 'I myself have next to no contact with people who live in what's nowadays referred to as "the precariat", except perhaps when I'm shopping or eating in a restaurant', noting that 'It's fatally easy, when you're in reasonably good circumstances, to overlook the millions of people stuck in casualised work and trapped in run-down areas'. He noted that 'the Remain campaign simply didn't engage with these people at all' and described a 'tipping point' in the Leave campaign when 'the precariat and the (as they would see it) neglected and patronised working class suddenly realised that they had a vehicle for airing their pent-up anger and grievance'.[117]

These expressions of sympathy, empathy, and even culpability not only positioned the writers as themselves 'good'; they also worked to, in Ahmed's terms, 'cover over' the bad feelings they encountered. In suggesting that this was simply a misattribution, a misunderstanding, such narratives simultaneously denied the agency of Leavers to accurately describe their own political actions *and* denied the actuality of racism, suggesting that 'residents in [deprived] areas partly blamed immigrants for their economic plight'.[118] In their attempts to empathise with the 'white working class', such Remain voters often positioned them as the true victims,[119] or at least as facing competition for resources from immigrants:

> I like to think of myself as not being racist ... I don't share the horrible views of Far Right groups, or of UKIP about immigration. I do, however, think that there does need to be better control because the UK ... does not have a bottomless pit of resources ... I don't think we even look after our own citizens that well sometimes, so how can we support vulnerable people who move here?[120]

> Immigration is a real problem ... It's impossible to have a sensible conversation about this issue because i) any-one who raises it is called a racist and it's not possible to dig beneath that to see what the concerns are, ii) there are areas of the country that have a high migrant population but not a lot of thought seems to have been given to integration and iii) freedom of movement has gotten mixed up with refugees and some-how [sic], in the popular public discourse Polish plumbers are lumped in with Syrian refugees (and the failure of the EU to deal with the refugee crisis).[121]

Judgements and stereotypes

As mentioned above, the myth that Brexit represented some form of working-class revolt in response to deindustrialisation, regional inequalities, and austerity is empirically misleading, yet incredibly powerful. The imagined pain and suffering of a politically constructed 'white working class' afford legitimacy to the resentful nationalism and racialised anti-immigration attitudes expressed by the older, white, propertied, pensioner class living in towns and rural areas who predominantly voted for Brexit. We see evidence of Steve Garner's 'moral economy of whiteness', whereby white Leave supporters' behaviour is judged as ethically sound on the basis of their purported pain and suffering, while racialised or migrantised 'others' are viewed not as emotional subjects but as the source of this bad feeling. The dynamics of this process within a single dual-nationality (albeit white) family are examined at the end of chapter 4. Yet, Schofield also reminds us that bad feeling has itself long been the target of anti-immigrant politics – which are imagined as a heroic resistance of the 'liberal "guilt complex"' that accompanied decolonisation.[122]

Neoliberal subjectivities

The descriptions of migrants to the UK which we have seen throughout this chapter should make us think twice about the idea that they were perceived as a threat on account of their entrepreneurialism and ability to navigate a neoliberal economy. On the contrary, migrants were repeatedly imagined to be 'vulnerable', or at least economically inactive. In the latter extract above, it was not 'Polish plumbers' that the public were believed to fear but 'Syrian refugees'. A museum manager and Remain voter shared his 'faint unease about immigration' and suggested that 'Christopher

Priest's 1970 novel *Fugue for a Darkening Island* maybe prophetically showed the country overrun with immigrants and racked with civil war. There must be a balance between doing our humanitarian duty as a nation and not being sunk by refugees flooding in.'[123]

Even those who carefully exempted refugees from their opposition to immigration imagined incomers as welfare recipients and criminals, not as the ideal neoliberal subject of a skilled young migrant. The comments below are all from Leave voters.

> We were fast becoming the dustbin of Europe. We were stopped [sic] deporting rapists and murderers. Our little island was fastly [sic] losing its identity. I'm all for helping people who have lost their homes because of wars and I wouldn't want that to stop. But other people who want to come here should be vetted. No more criminals. No more people who just want our benefits and not work for a living.[124]

> Would it be difficult to follow Australians and to vet those entering their country and to make sure they have a job and home to keep them equal to those inhabitants already there? The figures are out of hand and on top of that we have murders, terrorists ruining our way of life ... For our young people – I am afraid![125]

> We are being overtaken by foreigners, in particular Muslims. Everything they require is back home – dress, schools, customs – so why on earth do they come here? The answer – money and free housing! Every single one should have been sent back on arrival.[126]

These Leave voters were not rejecting neoliberal discourse; they were reinforcing it. Furthermore, some linked concerns about immigration to those about welfare dependency at home. A theatre usher in Blackpool emphasised that money currently wasted on immigrants and EU bureaucracy was needed at home not only to repair public services but also because of the 'one third of our population on state "charity" benefits'.[127] Alan Finlayson's recent work on the online alt-right suggests a similar pattern: here too, the rejection of neoliberalism is formed within, rather than against it.[128]

That the politics of even socially conservative Leave voters upheld a neoliberal common sense should not be surprising. And the account of a retired science teacher from Belfast can help us to resurrect its historical lineage. He approvingly summarised a Dominic Sandbrook article in the *Mail on Sunday* which itself drew a direct line back to Powellism. The chain of associations here is worth quoting at length:

> He [Sandbrook] cited the disquiet over immigration that was notoriously highlighted by Enoch Powell in 1968 as an early sign that something was felt to be wrong by the 'man in the street'. The Establishment and particularly the Left liberal metropolitan intelligentsia which controls the media have consistently portrayed such feelings as racist and intolerant. Every country in the world has some people whose views would be rightly condemned by all decent folk, but no one looking at Britain could in any way conclude that it is a bigoted or racist society – indeed it is a model of plurality. The denial of the legitimate expression of concern on such issues certainly contributed to the build-up of pressure which has finally erupted in this referendum. In fact I would go further than Mr Sandbrook and say that what we have witnessed is an expression, a profoundly deep expression, of the regaining of national confidence which took such a blow in the two world wars and the economic malaise under Labour and the unions in the 1960s and '70s. In that sense the EEC/EU era is just a phase in the longer cycle of the renewal of the British psyche.[129]

There is a lot to unpack here. We might note the way that good and bad feeling function in the distancing from 'people whose views would be rightly condemned by all decent folk' (but who do not, presumably, include Powell or his followers) and the declared pride in Britain's lack of racism and 'plurality' – followed swiftly by the repression of 'the legitimate expression of concern' (what are these concerns, if the presumed lack of bigotry and racism does, indeed, provide a 'model'?).

Even more significant, though, is the seamless linking of this to a far more expansive narrative of national decline, which takes in not only industrial relations but also – and more surprisingly – 'the two world wars'. The narrative here is familiar from the works of declinist commentators, such as Corelli Barnett,[130] and, as we might expect, is linked to Thatcherism: 'This astonishing and wonderful referendum result is the child of 1979 which was in itself an initial reassertion of national self-confidence and the rejection of socialist apathy and dependency culture.'[131] As we noted above, one of the key narratives of Brexit analysis has been that it represented a backlash against neoliberal values in favour of ethno-centrist communitarianism. But – as we see in this account, and as we might expect from Stuart Hall's analysis of Thatcherism – the two strands were in fact bound tightly together. Indeed, counter to Hay's point that Leave.EU and Vote Leave represented two irreconcilable political strains – socially conservative and globalising deregulationist – this voter praised Nigel Farage and Daniel Hannan in the same breath: 'they "spoke for England" and now they have been vindicated by the roar of the yeoman (and yeowomen) ... arise Sir Nigel and Sir Daniel!'[132] Similarly, a 38-year-old carer in Sunderland, who strongly rejected the media's portrayal of 'northern voters as bigots', condemned anti-immigration Leave voters as 'foolish and short-sighted in the extreme' and was energised by the possibility of

Judgements and stereotypes

greater trade and migration links 'with places like Mexico or Brazil', also stated: 'My only fear regarding immigration is that when we leave the EU and generate lots of employment here ... Britain could be swamped by migrant workers from economically failing countries in the EU'.[133]

It is worth exploring our retired teacher's political journey over the days surrounding the referendum. Shortly before the vote he was undecided and reluctant 'to reject the EU'. He did not mention immigration but wrote that EU bureaucracy, inefficiency, and lack of democracy were leading him towards voting Leave. He also bemoaned the lack of dispassionate facts and worried that 'most people will vote according to an inchoate gut-instinct rather than a clear rational analysis based on accurate information'. Just after the 'amazing' result, he was 'delighted' and 'astonished', and confirmed that his vote had been against the EU's 'vast, impersonal, and remote bureaucracy'. A few days later still, he was 'stunned, awed and overjoyed at the magnitude of the event', which he described as 'almost akin to a revolution' and celebrated on the grounds that 'the people have not been swayed by economics (or any other scare tactics) but by something much more important to them: a sense of what the country is and should be and also a sense that whatever the consequences, we will face them head on, stand on our own two feet, rule ourselves and be responsible for ourselves'. It was only then that he recounted his thoughts on Sandbrook's article and its invocation of Powellism.

We have dwelt on this commentator because his account enables us to connect themes which might otherwise appear disparate or contradictory. Immigration was not, for this voter, a primary issue of concern; but it featured within a constellation of national pride, self-reliance, and sovereignty, and a historical narrative stretching back through various eras of declinism – beginning with the First World War and centring around the analyses of Enoch Powell and Margaret Thatcher. This was what enabled him to see both Farage and Hannan as offering a single authentic voice of England (and its yeopeople) and allowed him to call for 'clear rational analysis', while also insisting that patriotic sentiment was not only more important than economic reason but also represented a 'deep wisdom'.[134]

In terms of the broader literature on neoliberal subjectivities and affects, we see multiple – yet not necessarily competing – sensibilities, which are often understood as caused by neoliberalism but might be better understood as forming the conditions for neoliberalism. This fits with Janet Newman's analysis, which argues that 'the neoliberal project of constituting new forms of self-governing, responsible and perhaps moral citizens offers a range of discourses in which self and society, individual and community, are imagined and coupled in rather different ways'.[135] The contradictions highlighted in the MO testimony show how neoliberal common sense – at the level of ideas or ideology – is often incoherent, multi-faceted. But, as Ben Anderson argues, it is at the level of feelings that common sense feels coherent, becomes intuitive, and appears natural.[136]

Conclusion

It is difficult to avoid discussing Brexit as a clash between two opposing groups, imagined in Sobolewska and Ford's terms as 'identity liberals', who have embraced ethnic and racial diversity, believe in non-discrimination, and see immigration as positive, and 'identity conservatives', who believe that diversity has 'gone too far' in favouring

Judgements and stereotypes

minorities or equalising rights and that immigration is bad for the economy, crime, and solidarity, and hollows out national culture.[137] In this chapter, and throughout the book, we have tried to complicate this narrative, showing that voters cannot be divided so neatly into these two categories. Although many of the Leave voters in our sources explained their votes in deeply racist and anti-immigrant terms, it is also true that many of those who ended up voting Remain also expressed discomfort about the impact of immigration and that others who voted Leave disavowed it. At the outset of this chapter, we expressed unease, not only at the veracity of these narratives but at their role in shaping public attitudes. The evidence we have examined confirms their power. Mass Observers reached for these frameworks as they sought to explain the divisions they felt were emerging around them. Even as their own lived experience spoke of a more complicated story, these tropes and stereotypes seemed to explain the views of others.

We have examined how Remain voters often apologised for others as a way of feeling better – both about themselves and about the nation. And while we focused in this chapter on specific apologies to EU nationals and other migrants, and supposedly 'left behind' Leave voters, expressions of guilt and shame for Brexit itself were also common. For instance, a retired civil servant in West Yorkshire said that, a year on, 'the country's decision to leave the EU still fills me with anger and shame'; a student mental health nurse in London felt 'ashamed of what "we" had done' despite having voted Remain herself.[138] Such statements served not only to underline the good intentions and civility of the writer; they also made the implicit argument that those on whose behalf they were apologising were themselves incapable (cognitively, morally) of speaking for themselves.

Beyond 'heads vs hearts'

They denied their agency as political actors and thus minimised their culpability for racism.

This narrative was – unsurprisingly – resisted by Leave voters, who insisted that they knew exactly what they had voted for, did not regret it, and had nothing for which to apologise. A retired civil servant in South Tyneside, for instance, noted that 'The more insulting the media is about the Brexit voter ... the more pride I have in myself and my country and I throw back my shoulders and face it with determination and defiance, and truly believe we will come through it all eventually as a stronger and happier nation.'[139] Yet, one of the surprising findings of our research is that the popular stereotype of the rational, cold, and calculating Remain voter had little purchase among Leave voters. Instead, they turned the idea of unruly emotion back on their accusers – emphasising Remainers' unwillingness to abide by the rules of civil democratic discourse and casting them as 'spoilt children'.

In the next section of the book, we will dig down from this level of imagined others into how differences were navigated in the intimate encounters of daily life.

Part II

Stories of excessive emotions: political feelings in personal life

> ...the meaning of Brexit is not confined to its literal definition. There's both more and less to it than mere advocacy of a British exit from the EU. It is, in a formulation first used, it seems, by the novelist Nick Harkaway, more of a mood than a policy.
>
> Jonathan Freedland, 'Brexit is a mood, not a policy – and Liz Truss captures it in all its delusion', *Guardian*, 22 July 2022

> One year on there is a nasty atmosphere everywhere. There's uncaring, snide remarks, rudeness, prickly self-defence and general outrage and huffiness about nothing.
>
> A1706, F, 71, artist, West Sussex, Remain, 2017

In calling Brexit 'more of a mood than a policy', Jonathan Freedland attempted to capture its symbolic nature, which exceeded, in his account, 'its literal definition'. And yet, he also gestured at its perceived irrationality, in which political facts and actions had become untethered from their meanings. This analysis reflected a wider body of popular and scholarly political writing, developed in the aftermath of the referendum.[1] This work was noteworthy for the way it transcended the more common use of 'mood' within political studies as a proxy for collective attitudes or opinions, and attempted instead to capture its nebulous, intangible nature. And yet, in the context of Brexit, this attention to the irrationality of mood had political implications, serving to underline the judgements we examined in the first half of this book.

In this next part, we turn to another narrative about the feelings of Brexit, which is that they were excessive. The period of the referendum campaign, and its aftermath, were experienced as a peculiarly emotional time, in which feelings carried both greater power and greater danger than usual. It seemed that just as feelings were shaping political decisions and attitudes so politics was intruding into the most intimate areas of affective life. In the aftermath of the referendum, studies commissioned by the Mental Health Foundation, the NHS Confederation's Mental Health Network, and the British Association for Counselling all found evidence of individuals claiming Brexit had negatively affected their mental health.[2] Findings from these studies were shared in various newspaper stories, pointing out how Brexit had left people feeling anxious, angry, and powerless.[3] Brexit-related conflict between family and friends was also reported as a common experience. Many Mass Observers experienced the prolonged campaign and its aftermath as something of an onslaught. They described the strain of managing their own feelings, and those of others, as well as their fears about the impact of emotions on political debate, public civility, and the safety of minorities. As time wore on, many disengaged completely.

In this section of the book, we turn our attention away from the role of feelings in voters' decision-making and identity formation. We look at emotions not as exemplars of particular political positions, or indications of public opinion, but as the subject of intense feelings in their own

Stories of excessive emotions

right. First, we examine how the feelings of Brexit were experienced at an individual and collective level as a particular public 'mood' or 'atmosphere'. In the final chapter of the book, we turn to the ways in which feelings were negotiated (and the concerns around how they *should* be negotiated) in intimate relationships. In doing so, we continue to complicate general narratives that link specific emotions with identities or behaviour, or suggest we are living in an age of heightened emotion, by listening to people's accounts of their political experiences in their own terms.

3
Moods

In political studies, 'mood' is often used as a proxy for political views. In the case of Brexit, as we have seen already in this book, this has been taken a step further. Political views have been reduced to *only* matters of 'mood', or of excessive feeling, directly contrasted with rationality – as with the quotation from Jonathan Freedland with which we opened this section. This not only diminishes individual agency; it also underestimates the complexity of moods. In this chapter, we want to look at mood on its own terms, as part of the way that Brexit was experienced, and the atmospheres it engendered. We draw on the work of scholars who show that mood is elusive, tricky, but does not absolve us from political responsibility. Both personal and collective, it is something we can be *in* and something we can *create*. It can align us with others or separate us from them. And it is not stable but nebulous and unpredictable. Moods shape how experiences are *felt*; they are 'ambient, vague, diffuse, hazy, and intangible'.[1] Less 'intense' and immediate than emotions, 'a mood lingers, tarries, settles in, accumulates, and sticks around'.[2] But while moods might seem 'less volitional than a feeling',[3] and can catch us unawares, there is also labour involved in setting, lifting, and shifting moods – as we will see in the next chapter when we examine the 'mood work' individuals undertook in their intimate relationships.[4]

These approaches have been very effectively applied to Brexit, helping us to understand it as a prolonged and ambiguous experience, embedded in daily life: 'at once ordinary and eruptive, innocuous and dramatic'.[5] Ben Anderson and Helen Wilson have tried to get at 'what kind of thing is Brexit?' by 'mapping how Brexit surfaces and becomes with everyday life and in everyday spaces, as it shifts from a dramatic disruption to something that touches people and becomes personal as it oscillates between the foreground and background of their lives – occasionally intensifying in moments of contestation and dissensus'.[6] And Stephen Coleman has teased out the 'mood stories' embedded in interviews he conducted in the aftermath of the result, highlighting that they disrupt conventional forms of political analysis because they respond to triggers in ways 'that are objectively opaque, causally untraceable and temporally unstable'.[7] Similarly, in her analysis of Ali Smith's Brexit-themed novel, *Autumn*, literary scholar Sibyl Adam emphasises that mood is cumulative and collective. It transcends individual feelings, rather than simply aggregating them:

> A collision of feeling underlies any mood because by definition a particular mood is something new that adds to what came before it. For instance, in a chapter of *Autumn* describing the collective national mood after the Brexit vote, each sentence brings a new element to the mood, where 'all across the country, people felt unsafe' and in the next sentence 'all across the county, people were laughing their heads off' ... It would be incorrect, then, to characterize a Brexit literary mood in terms of a specific emotion and instead more effective to describe this mood as a structure, as an ongoing sense of crisis.[8]

Moods

While Smith's novel reflects a broadly Remain-oriented perspective, this characterisation of the mood of Brexit as one of 'crisis' chimes with the findings of ethnographers working in predominately Leave-voting communities. Sarah Marie Hall, for instance, found that in Gorse Hill, Greater Manchester, 'waiting for Brexit is understood as a crisis-in-waiting, crisis-like, or a form of nested crises'.[9]

In this chapter, then, we pay attention to Mass Observers' own stories of the moods they encountered as they moved through the weeks, months, and years after the referendum – whether they found themselves caught up (perhaps involuntarily) in shared feelings or excluded by them. These narratives of public moods provided a discursive frame through which individuals interpreted their experiences of Brexit. They contributed to the sense of polarisation we explored in the previous chapter and shaped responses to interpersonal divisions, as we will see in the next. But moods were also messy and unpredictable. They could take individuals by surprise, reshaping their political choices and identities. This fluidity matters. It cuts across the idea of fixed and irreconcilable political positions.

The public mood

In both political studies and public discourse, 'mood' is frequently used as a proxy for attitudes. The 'mood' or 'temperature' of the country is assessed by polling techniques which might ask how people 'feel' about issues but really aim to discover which policy positions, leaders, or political parties they support.[10] In the US, political scientists have used an algorithm to standardise responses to hundreds of survey questions related to tax, spending, and welfare asked since the 1960s, which have been used to establish the prevailing 'policy mood'.[11]

Over recent years, polling companies in the UK have begun more directly to assess 'mood'. Since 2018, the polling company BritainThinks has been producing an annual report of the nation's mood. In this, questions about emotions sit alongside political judgements and predictions. And in 2019, YouGov launched its own 'mood tracker', asking people to 'describe your mood and/or how you have felt in the past week'. The lines signifying happiness, sadness, contentment, fear, frustration, boredom, and stress rise and fall as the months progress.[12] While this interest in mood is partly informed by a post-Brexit concern with public feeling, it also developed from a slightly longer interest in 'well-being' as a responsibility of government, typically measured by asking people to assess their levels of happiness, anxiety, and satisfaction. The UK Office of National Statistics has been tracking this since the then-prime minister David Cameron called for a national 'Happiness Index' in early 2011, and the UN has been producing a World Happiness Report since 2012.[13] The effects of the perpetual emotional (self) surveillance engendered by 'happiness economics' have been identified as one of the defining features of early twenty-first-century political culture.[14]

Of course, governments are not the only ones with an interest in assessing and altering public mood. This became notoriously apparent in the case of Brexit when the social media company Cambridge Analytica used Facebook data to psychologically profile millions of users. This allowed campaigners (for both Brexit and Trump) to target voters based not only on their demographic characteristics, or even their political views, but on personality traits. It also allowed them to attempt to manipulate users' feelings and to create new public moods – building on previous experiments with 'emotional contagion'.[15] This made the idea of 'public mood' even more difficult to ascertain as it operated below the level of the 'public realm', with voters in different algorithmic categories exposed to very different political advertising. This is partly why opinion polls were notoriously inaccurate and largely predicted a Remain vote.[16]

Social media also provides a source for academic analyses of shifting public mood. Typically, big data sets of tweets (for instance using particular hashtags or around particular dates) are scanned for emotional words, which are used to map aggregate feelings.[17] These are commonly used to predict anything from movie box office takings and stock market movements to election results.[18] And, of course, the EU referendum.[19] But they can also be used as part of wider attempts to measure the mood of public life.[20] In the case of Brexit, a study which tracked mood on Twitter found spikes in negative affect (anger, sadness, anxiety) and dips in positive affect (unspecified) uniformly across all regions of the UK, at key points before the referendum, such as the murder of Jo Cox MP (as well as incidents unrelated to Brexit, such as the Orlando terror attack and football violence among England supporters in Marseille). These peaked on the night of the Brexit results, with the collapse in positive affects mirroring the collapse of the pound sterling.[21] It is not clear from this study whether the uniformity reflects the particular political demographics of Twitter (would a study of Facebook, for instance, have given a more mixed picture?) or whether this negative affective response was uniform across Leave as well as Remain voters.

As with opinion polling, the way that such mood tracking is reported gives the impression of national unity – telling us that 'the public' or 'the nation' feels a particular way.

Stories of excessive emotions

These studies are driven by a positivist epistemology that seeks to aggregate individual feelings in order to establish a collective, public mood. This is necessarily artificial, belying innumerable gradations, ambivalences, and dissenting experiences. But as Pierre Bourdieu pointed out in 1973 (and was recently restated by Aurelien Mondon) polls don't neutrally record public opinion; they *shape* it. And in creating 'the illusion that a public opinion exists' they also create the necessity for the individual to locate themselves either within or without this illusory consensus.[22] In Sara Ahmed's words, 'when a citizen reads such an account, they can feel themselves to be or not in tune with the public'.[23]

Narrating the national mood

Mass Observation is itself a technology for assessing public mood, albeit one which explicitly encourages participants to bridge this gap between individual and collective experience. It was created partly in response to the 1936 Abdication Crisis, with the intention of understanding the mood of the nation. During the Second World War, it was used by Home Intelligence as a central part of its investigations into public morale (alongside the Wartime Social Survey). In 1944 these investigations even included a 'mood barometer'.[24] Mass Observers are aware that their responses will form part of this national picture, in ways that place them somewhere between the individuality of a focus group participant and the attempted overview of a social researcher. They are regularly prompted to reflect on the national mood, as well as examining – and telling stories about – their own feelings.

In 2016, Observers were asked to report 'the mood of your local area' in relation to the upcoming EU referendum. Many took this as a proxy for 'attitude' or 'voting intention';

others attempted to summarise collective feelings, telling us, for instance, that 'The moods I've detected among my friends and colleagues are uncertainty, worry, and some people trying to be optimistic, feeling that there's not much more we can do' or (afterwards) that 'People can't believe it. People are sad, but people are beginning to move on.'[25]

And yet, it is not always easy to separate these two approaches. Where does the voting intention end and the atmosphere, vibe, or tone begin in these two accounts?

> Perhaps I wasn't surprised at the result because I work in the North West. But I live in West Yorks – the mood either side of the hill was tense but our side seemed more confident of a Remain. So perhaps I was picking up a vibe over the hill.[26]

> the mood in Scotland is significantly more in favour of remaining; indeed the tone appears much less excitable and aggressive here than elsewhere in the UK.[27]

In some cases, the very act of writing about Brexit could trigger (or perpetuate) an unwanted mood. A charity worker in Newcastle commented, 'when I signed up for Mass Observation, I did not know I was going to have to do this. If I had done, I wouldn't have signed up. This is depressing and it is pointless. I would like them all to lose.'[28] A year later, a fundraising manager in Watford wrote, 'The whole thing stinks! Writing this has got me really worked up. Thanks MOP!'[29] Others relished the opportunity for self-reflection. A 23-year-old Remain voter in Stockport put this particularly clearly: 'this situation ultimately presents a golden opportunity to examine the constant traffic of my own thoughts and feelings. These feelings will pass and life will continue as it always does. Now, however, it feels as though we are living through an extraordinary age in which the over-arching meta-narratives of the day are aligning with my everyday life.'[30] In the run-up to the referendum, this

Stories of excessive emotions

sense of being part of something bigger, of witnessing historical forces at work, created a mood of tension and anticipation, whether this was greeted with excitement or dread.

By the time of the vote itself, many Mass Observers recounted a heightened sense of agency, reflected by the shared story that they were living through history. A retired nursery teacher described how she woke at 5.45 a.m. and 'stayed glued to [the TV] for the next four hours while history was made and unfolded'.[31] And a retired science teacher in Belfast explained how 'It is not very often in a lifetime that one feels that events of an epic and altogether extraordinary nature are unfolding before one's astonished eyes.'[32] A Leave voter in Sunderland who 'felt like cheering' at the result went on to say, 'The political fallout from the EU result is astounding. I've never known British politics to be so interesting.'[33] As a teacher from Kingston upon Thames put it:

> Whilst the future of the UK's relationship with the EU is unclear and I feel sad about the outcome of the vote, I believe the knock on effect on domestic politics is fascinating ... it is better than any soap opera and if a script writer had written out what has happened and presented it to a TV company as a plot for a political drama no company would have taken it up.[34]

In the aftermath of the results, individual Observers found themselves either in alignment or opposition to the now-official 'mood of the country'. The experience of hearing the results was therefore extremely powerful – both for those who found their own feelings reflected and for those who did not. As one retired teaching assistant put it: 'At last the people of Britain have truly spoken for themselves.' She was 'delighted' with the result and took pleasure in imagining how 'shocked' and 'worried' the rest of the EU would be.[35]

Another Leave voter who had prepared for the worst – 'I can already feel the disappointment, resentment and resignation of Friday morning' – instead woke to find that 'the reality was cataclysmic, a political firestorm'. Although this was 'the reality', it was 'so unexpected' that it 'fe[lt] like a weird dream'.[36]

Remain voters also described visceral reactions to hearing the result. These were often startlingly embodied, evoking a physical sense of shock and disorientation. One communications officer in Brighton, who had woken at 5.15 and checked her phone, 'spent the morning of June 24th feeling as though the world, or rather my world, was on a precipice, looking over into some kind of abyss which we were now doomed to fall into. I simply couldn't believe the result. I felt defeated. I felt insignificant. I felt like I'd been shouted down into submission by people who were just screaming nonsense and inaccuracies and lies at us.'[37] An elderly woman in London, who heard the results on the 'wireless' at 6 a.m., 'was upset for the whole of the day' and described feeling 'as though a rug had been pulled from under us'.[38] A retired civil servant described 'a feeling almost of nausea, real physical sickness, brought on by watching Farage's disgusting victory speech' followed by 'the vertiginous sense of collapse that went with seeing the first trading figures coming in'.[39] The physical instability of these reactions – the sense of falling, of vertigo – mirrors the findings of other research. For instance, Rosa Mas Giralt has found that long-standing EU migrants in the UK similarly described the result as having 'taken the solid ground I was standing on' or feeling like 'someone had pulled the rug from under my life'.[40]

The account of a Remain voter in North Shields is worth quoting at length. Its reflections on the very personal feelings generated by the result and wider sense of historical change were shared by many. But the hesitancy of the writer, her discomfort with the grand statements she twice downplays as 'melodramatic' but makes nevertheless, is particularly noteworthy. It indicates the way in which people were grappling for both a historical framework and a language appropriate to make sense of their responses. Again, the physicality of her response is striking:

> I've been thinking about how to describe the feeling I had. Because, I don't think pure politics has ever made me cry before. I have cried over the plight of people, of disabled people driven to suicide by benefit cuts, of refugees talking about fleeing their homes; but a referendum result is hardly something to tug at the heartstrings. I think I was crying out of desperation and helplessness. I think I felt, on a very tiny level, how it must feel to hear a declaration of war. I know that sounds melodramatic, but its [sic] all I can think of to compare it to because it felt like the world – my world – was changing in a way I didn't understand, that I couldn't control, that I was no part of but by which I was fundamentally affected. I felt like the world is changing in a way I can't understand, that I fear. The feeling I felt over the next few days made me think about what it must be like to live through a civil war – again, a melodramatic comparison – because more than anything I felt I don't recognise the people who voted for this in my own life.[41]

We examined the political implications of these stories of Remainers' disorientation at being cut adrift from the public mood, of feeling that the familiar had suddenly become strange, in chapter 2. Here, we are interested in the way this itself contributed to a shared mood of disorientation. As we will see in the next section, this story was resisted by some Leave voters, who insisted that nothing had changed. As this indicates, moods – and the stories we tell about them – are not entirely involuntary or passively internalised; we can choose to make ourselves available to them. One Remain voter, for instance, seized with relief on the opportunity to be caught up in a different public mood: 'Returning from holiday I heard that Leicester had won the cup. I do not follow football but it was a joy to know that an underdog had won and to share the rejoicing instead of the misery about the referendum.'[42]

'A really strong, strange atmosphere'

In addition to their own responses to the result, Remain-voting Observers gave powerful accounts of an apparently shared – if intangible – sense that something was deeply wrong. A customer service administrator in Solihull described his train journey to work as 'surreal[,] everyone sat in silence and there was a tense atmosphere[,] everyone seemed angry'. Work was also 'awful' – 'no one really spoke all day and when they did it was short sharp answers, my partner said the same about their place too'.[43] A fundraising manager commuting to London also found a strange mood on the train: 'plenty of people, but quiet, like they were stunned'.[44] One freelance reward consultant compared it to 'being back at RBS in 2008', saying that everyone she 'talked to was in a daze'.[45] An 80-year-old described walking along her local high street in Birmingham: 'Shopping took a very long time because everyone wanted to express their unanimous horror at the result.'[46] A project manager in West Yorkshire described the fallout among those close to her: 'Everyone was upset about Brexit … S had cried, as had her teenage daughter … Other S was upset because she is expecting a baby and the world's gone mad and they'd had a falling out in their family with people who had voted out.'[47]

Stories of excessive emotions

In Brighton, a mother dropping her children at school described the mood of the playground: 'When something big has happened you often feel vibes from it as you walk in (after the general election, or a few times when a parent or child that's part of the community has died or is very ill there is a really strong, strange atmosphere). Today many people in tears.' She could not shake this mood. Later in the day, she was 'Trying to write emails about the project I'm working on, and be "normal" when nothing feels normal.' She compared it to a time when the intensity of her personal feelings had isolated her from others: 'I remember when a friend of mine died at university, going to the supermarket to buy food the day after and standing in the aisle thinking "why are all these people just walking around as if nothing's happened" and it feels just the same now.' It wasn't until 6 July that she was 'Beginning to make some sort of sense of it. Weird is the new normal.'[48]

One way Mass Observers sought to make sense of this unfamiliar public mood was by reaching for historical comparisons – making it part of a story they already knew. A charity worker from Harborough could 'only liken it to the days just after 9/11 – there suddenly felt to be a massive unexpected threat in the world'.[49] A 76-year-old in Worcestershire who reported feeling 'horrified by the result' commented on the loss of one historical narrative – 'We have decades of peace because of the links with Europe and have just thrown them away' – and also the slipping back into another: 'Right wing attacks from Britain First + the BNP are the slippery slope which have happened before with the National Front and Oswald Mosley. Of course we have seen it all before. I was reading a book about the 1950s + it all sounded so familiar.'[50] The young man in Stockport we heard from earlier also reflected on the historical import of events: 'If I had sat down a few days ago to write this, I don't know what I would have said. Then I was angry and fearful and truly alone. I felt as though I could appreciate how my countries [sic] past generation felt standing alone against the world in 1940. But now I feel like the unity is coming back, both mentally and nationally.' A few paragraphs later, he returned to history: 'the EU feels like it is going through a League of Nations moments [sic]. ... The resulting hole was filled by the far-right. I hope that I am exaggerating but I fear the same again.'[51]

There were fewer accounts of public mood in the responses of Leave voters. Some made metaphorical claims: 'What a cheer went up when "Leave" EU won in Suffolk.'[52] Another described the 'very cynical and funny' comments on the *Daily Mail* website, noting that 'it's so gratifying and brilliant to see people who feel exactly as I do, so much pent-up anger at the Metropolitan elite who have controlled us for so long'.[53] But their accounts of the wider public mood seemed to downplay its magnitude: 'I'm very hopeful for the future. The mood in my local area seems largely unchanged though. Life rolls on.'[54] A 69-year-old in rural Suffolk explained that the 'shock locally ... Had everyone talking locally for no more than a week or two'.[55] Others set themselves and those immediately around them apart from a wider public mood, which was implicitly deemed illegitimate:

> The young seem to think that this decision will ruin their lives but we were doing it for the future of this country, for the young people ... I have no idea of the mood in the local area, we rarely talk to anyone and those we do have rather more problems in their lives than worrying about politics. The only people I've mentioned it to are at coffee morning, they are mainly my age or considerably older, and generally they are happy about it.[56]

Brexit anxiety

One of the pervasive public narratives in the immediate aftermath of the referendum was of widespread emotional turmoil. Various news outlets ran stories about counsellors and psychiatrists witnessing a significant increase in the number of patients seeking help for 'Brexit anxiety'. Yet, as Dan Degerman has shown, there was limited empirical evidence to support these claims.[57] But if mental health practitioners were not inundated with additional patients, they were called upon to advise individuals how to manage the unpleasant feelings generated by what Degerman describes as 'one of the most emotional and vicious political campaigns in the history of British democracy'.[58] They ran counselling sessions in workplaces and universities, wrote advice columns, and made videos – themselves contributing to this mood, even as they sought to alleviate it. We will see in the next chapter that the way this topic seeped into personal and social relations was awkward, depressing, exhausting.

But this was not purely an interpersonal matter and cannot be examined just as a matter of mood. The material stakes of the situation were extremely high. It is perhaps not surprising, then, that there was evidence of a short-term increase in 'mental distress', for both Leave and Remain voters.[59] For those whose citizenship status was suddenly thrown into question, this was more than a short-term concern. Mass Observers with European citizenship 'worried greatly about what it will mean' for themselves and their families.[60] The same was true for UK citizens living in the EU: one student in Geneva accompanied a confession of crying at the result with an apology for being 'overly dramatic' and then reiterated her reasons for feeling 'lost and confused; what would this mean for my future?'[61] Although these voices are not well represented in our sources, there is a substantial and developing literature on the anxiety, grief, alienation, and betrayal experienced by EU migrants living in the UK,[62] and on UK migrants in the EU.[63] Marianela Barrios Aquino has described a 'migrantisation process through which Brexit turned the EU citizen in the UK into what [Engin F.] Isin calls a neurotic citizen' – for whom citizenship is defined by inherent fear, anxiety and neurosis.[64] Citizens of Northern Ireland were placed in a similarly precarious position – as with a Mass Observer in County Down, who explained that she was 'anxious about how it will affect us ... It is making me very anxious overall and worried for my job and our house and benefits.'[65]

For others, the consequences were less personally threatening but no less concerning. The 'mood of celebration' at a graduation ceremony in Edinburgh was 'tinged with fearfulness at the day's headlines, certainly among those yet to find a job'.[66] A retired nurse in Nottingham gave extended consideration to a series of 'fears', 'concerns', and 'risks', including war in Europe, conflict in Northern Ireland, the break-up of the UK, economic and financial decline, and serious challenges to public service provision and workers' rights. He viewed the contemporary world as precarious – 'becoming more unstable', 'still so fragile', 'vulnerable' – and feared that hard-won benefits would be lost.[67]

Like this latter respondent, many Remain voters were 'genuinely worried about what a "leave" vote would mean for the country'.[68] This could not be dissociated from a wider sense of ideological foreboding: 'I think it would mean our country would take a severe lurch to the right. The thought fills me with dread.'[69] Many reported feeling 'terrified, really terrified that we leave the EU as the UK will become a right wing fascist racist state'.[70] An IT consultant in Exeter described feeling 'increasingly despondent as I see the country turning its back on reform and openness and is descending into intolerance, hate, bigotry and a less socialist society – to one where money and power trumps any other consideration. I fear for the future of my children and their families in this country.'[71] A 51-year-old administrator was 'very scared about the outcome … and such a right wing ugly mood in the country',[72] while a library and resources officer in Cheshire noted, 'I was terrified when the Tories got in. Now I feel physically sick.'[73]

As Degerman argues, the dismissal of such concerns as a matter of 'Brexit anxiety', which could be treated through emotional management techniques – which primarily involved accepting the situation and moving on – served to medicalise them as individual psychological problems, rather than recognising them as very real political, material, and collective issues.[74] While Remain voters frequently used the language of grief (the psychological understanding of which ends in acceptance), Verena K. Brändle et al. have shown that those who took to the streets were in fact seeking political justice, primarily through a restoration of citizenship rights.[75] Reducing these political anxieties to personal problems not only minimised the import of these claims, it also had the effect of suggesting that the problems of Brexit were *merely* a matter of mood, of having the *right attitude*. As we saw in the previous chapter, dissent was refigured as moodiness, the childish sulking of – in Boris Johnson's words – 'the doubters, the doomsters, the gloomsters … who bet against Britain'.[76] In contrast, Brexit was imagined as a salutary change of mood – a correction to a supposed mood of pessimism, weakness, and national decline, which was imagined to have overtaken the country since the Second World War.[77]

Moods

Sara Ahmed has described those excluded from such official moods as 'affect aliens' – 'alienated from the nation by not being affected in the right way'. Taking the example of the 2011 royal wedding and subsequent diamond jubilee, she underlines how 'Not being in the mood for happiness becomes a political action ... to become not only unsympathetic but also hostile.'[78] The discourse of 'Brexit anxiety' (much of it well-meaning) seemed to make 'affect aliens' of those who were unable to accept the result and to be optimistic about the future. It was, however, far less easy to alienate such a large proportion of the population.

'A never-ending saga'

As we have seen in the previous section of this chapter, Remain and Leaver voters told quite different stories about the moods of the referendum. Yet, one mood was universal. Mass Observers across the political spectrum experienced the prolonged campaign and its aftermath as an onslaught. Many were 'heartily sick of hearing about it' by the time polling day arrived on 12 May 2016.[79] Nine weeks before the referendum, a charity worker in Newcastle-upon-Tyne commented that he 'would happily vote either way to make it stop now', yet also expressed 'an inchoate fear' about the possibility 'that Britain leaves and shuts the world out', noting that this tendency 'represents the darkest part of humanity'.[80] A year later, a teacher in Portsmouth complained, 'The only real element of life that the [sic] "Brexit" has impacted on is the frequency with which it is being reported! I cannot really remember a day, throughout the whole year when it hasn't been, at some point, on the news. In this way, but perhaps not really, it is dominating everyone's life.'[81] In 2019 an unemployed Leave voter in West Lancashire spoke for many when he said, 'I have noticed a lot of people just wish it was all sorted out and done with.'[82] In contrast, an administrator from Birmingham reflected, 'My interest in Brexit has fluctuated over the year, but in its current stage – which appears to be the end game, but I'm sure isn't – I am finding it absorbing. I always relish the sense of living through important historical events.'[83]

As this latter comment indicates, one of the defining features of Brexit was the way it stretched out in time.[84] Unlike the 1975 referendum, which had been similarly described as 'historic', Brexit was an event that *kept on happening*. Whereas the 1975 Yes vote ratified the status quo and ushered in a period of ambivalent acceptance in which the referendum was quickly forgotten, the Leave vote was only the first of a series of historic moments.[85] These took in the 'historic defeat' of Theresa May's Brexit Deal, the Supreme Court's 'historic ruling' that the 2019 suspension of Parliament was unlawful, the final agreement of a 'historic' trade deal, and of course the 'historic day' when Britain finally left the European Union.[86] The polarised moods of glee or despair at the result, which we examined above, soon gave way to a wider national mood of frustration and exhaustion as the negotiations dragged on.

The failure to leave the EU on 29 March 2019 was experienced by some as a 'damp squib'; 'a pretty normal day which could have been a very historic one'.[87] While individual emotions ranged from joy and relief to profound anger and sadness, the overwhelming mood was of exhaustion with the whole topic. This was common across those who had supported Remain ('the topic of Brexit is banned. No one wants to talk about it, that's how bad things have got'[88]) and Leave ('I refuse to comment. The world is sick of it'[89]). Both Leave and Remain voters were 'fed up'.[90] And both described retreating into apathy as a defence against futile rage. A charity worker in Harborough described how she 'lost all patience with hearing about Brexit about a year ago and have most of the hashtags muted on Twitter, and I turn over the news when they start talking about it. It falls squarely under the category of "things I cannot influence" so I'm not prepared to give it headspace, it's too frustrating. I'm so annoyed with David Cameron.'[91] A retired shop manager in Brentwood's 'disgust' at the lack of progress made her so 'ashamed to be English!' that she re-evaluated a lifetime of patriotism: 'As a girl and throughout the 1939–45 war, I was brain-washed to be so proud in this democratic country ... Democracy is DEAD!!' In this case, as in so many others, strength of feeling led to disengagement: 'So it drags on, and I am absolutely fed up with the word "BREXIT".'[92] This collective malaise was so powerful that some even saw it as bringing the unity that had been so lacking in recent politics:

> I think it wonderful that national frustration has united a previously divided nation. As we sit around the tables with our coffees, we pay scant attention to the goings on. Apathy and disinterest has set in. Everyone is fed up with the process and just wants to get on with it one way or another. It is here, a huge anti-climax and just another day in this seemingly never-ending saga.[93]

In the previous chapter we looked at how some Leave voters felt excluded from the national community by the tone of some media coverage. Here, in contrast, we see a mismatch between media and public appetites for continued discussion creating a sense of commonality among an imagined national community of 'ordinary' people.[94] As a retired civil servant in Nottingham, who claimed not to have discussed the vote with anyone except her husband, put it:

Stories of excessive emotions

The press and TV coverage seem to suggest that everyone is keenly interested and discussing nothing else, but I suspect that many people are sick of hearing about 'Europe', 'Brexit', and so on and would welcome a rest. As it's clear that the leaving process is going to be long winded and difficult, then a number of long silences may be exactly what they will get.[95]

If the referendum was initially experienced by some as a moment of heightened agency where citizens had a unique opportunity to pass their judgement on an issue of historical significance, we can see how this experience mutated through the campaign and its aftermath to one of passive fatalism. These findings challenge public opinion research that shows the Brexit debate stimulated 'voters' interest in politics', despite trust and confidence in how the country was being governed falling to a record low.[96] Mass Observation shows public attitudes are never so fixed. Respondents began to doubt their political efficacy as Brexit was seen to be increasingly complex and interminable. Many Observers expressed guilt at their inability to maintain political attention; they were not apathetic, but they were exhausted. These accounts also complicate simplistic binaries between active and passive models of citizenship and might be interpreted as further evidence of what recent scholarship has termed 'standby citizens', who are not disengaged but whose interest and willingness to participate in political life is limited to specific circumstances.[97]

A dangerous mood

Brexit was so exhausting not only because it dragged on and on but because it seemed peculiarly emotional. As one respondent noted in 2016, 'It seems to be an issue that is never resolved; evokes very powerful emotions in some people and leads to many fruitless hours of discussion and argument.'[98] And, another, in 2017: 'One year on there is a nasty atmosphere everywhere. There's uncaring, snide remarks, rudeness, prickly self-defence and general outrage and huffiness about nothing.'[99]

Beyond this sense of an ill, irritable mood, we can see very real fears about 'how much anger the campaigning is bringing up'.[100] While some of this was clearly generated by the media coverage (the woman just quoted, for instance, was watching from New Zealand), others reported personal experiences. As we saw in chapter 2, some knew people of colour who had been told to 'go home',[101] or even suffered racial attacks.[102] The Brighton mother we heard from earlier reported on the experience of an eight-year-old daughter of a Swedish friend: 'A couple of the boys in the class came up to her daughter this morning and said "so, when are you leaving"?'[103] There seemed to be 'much more of an us & them mood everywhere [which seemed to have] made racists worse & any bigot worse too'.[104]

As we saw in chapter 2, Leavers tended to downplay these narratives of an increasingly intolerant public mood, insisting that 'Prejudice has always been prominent in British society and there have always been racial slurs and attacks. They are now blamed on the referendum result but I think they would have occurred anyway.'[105] Further to this, some Leave voters responded to Mass Observation's question about prejudice with their own accounts of feeling victimised. An elderly woman complained about 'the anger and hatred directed at people who voted to leave, not in my personal circle but in the media generally. We have seen marches in the streets, the faces of people protesting are ugly with anger.'[106] An unemployed Leave voter in

Stories of excessive emotions

Cambridge reported a more direct experience of the febrile public mood: 'The atmosphere is oppressive and one has a feeling of impending violence ... I have personally been threatened with having my throat cut at a music gig ... I didn't rise to it but there is a feeling of lines being drawn I feel.' Yet he also seemed to relish the clash, ending a diatribe against Remain marchers with the words 'I don't fancy their chances... . [original punctuation] Civil war anyone?'[107]

He was not the only respondent to raise the prospect that 'we are verging on Civil War'.[108] Others felt this had effectively already happened: 'the legal wrangling in the press, on social media and in the streets has been tantamount to creating a civil war'.[109] Such comments spanned political divides; a Leave voter in 2016 felt 'I no longer live in a country I live in a battlefield'.[110] Another in 2019 who was 'fed up' and 'very angry' at the delay reflected, 'Who knows what will happen in the next few weeks? Possibly civil unrest if we don't leave the EU as expected.'[111] It is hard to know whether this was written with a sense of foreboding, fatalism, or as a provocation.

While this had begun earlier – 'Already, within a few weeks of the start of campaigning, the mood is turning sour'[112] – the murder of Jo Cox MP marked the descent into 'a particularly dark moment', which seemed to 'reveal something about the mood of the country at that point, which was bordering on hysterical'.[113] Remain voters were in no doubt that 'the death of Jo Cox is due to the fear and hatred that has been stirred up during this EU election campaign' and blamed the referendum in general, and the Leave campaign in particular, for 'unleash[ing] potent forces', which had seen 'a mushrooming of mindless and senseless acts of prejudice and violence'.[114] A retired civil servant suggested that her murderer wouldn't have acted 'if the Brexit camp hadn't already created so explosive an atmosphere and whipped up emotions that should have been kept damped down'. This 'febrile, hothouse atmosphere of nationalism and anti-immigrant xenophobia' had, in his words, 'conjured up a demon'.[115] Yet, one Leave voter in Salisbury turned these accusations around – describing the narrative *itself* as a contributing factor to the tensions: 'It's so dangerous the way they have pitched the Referendum, as racism vs tolerance, hate vs love.'[116]

While most Observers experienced the moods of *others* as dangerous, one Remain voter worried about the possibility of being swept along with a nationalist sentiment against her own better judgement:

> I don't like feeling that English people are being pushed out of belonging together. I don't like it because that's how people get into right-wing / nationalist extremism. I'm really not like that and I feel uncomfortable for having these feelings. But if I feel that way, what is that making someone less rational feel like?[117]

Feelings here were figured as somewhat artificial, in that they might run contrary to what someone is *really like*. In this case, the writer found herself attracted to emotional scripts associated with populism, disrupting her identity as a rational Remain voter. She consequently reaffirmed that identity by distancing herself from feelings she *felt uncomfortable for feeling* and drew a clear distinction between herself and 'someone less rational'. But she could not escape the sense of mood as something uncontrollable and dangerous, something not quite volitional, in which she might be caught up despite herself.

Stories of excessive emotions

'Feelings that are not our own'[118]

The moods of Brexit were fluid and unpredictable. People reported involuntary physical responses. A Remain voter in Brighton 'felt a bit teary as I put my cross in the box. Now I just feel sick'. She reported not only 'Feeling sick all day' on 23 June but being overtaken by her own feelings as the next day brought both the result and David Cameron's resignation: 'I sobbed into my tea towel as I was washing up. That's a first. Me feeling sad about a Conservative Prime Minister.'[119] The departure of Cameron was mentioned by several Observers. A student in the West Midlands similarly described that when he 'turned on the TV and saw that the stock markets were in turmoil and that David Cameron was stepping down as Prime Minister, I genuinely felt scared and worried for my future'.[120] And an artist in Lincolnshire described the disconcerting sense that the country was adrift: 'As I write, we now have no effective Prime Minister and no opposition. Politics in Britain have never been in such a state. It is deeply worrying … party politics are in chaos.'[121]

In discussing the way that moods 'are generated by those who are around, becoming something that can be picked up as well as put down by others', Ahmed turns to Heidegger's theory of 'attunement'.[122] This is not a case of individuals each bringing their own separate moods, which may or may not be identical, but of a shared mood accumulating, which those present may or may not find themselves feeling 'with'.[123] In this final part of the chapter, we examine how individuals participated in moods that shaped and shifted their experiences, and even their political views.

Let's take the account of a 50-year-old civil servant in Bath. Until shortly before the referendum, he was a reluctant

Moods

Remainer, citing the EU's failure to devise a convincing immigration policy and TTIP as reasons to leave the EU but the fear of economic 'chaos and uncertainty' as reasons to stay. He kept a diary over the period of the campaign, which recorded increasing levels of 'disgust' with the 'puerile tone of the debate'. It also shows oscillation between disengagement and partisanship across short time periods. For instance, on 3 June, he noted the 'bleak future' predicted by the Remain campaign and the 'positive changes' heralded by Leave, contrasting both with the 'general feeling amongst everyone I've spoken to is one of disenchantment and cynicism'. As a result, he had 'finally concluded that it doesn't matter which way the vote goes, there are pros and cons to either argument'. Yet, the very next entry, written a week later on 10 June, ran as follows:

> What a relief! My wife and I met with a group of friends for the first time in about a year, and talk inevitably turned to the referendum. Thankfully after weeks of listening to media warnings that the UK could leave the EU we met 8 people who agreed that this would be insane. We had this conversation while sailing down the Thames past the City and Canary Wharf financial district, a densely packed area of offices for many thousands of staff. We all agreed that surely all these people couldn't vote for an EU exit – let's hope that this is so.[124]

This passage speaks of more than political agreement. There is a sense of letting go, of relaxation, pleasure, and ease. This is enhanced by being outside his home environment, with rarely seen friends, and in a congenial (and classed) atmosphere.

After this experience, our Observer does not seem to have looked back. Indeed, after the referendum, his identification as a Remain voter intensified. This led to feelings of misattunement not only with Leave-voting friends (which we will examine in the next chapter) but with 'the UK population as a whole, and this is just another reason for withdrawing as far as possible from contact with them'. Again, he found comfort and ease in congenial social spaces, noting that his personal 'embarrassment at being associated with Brexit has been echoed at a number of arts events that I have attended', including one 'where a pro-Europe comment was met with a big cheer', noting that 'It's only really at times like that I feel a sense of belonging with others.' Most strikingly, this had caused him to rethink his views on immigration: 'in the last 12 months I've become an advocate for keeping it as it is. I like the fact that the UK is a melting pot of cultures with the ideas that they bring, and I would hate to see the country stagnate into a boring backwater.'[125] We might interpret this as the result of being exposed to alternative views, but the affective experience of feeling himself part of a pro-Europe, pro-immigration community was clearly also central.

As this example shows, mood is not something we simply catch from others or passively internalise – it is rather (in Ahmed's words) 'that we are caught up in feelings that are not our own'.[126] Being around Leave voters did not shift our Observer's position. Feelings of affinity, of shared identity, are created socially. His mood – his relief, his belonging – was a constitutive part of the mood he experienced. And the discomfort, or misattunement, he experienced around those who had voted differently is as significant. This was not an uncommon experience – particularly for Remain voters processing defeat. A fundraising manager in Watford, writing her MO diary in a museum café the day after the result, overheard other customers talking about having voted Leave and ended her entry, 'I might have to leave before I have an outburst!'[127] Even political agreement did not guarantee attunement. The woman whose description of a Brighton playground we heard earlier found attending a school fair to be draining because 'Brexit is all anyone can talk about'. And although she was as 'sad and angry' as the other parents, she found their characterisations of Leave voters as 'ignorant racists' simplistic and 'insulting'. This Observer found relief leaving her home turf and attending a village fair in rural Sussex with 'an odd mix of Brighton rockabillies and country village folk' – 'It was great. No-one mentioned the referendum.'[128]

The unpredictability of feeling – the way mood comes upon us, settles around us, sometimes unexpectedly – can be seen in the account of a Remain voter who heard the result while on holiday with her daughter and son-in-law, both strong Leave voters, and her sister, a non-voter who tended towards Remain. There was, she reported, 'a certain air of gloom around'. Surprisingly, this appeared to be generated by her daughter who 'seemed quite depressed. The voting had gone her way but she started wondering if she had done the right thing. ... It affected her so much that she couldn't eat and she didn't want to do anything. She wouldn't even go out for lunch and just fell asleep.' This mood took hold of the group – 'Everyone seemed tired and out of sorts or falling asleep' – until the writer made a deliberate attempt to remove herself from it. She and her sister 'had a walk and stopped at a little café and had an ice cream with strawberries and discussed the E.U. again. The vote hadn't gone our way but we were happy and we were not going to let it ruin our holiday.' On arriving home, on the other hand, she found that 'the present mood seems to be that many people are pleased with the result of leaving the E.U.'; in particular, her 'window cleaner was chatting to me today and he was overjoyed that we are leaving the EU'.[129]

A similar mismatch between mood and political outcome can be seen in the account of a Leave voter who (despite writing after the result had been declared) described the referendum as 'A trauma from start to ----?' Her agitation began with the process of travelling with her blind husband to the polling station and feeling inadequately provided for when they arrived. And it continued through confrontations with Remain-supporting loved ones and with her Polish matron at work. She did report feeling 'less anxious about the future', but still concluded, 'all in all, WHAT A MESS'.[130] As both examples make clear, we cannot straightforwardly read affective responses to the referendum from political preferences. They were produced in the complicated and unpredictable encounters between individuals, social spaces, and collective narratives. We see how moods are not distinct sensations that reside within individuals that can be collectively aggregated; rather, moods represent diffuse modes of shared feeling that ultimately shape how people experience and understand political events – like Brexit.

Conclusion

The 'mood of the country' was figured in many ways during the Brexit period – from a blunt description of the very marginal vote in favour of leaving the European Union to dramatic characterisations of a divided and angry national community. Before and after the event, polls attempted to keep track of the nation's mood and shifting attitudes towards the exit negotiations.[131] But mood is not so straightforward. As we see in these descriptions, moods are social, something 'in the air'. But they are also ephemeral, transient, unpredictable – they might suddenly sweep us up, or unexpectedly leave us cold.

The idea that Brexit was an excessively emotional event in British politics was pervasive. This emotionality became itself a mood – prickly, tense, febrile. The work of managing this mood, of being constantly on edge, was exhausting. We will see in the next chapter how it seeped into intimate spaces and personal relationships, and the work that was required to navigate or contain this.

But we have also seen that Brexit itself was imagined as a form of 'mood work', something which both required and might inculcate an 'optimistic' public mood. Those who resisted were deemed 'moody', 'anxious', 'bitter'. And yet, even amongst Brexit's staunchest supporters, hope soon gave way to frustration, fatalism, and disengagement. The government eventually tried to marshal this collective fatigue in its 2019 election slogan: 'Get Brexit Done'. But even though boredom with the whole affair was perhaps the most pervasive mood of all, it also felt like a deliberate action, a withdrawal from a collective situation.[132]

4
Relationships

In the previous chapter, we examined how Mass Observers experienced and narrated the moods of Brexit. We focused on the idea that public feeling was excessive and dangerous, creating a febrile mood in which civility and democratic norms were under threat. We also saw that this state of high alert was creating fatigue and disengagement. Many Mass Observers described feeling drained by the heightened public and private discourse and frightened by the feelings it unleashed, whether in themselves or others. In this chapter, we zoom in to examine the way that these stresses and strains were experienced in daily life and intimate relationships.

While academic research has highlighted examples of conviviality, the dominant public narrative was that Brexit was intruding into personal relationships, causing tension and divides.[1] In the three years after the referendum, the *Guardian* alone ran at least two pieces asking readers to submit their tales of relationship breakdown,[2] and a further two documenting its effects on various couples.[3] We would suggest that this became a new feeling rule, whereby individuals were prompted to re-examine their relationships and cued to feel discomfort with those around them. Articles advising readers how (not) to discuss Brexit at the dinner table became a staple of Christmas lifestyle features.[4] Much like the narrative of 'Brexit anxiety' that we examined in the previous chapter, this story of relationship breakdown drew on the expertise of psychological professionals. Many articles, for instance, cited a 2016 survey of 300 relationship counsellors which found that one in five had clients who had mentioned Brexit as a factor in their relationship problems.[5] By 2019, the Chief Executive of the UK Council for Psychotherapy noted that Brexit was 'ever-present in the consulting room'. She attributed this to tensions among families, and within workplaces and neighbourhoods, which meant that 'it is almost as if the therapeutic room has become the last place people can talk with any ease'.[6]

Mass Observation also played a part in reinforcing this feeling rule, with the 2017 directive explicitly prompting Mass Observers to reflect on Brexit's effect on their relationships. As with any feeling rule, this was consciously resisted by many respondents, who insisted that 'contrasting views have made no difference',[7] and that 'friendships are too important to be rent asunder by a policy difference'.[8] Others challenged it directly: 'Nothing has changed as far as I am concerned in relationships. I never came across any dreadful schisms within families that the newspapers were banging on about.'[9] Yet, as the examples discussed in this chapter will show, reports of heated discussions were common, as were attempts to avoid political discussion – or even conversations with certain people – altogether. Those who did not experience conflict themselves were aware this could be happening to others: 'Even within families and close knit groups of friends I'm told that there is disagreement.'[10] And while few Observers reported complete relationship breakdowns, some questioned whether they *should* break connections on political grounds.

The sense that Brexit was exceeding the realm of the political was reinforced by its treatment on TV, whether in long-standing formats like Channel 4's *Wife Swap* and *Gogglebox*, ITV's *Loose Women*, and BBC Radio 4's *The Listening Project*, or one-offs like Channel 4's *Brexit Britain on the Couch*, *How Europe Stole My Mum*, and *Grayson Perry's Divided Britain* and BBC2's *Brexit Blind Dates*. Such programmes portrayed Brexit as a matter for intimate exchange (often between irreconcilable identities) as much as public debate. While they explored ways of handling Brexit on a personal level, they also contributed to the sense that feelings on the topic were dangerous and volatile and needed careful treatment. This concern has frequently been heard in parliamentary debate and in media analyses, which have amplified the sense of a divided nation.[11] In all these sources, we see a clash between the belief that emotional expression and exchange are both healthy and necessary, and a competing sense that repression and avoidance are the only practical responses to deep divides. While public commentary insisted that it was 'good to talk' and modelled a therapeutic discourse of empathy and 'active listening', it also reinforced the idea that positions on Brexit reflected fixed and irreconcilable identities and that political talk was therefore risky.

It is striking that guidance on how to negotiate political differences was based on models drawn from psychotherapy and relationship counselling, rather than democratic theory.[12] Just as we saw in chapter 3, political divides were treated as psycho-social, rather than collective, political problems. Yet, it is analysts of political talk who are best placed to consider the implications for civic culture of a withdrawal from shared discursive norms.[13] Research into the experiences of deliberative processes – on the individuals who participate in them, on policy outcomes, and on wider political culture and democratic norms – is a long-established field.[14] This expertise was absent not only from consideration of the forms that the referendum should take but also from the public advice on managing its aftermath.

The EU referendum was, in many ways, an ideal candidate for deliberative processes. We saw in chapter 1 that many Observers were frustrated by the lack of opportunities to debate about Brexit and by the impossibility of accessing 'impartial' political information. But while there were some independent experiments with initiatives like citizens' assemblies, these were limited and had little impact on either political discussions or public debate. Indeed, as Stephen Coleman has noted, the idea that the referendum would stimulate a 'national conversation' not only failed to materialise but it had precisely the opposite effect.[15] Rather than seeking out opportunities to talk about Brexit, many people reported avoiding political discussion with those around them. As one Mass Observer put it: 'We don't talk politics. We never did, but we even more don't talk politics.'[16]

And yet, as we have already suggested, this is not quite the full story. While many Observers sought to preserve relationships by insulating them from politics, a small number felt newly obligated to confront others and 'speak out' about their principles. This approach was seen most clearly in the accounts of Remainers, who – as we saw in chapter 2 – had often become more aware of racism and prejudice around them and felt a duty to call it out, even in long-standing relationships, where they had previously found it possible to ignore. While this was relatively rare, a greater number of Observers silently withdrew from friends and relatives whose views they could no longer tolerate. They were avoiding talk *at the cost of* relationships, not in order to preserve them. While such practices departed from the public narrative of fostering reconciliation, they underline that individuals (rightly!) perceived the divides over Brexit to be political in nature and unsuited to a therapeutic solution. The few Observers who did engage in confrontation were taking what is described by democratic theorists as an 'agonistic' approach, giving voice to conflicts over identity, rather than suppressing them.[17] Yet, while such approaches engage directly with the realities of power relations, we will also see that they themselves have uneven effects – which can expose vulnerable members of the community to constant 'debate' over their very existence.

Building on the previous chapter, we examine the stories Mass Observers told about their personal relationships in the wake of Brexit and the strategies they deployed to manage them. The latter might be understood as a form of what Ben Highmore and Jenny Bourne Taylor call 'mood work'. This draws on the influential concept of 'emotional labour', developed by sociologist Arlie Hochschild, while recognising that moods are nebulous, unpredictable, and subject to many factors outside the control of those labouring to control them.[18] Mass Observers navigating the moods of Brexit were caught between the personal and the political. In the absence of workable models in popular or political culture, they muddled through – finding ways to balance love, duty, principle, and discomfort.

Couples counselling

One of the most striking features of the media discourse on Brexit was how frequently it drew on narratives of family breakdown. In these stories, individual families were made to stand in for the imagined collapse of the affective bonds of nationhood. In October 2019 the *Guardian* agony aunt Mariella Frostrup responded to a correspondent's concerns about the 'Brexit-related chasm' in her family with the words: 'Talk about the nation's debate in a microcosm! It was only a matter of time before this toxic political fracas, currently dividing us like the most bitter of divorces, came to haunt lifestyle pages as well as the headlines.'[19] In fact, this wasn't the first time this issue had appeared in Frostrup's column, or those of other agony aunts and uncles.[20] Not only was this issue intruding into the realm of the personal but this seemed to be the frame through which it could best be understood: whether bitter divorce or respectful co-habitation.

As Moira Peelo and Keith Soothill note, problem pages have long contributed to the working through of matters of public concern. They point to the role of agony aunts and uncles as moral arbiters and social barometers, and describe their work as turning 'private troubles' (in the cases they examine, underage sex and male rape) into 'public issues'.[21] In the case of Brexit, it seems that the relationship was inverted. Here, a self-evidently public issue was made into a matter of private trouble. And it was the perceived centrality of *emotion* to Brexit debates that facilitated this manoeuvre. As Frostrup put it in another column: 'the emotional energy around Brexit represents a toxic breakdown ... In the same way that "civilised divorce" is an oxymoron, you can't have a sensible conversation about leaving the EU. Even if you stay calm, others will weigh in and increase the emotional ante to unhelpful levels.'[22]

Throughout these pieces, we see a complicated interaction between the idea that Brexit was the *cause* of relationship breakdown and was *itself* a relationship breakdown. Frostrup's piece compared Remainers and Leavers to an unhappy couple – in this case, the 'complacent spouse' and 'serial adulterer', respectively.[23] In another piece, she aligned the correspondent's marriage problems with those of Britain in Europe: 'it seems to me that it's high time to push for reforms, including an extension to your right to have your voice heard ... And that's exactly what we should be doing in Brussels.'[24]

Such discourse was not limited to the lifestyle pages of the *Guardian*. An article by psychoanalyst Susanna Abse, published in *New Associations*, the journal of the British Psychoanalytic Council, took a similar line, imagining counselling 'a couple in the process of separating. Nigel Leaveson and Anna Romaine'. She diagnosed their problems as a symptom of 'large group, national trauma', brought on by lack of trust in political institutions compounded by the brutal insecurities of austerity.[25] Due to their differing personalities and past experiences, the couple react to this trauma in different ways:

> At the risk of being heteronormative and reinforcing gender norms, let's remind ourselves that Nigel Leaveson desperately wants autonomy; he fears being colonised and prizes his independence and hates to feel needy and out of control. Anna Romaine, on the other hand, wants to stay close and fears he will abandon her and the children. She is convinced unless she nails him down with financial and child contact agreements, her survival is at stake.[26]

In treating 'the divisions we see between Leave and Remain supporters' as 'a couple problem', Abse regretted the impossibility of achieving the necessary therapeutic work within the political arena:

> Sadly, however, politicians, unlike couple therapists are aligned to a particular standpoint and are also in the business

of creating hopes and dreams, rather than telling people about painful realities. It would be woefully naive to imagine this might change. Nevertheless, we should hope that our leaders can at least remember the universal human need for containment and security, so we can begin the process of really understanding each other and concern and empathy can re-emerge in our country.[27]

While this could be read as an attempt to depoliticise this topic, and to make it a matter of intimate exchange rather than political debate, there was an implicit political programme here. Abse not only named the problems of political distrust, financial insecurity, and austerity but also asked leaders to *remember* citizens' 'need for containment and security'. The unspoken contrast here was with the postwar welfare state, which Labour politicians (most notably Evan Durbin) explicitly conceptualised through attachment theory. The idea was that by creating material and psychic security at national level, it would be possible for individuals to develop as mentally healthy and democratically engaged citizens.[28] Yet, this argument did not come through explicitly in Abse's interventions or become a part of the wider discourse over healing Brexit divisions. Instead, the psychoanalytic approach seemed to be applied purely at an individual level.

In 2019, Abse fronted a series of three short segments for Channel 4 News which aimed to put *Brexit Britain on the Couch*. Two of the three pieces explored the feelings of Leave and Remain voters in very different areas of the country; the other was a single interview with former Conservative MP and ardent Remainer Nick Boles. The series modelled the understanding, concern, and empathy for which Abse had argued in her article – in the introductory voiceover, she expressed her 'hope that with a bit of psychoanalytic insight, we can bring ourselves back together'. She offered participants the chance to explore and explain their voting decisions and praised them for their 'thoughtful' answers. And, in line with the psychoanalytic approach outlined above, her questioning connected voting decisions with formative life experiences and individual psychic needs, particularly defining Leavers as 'battlers' and 'survivors' in search of 'freedom'.

The programmes thus suggested that a way through the crisis could be found in a process of empathetic and active listening but also reinforced the idea that divides were inescapable because they reflected voters' inner selves: 'people's sense of who they are defines their polarised relationship to Brussels'.[29] Yet, at least one of the participants pushed back on this narrative and insisted instead on the circumstantial contingency of his vote. Abse struggled to fit the determinedly self-reliant life narrative of self-employed Grimsby fish-salesman Nelson Sleight to his Remain vote. He explained that he was drawing on his professional expertise in connecting with people and noted, 'if I was doing something else, I might be a Leaver, if I'd been 50, I might have been a Leaver – but I'm not 50, I'm coming to the end of my sort of reign, and that's why I'm a Stayer.'[30]

'It's good to talk'?

While the idea that Brexit was altering intimate relationships became a new feeling rule, this was accompanied by widespread concern with fostering reconciliation through constructive conversation. The idea, drawn from psychoanalysis, that talking is the route to both self-knowledge and healthy relationships has long been present in both popular culture and public policy.[31] We can trace these ideas through the consciousness-raising groups of second-wave feminism, the principles of restorative justice, and the increasing familiarity of talking therapies.[32] The idea that, in the words of the 1995 BT advert, 'it's good to talk'[33] is present in everyday understandings of everything from sex therapy to child psychology and underpins public initiatives to facilitate conversations around difficult issues, from Death Cafes to Talk Money Week.[34] And yet, the very need for these initiatives indicates that it is an approach more easily recommended than followed. We can see this in BBC Radio 4's *The Listening Project*, which was developed in 2012 in collaboration with the British Library and local BBC radio stations and which drew inspiration from the US StoryCorps initiative. Although this is not emphasised in *The Listening Project*'s own material, StoryCorps is explicit about the political aims of its 'mission': 'to preserve and share humanity's stories in order to build connections between people and create a more just and compassionate world'.[35] *The Listening Project* describes its work as 'collecting intimate conversations between friends or relatives, to build a unique picture of our lives today'.[36] There are clear resonances here with Mass Observation's intention to 'create an anthropology of ourselves'. One of the features of *The Listening Project* is that the artificiality of the setting and the presence of a facilitator enables participants to have conversations with those closest to them in ways they would not normally do.

Over August and September 2016, *The Listening Project* collected a series of thirteen Brexit conversations, between pairs of friends, colleagues, and relatives. Some had voted differently from one another; others had not. In line with the approach of the programme, these were all undertaken in a spirit of sensitivity and care, yet some, nevertheless, revealed deep divides. The way participants negotiated their own and each other's feelings in these encounters is instructive. Some used the opportunity to affirm their similar worldviews, cemented by their shared response.[37] Others had to try a little harder to bridge the gap. The conversation between young siblings Mairi-Frances and Rory is particularly instructive here. She was managing the conversation, trying to understand his and other Brexiters' feelings (including their dad's), while also gently expressing her own. This aligns with long-established research showing that women assume greater responsibility for the 'emotion work' required in intimate relationships.[38] The staged nature of the conversation seemed to aid Mairi-Frances in this task, allowing her to ask, for instance, 'do you remember when I was very upset?' Even so, it took the intervention of the facilitator to make Rory really acknowledge what she was saying. The siblings were eventually able to find common ground over their shared rejection of racism and celebration of Leicester's multiculturalism and spent much of the latter part of the interview recounting their joy over Leicester City's recent Premier League win.[39]

Conversely, some conversations revealed deep differences, despite similar votes. For instance, Ben and his father Kenneth both voted to Remain, which clearly made their conversation easier than it might otherwise have been, not least because Kenneth seemed to be expressing some of his own sympathies with the Leave case by voicing what 'other people' might think. This allowed them to have a difficult conversation at a safe distance, edging round each other's views with great care, but this also seemed to be a little frustrating to Ben, who sounded as though he was seeking a deeper exchange.[40] Likewise Denise and her son Ben also both voted Remain, from a more similar political position, but were tentative about each other's feelings in the aftermath, often using hypotheticals to test the ground. While Denise was 'heartbroken' and 'scared' but keen to instil in her son a sense of responsibility, he was despondent, angry, and keen to give up on the UK altogether.[41]

In August 2016, *The Listening Project*'s Fi Glover also presented a radio programme which took this approach to a community level. *Two Rooms* focused on conversations in the strongest Leave- and Remain-voting areas of the country: Boston and Brixton, respectively. After the programme, residents of the two areas apparently developed links, cemented through reciprocal visits in October 2017 and March 2018.[42] This was organised through More in Common, a social enterprise established in the memory of Jo Cox MP which has become best known for its Great Get Together community events.[43] All these initiatives were driven by the belief that intimacy could bridge disagreement; we just needed to understand one another better.

However, the idea that 'it's good to talk' also rubbed up against the long-standing cultural assumption that certain matters – particularly politics – are beyond the limits of civil conversation. Party politics, in particular, was a proscribed topic in many inter- and post-war civil society organisations, exemplified in the motto of one club in post-war Banbury: 'No religion, no politics, good comrades all'.[44] Other media formats demonstrated the rationale for such a proscription. The hosts of ITV's *Loose Women*, for instance, repeatedly returned to the topic of Brexit, on which they were apparently evenly split, revealing that it had caused tensions between them and that they were scared to reveal their votes publicly, for fear of abuse.[45] This was explicitly framed in terms of feelings. On one occasion, host Saira Khan complained that 'all the people who voted out were labelled racist, and that was really awful, everyone was becoming so emotional and horrendous', while a phone-in linked this to our feeling rule by asking, 'Has Brexit caused ructions in your relationship?'[46] The wider context was also painfully present. Just days after the referendum, Jamelia, then a presenter on the show, spoke about her experience of being racially abused in the street by a man she thought was a policeman, though she resisted linking it to the wider surge in racial abuse post-Brexit.[47] The hosts also grappled explicitly with the question of whether or not to talk through their differences, linking their 'huge barney' both to the everyday experience of 'people around their dinner tables', finding it difficult 'to talk about this without passion and rage', and to democratic norms: 'We came out of our meeting this morning and said "oh, sorry if I was a bit heated but actually we want to talk". That's what they need to do in Parliament.'[48] It was striking that Parliament was the only point of reference here, underlining how few models there are for *the public* to engage in political talk. This comparison was particularly awkward because parliamentary politics had been the direct cause of the 'Brexit rage' and 'Brexit fatigue', which had resurfaced in the aftermath of the government's illegal prorogation of Parliament and which had been discussed at length the previous week.[49] And the feelings of parliamentarians were also seen to have 'hit boiling point' at this time, as a BBC Radio 4 show put it.[50]

While *Loose Women* grappled with the tensions that Brexit had introduced to long-standing relationships, other shows engineered confrontations between strangers. In late 2018 the Victoria Derbyshire current affairs show ran a series of *Brexit Blind Date* segments, in which Leave- and Remain-voting celebrities were paired up for a meal and a chat. The tone was light-hearted and publicity material

Relationships

traded on the potential for fireworks, while also insisting that the show modelled constructive conversation: 'The way to do politics is to sit down and talk about things, try and find common ground and listen rather than ... shouting across the divide.'[51] While the conversations on the show were mostly amicable and humorous, the introduction asked 'will daggers be drawn or deals done?', featured an image of boxing gloves, and showed one of the participants pretending to leave the table, without revealing this was a joke. Similarly, the Channel 4 series *Wife Swap*, which originally ran from 2003 to 2009, re-formed for a one-off Brexit special a year after the referendum. As has been common with reality television more broadly, these programmes were caught between their producers' competing desires to showcase tension and to model constructive conversation. The effects of such programming in forming and transmitting ideas of good citizenship have been noted by scholars.[52] Yet, *Wife Swap: Brexit Special* also worked to reinforce the classed stereotypes about the Leave vote, which we examined in chapter 2 – pitching a 'white working class' family on Canvey Island against a 'prosperous' dual-nationality family from rural Nottinghamshire. Predictably, set piece disagreements centred on immigration and racism, with social exclusion and poverty used to explain nativist prejudice.[53] Again, the message was that political disagreement could be healed through intimate exchange.

In 2019, the BBC ran a Crossing Divides season, promoting 'Extraordinary conversations across the fault lines of ethnicity, class, faith, generation and politics'.[54] This was accompanied by a website, which included more stories of how Brexit was dividing families,[55] as well as initiatives to encourage conversations on public transport,[56] an interactive website in which participants were urged to 'have a different conversation' by playing characters in various scenarios – the first of which related to Brexit,[57] and advice from relationship counsellors, rhetoricians, mediators, and conflict resolution experts on 'How to argue constructively about Brexit'. The latter emphasised being curious about the other person's position and seeking to understand, rather than to convince. It also counselled about the need to 'know when to stop ... and realise your relationships are more valuable', suggested that 'If you know the person you are talking to gets very upset very quickly, it may be best to avoid the subject', and recommended setting aside time for discussion in 'small bitesize chunks'.[58] The message here balanced the two competing approaches we have noted: while talk is important, it is also dangerous and should be handled with caution. Yet, the article gave the final word not to a mediator or counsellor but to professional contrarian and Brexit Party representative Claire Fox: 'On the one hand I understand why people are retreating but it's important people don't [stop] influencing fellow citizens and put forward their ideas ... I would never say don't have an argument.'[59]

Democratic talk

Fox's words remind us that the context here was political, not personal. Deliberative democratic theorists identify a vicious circle whereby people withdraw from political debates they find 'unedifying and bewildering'. Simultaneously, public debates are superficial – often focused on attention-grabbing headlines – precisely because engagement is low and mechanisms for ensuring accountability are limited.[60] Meanwhile, contentious issues (particularly those that cut across established political positions and social networks) lead individuals to avoid casual political talk, further removing it from

Relationships

their daily lives, thus eroding civic culture.[61] Proponents of deliberative democracy argue that democratic interventions – such as citizens' assemblies and other deliberative mini-publics – can break this cycle by improving the quality of discussion, engagement, and outcomes that command wider public legitimacy.[62] For example, the Irish national assembly on abortion was widely regarded as a success, not just for establishing a clear and just policy recommendation but because of how the discussions that took place within the assembly were reported in the news and served to heighten the wider public's knowledge and understanding of the issue outside of the assembly too.[63]

In 2017, UCL's Constitution Unit gathered fifty randomly selected members of the electorate into an unofficial Citizens' Assembly on Brexit. This 'mini-public' met over two weekends in Manchester to consider what kind of Brexit the UK government should seek. Members were asked to reflect on their own views, engage with information and arguments surrounding different options from experts and other assembly members, and then reach recommendations based on these discussions. The assembly was driven by the rationale that greater deliberation and discussion between Leave and Remain supporters was essential for fostering more informed and considered decision-making within the Brexit process. The assembly was deemed a success by the organisers because it stimulated informed debate, built connections between policymakers, experts, and voters, and led to clear and consistent recommendations. And yet it had no impact on the wider political sphere. As the report concluded: 'Rich intense discussion can be a wonderful experience for those who are in the room. But this has little wider value if people outside the room – especially policy-makers – pay it no heed.'[64] While the Citizens' Assembly on Brexit did not have official status, there are indications that such methods are becoming more embedded in UK politics: both the Westminster and Scottish governments have recently established citizens' assemblies.[65]

Such processes have, however, received criticism from some democratic theorists, precisely because they privilege dispassionate information, expert opinion, and rational discussion. Rather than enabling citizens to engage politically and ideologically, they sidestep the emotional investments and power relations that make politics so difficult.[66] In contrast, proponents of agonistic pluralism argue that we need to allow space for constructive conflict. Chantal Mouffe argues that antagonism between different voices becomes agonism – a productive, ongoing struggle of political identities – when debated in public space, which is essential to democratic politics:

> The prime task of democratic politics is not to eliminate passions or relegate them to the private sphere in order to establish a rational consensus in a public sphere. Rather, it is to 'sublimate' those passions by mobilizing them towards democratic designs, by creating collective forms of identification around democratic objectives.[67]

The idea here is that if democratic consensus ultimately fails to allow individuals to articulate their antagonisms – their points of difference – then those suppressed feelings ('ressentiment') re-emerge in ways that can be seized upon by nativist actors and directed against targets like the EU or immigration. It is this suppression of feeling, rather than the populism to which it gives rise, which such theorists believe to be the real problem. The perception of limited differences between mainstream parties and the idea that there is no alternative to neoliberal globalisation limit the space for ideological clashes within politics, and provide 'the breeding ground for such ressentiment'. A vicious cycle emerges when politicians, scared of populism, dismiss these feelings as irrational or unreasonable and propose more technocratic and deliberative alternatives, thus further limiting the space for conflict and choice. Antagonism must be aired to avoid the build-up of xenophobia, nationalism, and nativism.[68] The answer, then, is to legitimate the expression of difficult feelings in political life, not to suppress them.

Recent critiques have, however, noted that this may be too optimistic about the capacity of debate to combat deliberate misinformation (particularly pseudo-science) and also that it places a heavy emotional burden on those at the sharp end of such antagonism, constantly having to justify their very presence – or even existence.[69] We should also pay attention to the way that calls for 'debate' are being deployed to promote discriminatory positions on everything from trans rights to imperial history.[70] Legitimating antagonism is not easy when the stakes are so high. But, for agonists, this is evidence for the need for *more* space for disagreement, not less. As we saw in chapter 2, there is plenty of evidence of ressentiment in our sources, as well as plenty of disquiet about how to respond to it – whether it should be treated as legitimate, engaged with, or suppressed.

So far in this chapter, we have shown the widespread concern that Brexit had produced new divisions that penetrated personal relationships, which we have suggested amounted to a new feeling rule. The focus of these narratives was on healing divisions, but they showed uncertainty about whether this could best be done through facilitating or avoiding debate. In the rest of this chapter, we consider the extent to which this played out at a grassroots, everyday level by returning to the personal testimony of Mass Observers.

Stories of excessive emotions

We explore the stories they told about Brexit-related conflict with their friends, colleagues, and family members, and how they struggled to balance these two approaches. We note the uneven burdens that an expectation of reconciliation placed on those most directly impacted by Brexit. And we also highlight that some Observers interpreted the new feeling rule as an obligation to place politics above personal relationships – though this mainly took the form of silent withdrawal, rather than engaged confrontation.

Preserving relationships

If there was anxiety at national level about the extent to which it was 'good to talk' about Brexit, this was no less apparent in the writings of Mass Observers. As they wondered whether and how to interact with those who had taken a different position in the referendum, they came up against the contradictory approaches we examined above. While intimate exchanges might enable understanding, they could also be raw, difficult, dangerous. Many reported avoiding not only confrontation but discussion of any kind, on the grounds that 'People can get quite heated about it' and it was best to avoid 'a possibly acrimonious debate'.[71] One 36-year-old Remain voter described how her mum's Leave vote 'did cause arguments and strong feelings between us' and that, despite still feeling 'very angry about it', she had 'now decided not to talk about the issue with her'.[72] A 24-year-old PhD student simply noted that 'it's best to avoid discussing the topic with a few of my older family members'.[73] This desire to avoid the subject, so as to preserve relationships, runs through the sources. Katherine Davies has described such silences as 'an act of care'.[74]

Relationships

An online jewellery retailer with strongly Leave views explained, 'I never mention my political views to anyone because it is such a contentious issue right now. Everyone is very judgemental about whether you were "in" or "out". It just makes me want to hide my views even more.'[75] But, as well as worrying about being judged, she was wary of evoking strong *feelings* in others – whether upsetting them or attracting their hatred:

> I have an aunt and uncles who are all fervently pro-EU, so I have to watch myself, that I don't say anything that would upset them. Mostly I just smile and nod and say I'm bored of the whole thing.
> ... Soon after the referendum took place, I saw on Facebook that one of our neighbours is massively anti-Brexit and had posted about being heartbroken. That has made me wary of her, that I might say the wrong thing, or she might hate all of us if she found out my whole family voted Out.[76]

Although the rest of her account shows that she herself had very strong views (which did shape her personal judgements), here she weighed them against those of others who she judged to feel more strongly. Conversely, others suggested those with stronger views bore a greater responsibility to manage the feelings of others. One elderly Remainer who described herself as 'astonished', 'shocked', and 'angry' about the result also noted that 'when I am with friends I suspect might feel that Brexit is the right way forward I don't mention the subject! I would be in danger of upsetting them with my strong opinions!'[77]

These Observers worried about the *feelings* their *views* might occasion in others. But feelings and views were also often seen as interchangeable. To return to our jewellery retailer, writing a year earlier, she expressed much the same position but in the language of 'feelings', rather than 'views'.

Stories of excessive emotions

Explaining her fear of 'insults and bullying' on Twitter, she commented, 'it doesn't change what I feel, it just makes me hide what I feel from anyone outside my family'. She went on, 'It's wrong that I have to hide it – we should all be able to express how we feel.'[78] This suggests not only that political views are understood to be indistinguishable from feelings but that both are seen to emanate from an inner truth – which could be either expressed or suppressed. For some, silence was explicitly imagined as a way of repressing an inner self that might otherwise burst free: 'this subject and anything relating to our "government" has me frothing at the mouth and on the whole I generally avoid talking about politics as I become like a cross between Citizen Smith and the Hulk'.[79]

Stephen Coleman argues that this perception lies at the root of the contemporary perception that political talk, 'once regarded as a defining expression of popular sovereignty, has come to be thought of as a feel-bad activity – a nervous, cacophonous, resentful flow of public grumpiness'.[80] Coleman notes the mismatch between modernist democratic norms, constructed around civility and consensus, and contemporary feeling rules, based on self-expression and authenticity. But, he cautions, 'Contrary to the romantic notion of self-expression as an authentic baring of the unique self, what one says can never fully reflect who one is and what one means.' It is the frustration this engenders, the misrecognition and misrepresentation to which it gives rise, that lies at the heart of many of our problems with political talk.[81] Frustration at being misinterpreted is clearly present in our sources, as we saw with Leave voters' complaints at being labelled as racists in chapter 2, despite expressing views that were plainly racist, because this was either not how they interpreted such narratives themselves

Relationships

or not how they saw their 'true selves'. Attempting to explain oneself could also be overwhelming. As our online jewellery retailer put it: 'it was all getting so tiresome ... I didn't want to have to explain the way I see things.'[82]

The struggle between civility and authenticity can be seen in the account of a library assistant in Newport. She described feeling angry with a customer wearing a 'Get Britain Out' t-shirt, while 'printing off his cheap flight tickets to Fuertaventura [sic]' four days after the referendum. She not only performed the required 'emotional labour' of being civil to him in the moment[83] but also attempted to regulate the way she narrated her feelings in her written account: 'I'm sure he's a much more complex being than that, but right now he's a symbol to me of a very English attitude that I dislike'; 'I'm having an angry day, and this makes me angry'.[84] This seemed to be a way for the writer to maintain her self-identity as a rational and tolerant person, able to subdue her passions and prejudices, while also practising the anger and judgement consonant with her political views. As we have already seen in previous chapters, such strategies both reflected and reinforced the popular story that prejudice was the preserve of the Leave camp.[85]

Navigating uncertainty

One of the features of the referendum was that it required all voting citizens to align themselves with one of two blunt alternatives, each of which cut across traditional party and ideological lines. It therefore had the potential to disrupt established norms within personal relationships. Mass Observers were often unsure even of their own opinions and feelings, let alone those of friends and family. Their ability to manage the unexpected intensity of this situation was not only (as we saw in chapter 3) exhausting but confusing. Silence was the result of weariness or cowardice as much as care, and talking was only rarely therapeutic.

One unusually long account from a Remain-voting community health worker in Nottingham is worth examining in some detail. Throughout the long campaign, she described her exhaustion with the topic and her attempts to avoid conversation with (like-minded) colleagues, as well as with her vocally Leave-supporting parents (from whom she dreaded a birthday phone call) and even her school-age children, who were upset and anxious about the result and seeking reassurance that she voted Remain. Throughout this woman's account, we see her desperately trying – and mainly succeeding – to keep the issue out of her personal relationships. The effort of explaining her views and the risks of being misinterpreted seemed too high. But it is difficult to interpret this as a straightforward 'act of care', particularly in the case of her children. It seems to have been born of something closer to fatigue. Perhaps surprisingly, then, it was talking which finally brought some relief:

> Actually, 3 weeks later I finally discuss it with my parents. My mum brings it up. She admits to having a sleepless night worrying that her Leave vote was the wrong thing to do. She didn't just vote over immigration, it turns out. She also voted because she was sick of the UK having to bail out countries like Greece who got themselves into an economic mess. I was never going to fall out with her about this anyway, but I can see her point of view, and I accept her crisis of conscience.[86]

This is a particularly clear (and, in our sources, rare!) example of the value of political talk. Mother and daughter were able to hear and acknowledge each other's positions and to establish some shared values. It supports both Coleman's and Davies's arguments about the desire to be recognised

Relationships

as fundamental to affective politics. It also models the kind of frank exchange promoted by the media initiatives we examined earlier.

And yet, it is not the full story. While this Observer did grudgingly reconcile with her mother, the role of political talk in her marriage was more complex. In her 2016 account, she reported 'barely discuss[ing] the referendum' with her husband: 'We have opposing views but we just don't discuss it. I don't know why, perhaps because everyday life is more pressing.' On polling day, she noted, 'We don't discuss what he did, but I think I know he voted Leave. No point falling out over it.' On hearing the result, they still 'don't discuss it at all' – she speculated that 'he just wants to avoid a row and more tears' and wondered 'Maybe he is having second thoughts?'[87] Yet, her 2017 account of the same events told a different story, in which she 'shouted at him angrily when he told me the result and had a rant about being selfish'. She also reported that 'It hasn't affected our relationship … We haven't discussed it since.'[88] While she constantly downplayed the significance of the vote to their marriage, it was clearly playing on her mind, to the extent that she told two contradictory stories. Yet, it is also striking that in neither of these scenarios was it either particularly good or particularly dangerous to talk. Even the reported argument apparently did not clear the air but brought the couple back to silently avoiding the issue.

We can only speculate on the reasons for this narrative disjuncture. Perhaps in 2016 she had not yet processed their disagreement and preferred to suppress it, or perhaps the 2017 account was an attempt to imaginatively correct the previous silence. It might be an example of what Coleman calls 'silent, counterfactual thought: "This is what I would say if I were to say it. This is how I would say it if I were to be able to say it that way'", in which Mass Observation functioned as an externalised form of 'voiceless rehearsal spaces of the mind'.[89] It also seems significant that the Observer claimed not to be entirely sure how her husband voted. A lack of discussion seemed to enable this woman to avoid recognising parts of her husband that she would rather not see – or, indeed, acknowledging the part of herself to which this mattered.

The limits of tolerance

As we saw above, official advice about managing Brexit talk in personal relationships stressed curiosity, understanding, and avoiding 'upset'. We have also seen that many Mass Observers followed the third of these recommendations – avoiding talk in order to preserve relationships. Yet, there was little evidence of curiosity or the search for understanding. Those who did explicitly express tolerance towards friends and relations with different views treated this as something best laid to one side, rather than worked through. As one put it, 'they didn't make their decision lightly – they are sensible people of a wide range of ages and I honour their opinions and must abide by the majority vote'.[90] The civil servant whose journey towards identifying with the mood of the Remain camp we examined in chapter 3 reported in 2017 that he had maintained regular contact with three Leave-voting friends, noting, 'I hope it won't damage our friendship, as I respect their right to vote how they wish, but I can't help thinking about how they voted every time I see them.' He was 'furious at their stupidity', compounded by their previous lack of interest in politics.[91]

Even those who seemed to be following the BBC's advice to be curious about other's positions betrayed a great deal of judgement. For instance, a Leave voter, who described her 'initial surprise' at her daughter's Remain vote and then narrated her attempts to understand it, ended up explaining this through her daughter's desire to avoid professional difficulty, fear of the unknown, and lack of hardship – contrasted unfavourably with the Observer's more difficult life, which had made her 'resilient'.[92] Similarly a 21-year-old Remain voter living in Brighton described his willingness 'to debate my views and to see if they still hold water', while affirming that he hasn't 'met anyone who's put forward a single "good" argument for Brexit' and that his opponents were usually 'left with either mere racial discrimination or incorrect assumptions based on political lies'.[93]

There were very few accounts of exchanges of divergent opinions which were both respectful and open to being influenced. One which stands out came from a member of a church homegroup, who described 'a very measured and informative discussion', the evening before the referendum, 'very much bound in mutual love and respect for each other'. The group included 'some very professional folks' in finance and engineering, as well as teachers, students, and a former midwife. Crucially, though, this 'very useful insight and a range of opinions' was approached through a common interpretative framework. The group attempted to weigh the Biblical exhortation 'to follow and support those in power' against its injunction 'to remind our leaders they are in a privileged position, we believe, given by God' and thus to 'hold our leaders to account'. Framing the referendum as a question of how best to apply shared principles seems to have depersonalised the discussion among this group, who were able to 'recognis[e] the potential for this to have been divisive and the over-riding desire to remain friends'.[94]

Stories of excessive emotions

After the result, however, the same Observer experienced 'some quite sharp disagreements among friends which has been unpleasant and upsetting' and which caused him to 'have had to work hard and make amends for some of the things I have said'.[95] A year later he was surprised by the strength of his own feelings and those of others, which 'got to a point where it threatened one longstanding friendship'. Even this advocate of respectful discussion found it easier to 'agree ... to disagree, and not discuss it anymore'; he also 'stopped following one or two people on Facebook whose rhetoric became worryingly unpleasant' and reported general disillusionment with 'the voting public'.[96]

Reported exchanges were often very far from the ideals of constructive or therapeutic talk. This was particularly common from Remain voters upset with older family members:

> I was not surprised that my father, for example, voted to leave, but that he would try and defend his position, uninvited whilst in my home caught me off guard ... Rarely have my parents and I discussed politics, however the referendum did generate discussion ... Rarely does a child express shame as I did to my father when he suggested he voted leave. We stick to sport and his grandchildren as safer topics now.[97]

> whereas I used to avoid political discussion with [my parents], I now remind them constantly that the mess in this country is their fault ... they have condemned their grandchildren and great grandchildren to uncertainty and probably penury ... they actually said, 'Well then they'll know what it was like for us in the 1930s!' I couldn't believe my ears. To have been through such hardship and then want to visit that upon innocent future generations is beyond my understanding.[98]

In both cases, these writers felt newly emboldened – perhaps even obligated – to speak about politics in family

Relationships

spaces. But this took a confrontational, judgemental form, in which the writers described deliberately expressing their own feelings in order to evoke particular emotional responses in their parents – though this was (unsurprisingly!) unsuccessful.

Other Observers reported *avoiding* talk in ways that similarly seemed to further, rather than to avert, relationship breakdown. A 21-year-old Remainer reported 'avoid[ing] going home for 90% of the year' and having to 'numb my mind when I'm around them because it's toxic their political views'.[99] A 43-year-old writer recounted the rifts in her family:

> I was horrified to learn that my own mother had voted to leave, despite the fact that at the time she and her husband were looking for a place to live in Majorca ... Her husband was furious with her. They barely spoke for a while. I couldn't think of anything polite to say to her. I asked her why she'd done it ... Since then the rest of us have not referred to Mum's vote ... I have hardly seen my mother since the referendum. There are other reasons, but I am still angry with her about her vote.[100]

Confronting racism

Although, as we have already seen, the referendum led many people to disengage from political discussion, for a few it had the opposite effect. One 51-year-old Remain voter said that, although the referendum hadn't changed any of his relationships, 'partly because (like religion and politics) it is a subject best avoided with certain people', it had, however, been 'a common topic of conversation' and had made him 'feel more engaged in politics' as a result.[101] A 91-year-old Remainer was disappointed not to find anyone who wanted to discuss Brexit when he moved into residential care, adding, 'It surprises me as this age group have been brought up in an atmosphere of Empire and the union flag and I thought they would have strong opinions on it.' As a peace-seeking Remainer with a multicultural family, he probably wasn't expecting to agree with his companions but would have relished the discussion nevertheless.[102] At the other end of the age spectrum, a young man noted that, in the short period since he had left school, people who knew about politics and were able to 'fight their corners on the EU debate' had become 'popular and interesting' rather than 'unpopular and nerdy'. Interestingly, he attributed this to the bluntness of the question: 'When it's put down to a simple "in" or "out" people can work that out and decide which way to vote. But having to sift through tens [of] political parties and hundreds of policies to decide which one you believe in most just so you can talk about it on the bus? That's too much work dude.'[103]

Several Observers also noted that they felt 'more motivated to help encourage people to talk and think about what is going on in the world, to help those in need and to prevent things like this from happening again'.[104] A 65-year-old, who noted that she didn't 'have the confidence' to counter views she disagreed with, also noted that her 'views on UK politics have changed yes I think we really need to do something about societies [sic] divisions. We need to speak out and say what is right and wrong.'[105] The 'need to speak out' is not the same as therapeutic talking. Indeed, it might emphasise rifts, rather than bridging them. Some Observers noted that the referendum had forced them to confront political and ethical differences in ways that might have been uncomfortable but which were also principled. For instance, a 76-year-old retired librarian reflected:

Relationships

> A close friend voted to leave and I worry about my attitude towards her – should I distance myself from her? I have thought a lot about this and I think that I will politely say that I don't want to discuss politics with her; should she express unpleasant/unacceptable views about immigrants I will have to say that I don't want to listen to such comments.[106]

As this example suggests, the conflict wasn't limited to the topic of Brexit itself but introduced new dynamics into long-established relationships, whether seeming to legitimate (or even necessitate) conversations on topics which had previously been off-limits or pushing others to draw lines around them. We saw in chapter 2 that many Remain voters suddenly became aware of the experiences of migrant (or racialised British) friends, colleagues, and acquaintances, and felt newly compelled to reach out to them. The flip side of this was that they also felt newly obligated to confront the racism they had previously ignored:

> the referendum revealed some people I already knew, especially via social media, to be racists. I already knew one of my brothers was racist, but the referendum caused me to block or unfriend him and others who believed the vote to be entirely about immigration.[107]

> the referendum did change the way I view others. Arguments waged and positions were entrenched, ultimately members of my family and close friends voted to leave, in my eyes they are nothing short of bigots, and I had to adjust to how and why I would engage with them.[108]

Some Observers felt a moral duty to engage in these situations: 'I would elaborate, not stopping their speech, but showing it to be false, and purely based on stereotypes, assumptions and fear-mongering'.[109] Others preferred to avoid direct confrontation. A 30-year-old university lecturer described feeling 'really uncomfortable' when her

'Brexiteer' aunt 'posts things which are racist online' but responded with (limited) avoidance rather than confrontation: 'over the last year I would say I have tried to distance myself a little from her'.[110] Similarly, a 63-year-old Remain voter reflected on his attitude to his older sister, whom he suspected of voting Leave, noting that 'she still refers to people from India and Pakistan as "Pakies" [sic] a term which I despise and she does not like many foreigners in our country. While our relationship has not suffered she is 75 years old and if I and she had been younger I may well have cut ties to this relationship.'[111] While the writer felt his sister's views were morally repugnant, there was no indication that this affected his behaviour towards her. In both of these cases, it was unclear whether the referendum intensified the racism on display or whether the writers simply became more aware of the stakes of tolerating it.

An agonistic approach would insist on these latter two writers confronting their relatives. But this is hard work. Bart van Leeuwen has recognised the unrealistic burden that such an approach might impose. He cites 'The dictum that one should refrain from talk about politics or religion when visiting friends', and the respite it offers from the pain of having one's identity made a matter for debate: 'some things are too important to discuss with those who might be ready to question and criticise them. In that sense there is a prudence hidden in some cultural practices.' Yet, he also excludes certain situations from such a pragmatic approach. The first of these is 'if the expression of someone's identity constitutes an explicit disrespect towards other citizens'; in such instances, 'a critical response is appropriate and required. Conflict avoidance in these situations is wrong.'[112] The Mass Observers who felt newly uncomfortable in avoiding conflict with (in van Leeuwen's terms) 'exclusivist interpretations of identity' recognised this intuitively. And yet, the price of acting on it seemed too high. While their descriptions of their dilemmas suggest they were grappling with a new feeling rule, political or ethical discomfort did not outweigh the desire to maintain personal comfort for those with the privilege of being able to separate the two.

The burdens of reconciliation

One of the criticisms of agonistic approaches to Brexit is that they have paid rather more attention to the feelings of those expressing nativist views than those affected by them. We would like to end this chapter by considering the account of a Leave voter and her reported interactions with her son and daughter-in-law in the immediate aftermath of the referendum:

> I'd invited my son and [EU nationality] daughter-in-law to come for Sunday tea – my son left a message on the answer phone to say they were very upset over the referendum and could they come another time!!
> Some news reports suggested that some immigrants had the feeling that they were not welcome here.
> I'll write again when I've discovered more –
> My son came to see us on the Tuesday Eve 28th June. Very upset – he blamed 'you oldies' for voting out. He wanted his family to be European!! (Which really unsettled me as I envisaged mass migration from our country ...)
> My daughter-in-law ... was not happy with the result. So a couple of days (Fri) later I went round to see her – (feeling quite fearful of another tirade) – but after I said I was sorry to upset her, she said my comment 'at last we have our country back' made her think I'd voted to come out of Europe!!
> I plucked up courage and went round to see my daughter-in-law and granddaughter on the Friday morning and said

Stories of excessive emotions

I was so sorry if I'd hurt her (but I couldn't remember saying it – possibly I thought everyone would feel the same way as me – obviously not), but I never tell anyone how I vote. I hope things between us are ok?[113]

This is a particularly interesting account because it allows us direct access to the way that self-preserving strategies on the part of those most directly impacted by the Leave vote were interpreted, undermined, and redirected by those responsible for it. We see the son's attempt to avoid exposing his wife and daughters to harmful talk in the immediate aftermath – but also his mother's implicit delegitimising of this through the double exclamation marks. The writer shows she knows the cause with her qualified reference to *some* news reports on *some* immigrants' *feelings*, but also disavows this with the faux-innocent 'I'll write again when I've discovered more –'. The confrontation between mother and son is presented as an unexpected and unsettling attack on the former, and her subsequent visit to her daughter-in-law and granddaughter is narrated in a confusingly circular way, which privileges her own 'courage' in the face of 'fear' at a 'tirade'. She repeatedly describes her son's and daughter-in-law's feelings as mere 'upset' and declares confusion over how she could have caused offence, while simultaneously making clear that she was not only glad 'to have our country back' but assumed 'everyone would feel the same way', and excludes her daughter-in-law from this imagined affective national community with the sardonic aside, 'obviously not'.

We can only glimpse the daughter-in-law's experience of this encounter between the lines of the account. But the writer's insistence on talking, despite her family's clear attempts to avoid this, makes for uncomfortable reading. There are familial as well as political power dynamics at work. And we should set this in the context of research which has shown the intense emotional labour required of migrants in responding to Brexit.[114] Rosa Mas Giralt has examined the 'sense of betrayal ... in their everyday interpersonal relationships' that many EU citizens experienced, particularly the 'deeply felt rejection' when close friends or family members had voted to leave or did not support them in the immediate aftermath.[115] In our case, this talk was engineered to make the Leave-voting writer feel 'ok' about her actions, not to understand, reassure, or comfort her family at a time of vulnerability. No amount of talk (therapeutic or otherwise) could disguise the fact that she had voted for them to be cut off from her political community. Despite her attempts to reduce this to a matter of 'hurt' feelings and misrepresented 'comments', the awkwardness of the writing betrays that she knew her family (rightly!) suspected that this was really a matter of political actions and their all-too-real material effects.

A year later, her strategy of underplaying the significance of the matter, and trivialising the responses of her family, was still apparent. She explained that 'the issue seems to have been "slightly" buried – we get the odd "dig" during conversations' and acknowledged that 'freedom of movement will be an issue eventually' for her son's dual-nationality family. Yet, she claimed to have no regrets and responded to a prompt asking whether the referendum had changed her relationships only by saying it had shown her that 'other people had thoughts like me!!' and by awkwardly shifting the topic to 'the hatred they [the EU] feel towards us'.[116]

We have lingered over this account because it is particularly revealing of the way that the feelings of certain groups of voters were leveraged during the referendum, while others were simultaneously ignored, dismissed, and mocked.

Stories of excessive emotions

The dynamics within this individual family might be a microcosm of the politics of feeling on a national scale, and the desire to 'talk' was governed by similar power relations. The son's angry confrontation with his mother might be the mirror image of some of the accounts we examined earlier of writers attempting to shame their Leave-voting parents. But his wife and daughter were not able to choose their battles. Despite their attempts to avoid confrontation, the topic presented itself in their living room – and demanded that they understand, absolve, and reconcile with those who had unsettled their lives.

Conclusion

In this chapter, we have explored the prominent narrative that the stresses produced by Brexit created strains in personal relationships. On the one hand, this was seen to be a problem of politics exceeding its limits and intruding into spaces of private and intimate life; on the other, it was a matter of personal feelings getting in the way of politics and making civic discourse too fraught to sustain. These were not mutually exclusive positions, but seemed to reinforce as well as complicate each other. Both popular psychological discourse and democratic theory agree that talking is the way to resolve differences. But as we see, there are competing views within both spheres about the extent to which such talk should embrace or avoid conflict and how far speakers should express or suppress their feelings.

The evidence from Mass Observation analysed in this chapter suggests that such concerns also deeply affected people navigating their everyday lives. They worried about how – and even whether – to speak to those who had voted

Relationships

differently from themselves and about the competing obligations to maintain civility, correct misperceptions, and confront differences. The public discourse seemed to add to these worries rather than assuage them. We have suggested that individuals found themselves caught between two long-established but competing approaches. On the one hand, they were told that 'it's good to talk'; on the other, warned that political talk is dangerous. But, as we saw in the final section, the decision of whether or not to engage in intimate talk was not politically neutral but replicated the power differentials already seen in public debate.

We did not come across any reports of Observers self-consciously following public advice about healing Brexit divisions but did find some wondering whether they should cut off long-standing relationships in the wake of the referendum. We suggested that this might be understood as an emerging feeling rule, which obligated individuals to re-evaluate personal relationships on moral and political grounds. While this inverted existing norms, by placing the political above the personal, it did not resolve the question of whether it was better to seek or to avoid talk – with strategies for managing these divides split between vocal confrontation and silent withdrawal. But whether they sought to preserve their relationships or to leave them, it is striking that most Observers took the approach of avoiding political talk.

The decision to hold a referendum was framed by some as the beginning of a 'national conversation'.[117] Underpinning this narrative was the vision of a spirited democratic debate that would allow people to confront their differences and collectively establish a conclusive decision about a polarising issue. Yet, without any structures to facilitate such a conversation, the burden of this fell on individuals and an already attenuated civic culture. As we saw in chapter 1, at the macro-level, Mass Observers expressed widespread disdain for the campaign, which they found confusing and unhelpful. They regularly called for more dispassionate information, undisputed facts, and reasoned debate, in ways that suggest a desire for an idealised form of democratic discourse. And yet, as we have seen in this chapter, at the micro-level, Mass Observers rarely engaged in meaningful or productive discussions about Brexit with those around them. The affective experience of dealing with difference is uncomfortable, and individuals have few cultural models to draw on. Finding that respectful and open debate was impossible, they withdrew from political talk altogether.

Conclusion

Throughout this book, we have seen the power of two widespread narratives about the politics of feeling surrounding Brexit. First, that the Leave vote was the product of an emotional context in which feelings had become more important than facts, freeing voters to follow their 'hearts' rather than their 'heads'. This positioned leaving the European Union not only as the more emotional but, consequently, as the more authentic choice. Second, that the EU referendum inaugurated an excessively emotional period in modern British history, in which the passions unleashed by direct democracy threatened to destabilise the Westminster system and political disagreements poisoned intimate life. These two stories were inextricably linked. It was because political feelings were taken to reflect personal identities that they were so explosive, while their apparent dangerousness reinforced their status as the authentic 'will of the people', which could no longer be contained by polite democratic norms. While these narratives did not accurately describe the politics of feeling in Brexit Britain, they played a significant role in shaping them.

In this concluding chapter, we want to think about the role of political studies in contributing to these broader narratives. Various scholars have suggested British political science has a problem with accounting for politics that don't fit with its practitioners' normative commitments. For instance, Bice Maiguashca and Jonathan Dean have argued that the 'repeated denigration and infantilising of Corbyn-supporting activists, either as "populists" or as simply a bunch of "deluded" lefties ... reflects badly on the affective and normative orientations that underpin British political studies'.[1] Peter Allen and David Moon have described this as an epistemic snobbery whereby political scientists saw support for Corbyn as unworthy of intellectual attention or analytical efforts. They also argue that political scientists have been unwilling to acknowledge the key role they play in shaping how political events are discussed and interpreted. Central to these arguments is the use of quantitative data to support what are broadly conceived as centrist or centre-right political views that are subsequently presented as objective and non-ideological.[2] Sadiya Akram has made a similar argument about British political studies' failure to account for race and racism, and its perpetuation of a universalising approach that implicitly normalises whiteness as a stable uncritical concept. As she writes: 'The neglect of race in the discipline affirms the dominance of whiteness in the discipline; a point which is little commented on or questioned.'[3]

We want to suggest that British political studies has lacked a similarly reflexive approach to understanding the politics of feeling of Brexit – and its own part in shaping this. In recent decades, modern British historians have demonstrated the broader cultural throw and impact of social science on British politics and culture, particularly on popular understandings of class.[4] It seems clear that political science has a similar capacity to produce categories, stereotypes, and

Conclusion

narratives that shape vernacular understandings of political events, and that this is particularly clear in its treatment of feelings. While some political scientists have, at face value, appeared to follow Grayson Perry's injunction (quoted in our Introduction) to be more emotionally literate and have turned their attention to the impact of feelings on political behaviour, their approaches have worked to reinforce damaging stereotypes and divisions. By looking at emotions as involuntary physiological responses whose impact on political behaviour can be objectively measured, for instance, political studies has contributed to the misleading public narratives that positioned Leave supporters as motivated by passion and Remain supporters as motivated by reason. Subsequent studies that aimed to identify the instrumental nature of emotions in political decision-making so as to understand why people appear to vote against their own material interests have continued to implicitly reinforce the division between emotional and rational actors,[5] as have those which identify excessive emotion as a threat to democratic norms.[6]

As Emmy Eklundh argues, such studies work to exclude supporters of movements and political parties labelled as populist from the bounds of democratic politics, on the grounds that they are irrational, misled, or manipulated.[7] Yet, even those political scientists who have been most concerned with understanding and giving voice to the 'left behind' voter have done so in terms which reinforce this binary: pitting 'isolated, insecure, pessimistic ... and resentful' blue-collar workers against 'the younger, university-educated, more socially liberal elites who define the political consensus of twenty-first-century Britain'.[8] As we have seen throughout this book, this was one of the most pervasive narratives of the referendum, which shaped (but did not determine) the way individuals experienced their own feelings and interpreted those around them.

In discussing the way these narratives shaped popular understandings of the referendum, and of British politics more widely, we are not saying that they had no basis in the reality of people's lives or that these divisions did not pre-exist the act of writing about them. But it is also important to recognise the interaction between interpretation and experience. Attempts to reckon with the 'left behind' were particularly prominent in the left-liberal broadsheets.[9] Journalists such as the *Guardian's* John Harris and Jon Domekos deliberately sought out the voices of 'left behind' citizens as a corrective to the perception that mainstream political analysis was out of sync with public sentiment.[10] This clearly fed through into the expressions of empathy, and also the judgements, from Remain voters that we examined in chapter 2.

Yet, as we have already seen, public opinion is not a stable entity, able to be neutrally measured and represented. Representations of public views themselves *shape* those views, providing cues for individuals to orient themselves within the national community. Vox pops, in particular, provide emotional cues, modelling possible *feelings* as well as views on a given subject.[11] In the case of the Brexit referendum, and the anti-immigration sentiments with which it was entwined, the effects of this process were particularly clear to see. Aurelien Mondon has examined how elite actors (including political scientists as well as journalists and politicians) used opinion polls in ways that actively constructed an illiberal populace, whose demands must be satisfied.[12] We can also see this process at work in more emotive formats, like BBC's *Question Time* and vox pop interviews in news reporting, both of which gave

Conclusion

prominence to the voices of 'left behind' voters. Neither of these formats is new – indeed, both came to prominence in the 1970s and are part of the longer historical story of the political legitimacy of 'ordinariness' we outlined in the Introduction[13] – but they took on a particular significance in the context of a referendum in which the matter of what 'the public' thought was deeply contested. And there is some evidence that voters themselves resisted this as an over-correction, which prioritised 'extreme' views over the 'middle ground'.[14]

In this book, we have sought to get past accounts of the politics of feeling in Brexit Britain that either dismiss or valorise the feelings of Leave supporters without accounting for the normative political implications of doing so. Instead, we have listened to 'ordinary' people in a way that systematically identifies *their own* discursive frames and subjective understandings of the place of feeling in Brexit Britain. This approach has allowed us to consider the twin narratives of 'heads vs hearts' and 'excessive emotions' from a more critical angle, showing that, while they certainly permeated our sources, they were actively resisted as much as they were straightforwardly reproduced. We have also shown that these narratives misrepresent the complexities, contradictions, and contingencies of the role that feelings played in both the Brexit vote and the 'mood work' that followed. And yet, they do provide a key to understanding the particularities of that political moment. They help us to see that the toxicity of political debate was born of a clash between understandings of emotion in which people *both* valorised individual feelings *and also* maintained the belief that they are separate from, and inferior to, reason.

Our argument

As we have suggested, the idea that politics has become increasingly – and worryingly – emotional rests on a simplistic, yet disproven, reason–passion dichotomy that disregards a significant body of literature showing that feelings are (and always have been) an intrinsic part of political life. We proposed moving away from political analyses of feelings as a set of involuntary physiological responses driving individuals' behaviour, towards an approach inspired by historians of emotion, which focuses on the established norms for acceptable emotional thought and expression. We turned to three 'directives' issued by the social research organisation, Mass Observation, in 2016, 2017, and 2019, which asked members of the public to reflect on their 'thoughts', 'feelings', 'hopes' and 'fears' about the campaign and its aftermath. We read these richly subjective accounts for empirical evidence of the cultural resources – the stereotypes and shared storylines – that respondents were using to understand the politics, and the feelings, around them. Such evidence suggests we should be wary of ahistorical ideas that imply specific emotions – anger, anxiety – were more prevalent than in previous decades. Instead, it allows us to examine the discursive frames, scripts and 'feeling rules' that people of all political persuasions used to weigh, deploy, and disavow emotion as a legitimate basis for political judgement, within the specific cultural and political context in which they found themselves. Here we want to highlight the ways that these findings help us to understand the contemporary politics of feeling, and to examine its implications for public life and democratic politics.

The first part of the book focused on how people understood the role of feelings in their own decision-making and

Conclusion

how they deployed judgements about the feelings of others to make sense of the political divisions produced by Brexit. In chapter 1, we found that, contrary to public narratives, people rarely distinguished between the head and heart. Instead, we identified two prominent cultural resources of 'gut feeling' and the 'unhelpful campaign' which dominated Mass Observers' accounts of how they voted in the referendum. The recourse to 'gut feeling' highlighted a feeling rule which legitimated emotions as apolitical, morally neutral sources of knowledge, which are difficult to dispute. We historicised this in terms of long-standing conservative discourses emphasising the natural authority of feeling (where sensation takes priority over reason), and newer neoliberal subjectivities (which stress individual morality over social and political intervention). We also set the recourse to gut feeling in the context of the cultural value of 'ordinariness', with its implicit disavowal of being 'political'. Since the post-war years, the 'ordinary citizen' has carried a powerful political weight, as a supposedly independent, apolitical, individual, who is willing to trust their unmediated feelings rather than be manipulated by group, collective, or corporate interests.[15] The turn to 'gut feeling' can, therefore, also be imagined as a bulwark against inauthentic feelings, stirred up by dangerous political actors.

The second of our cultural resources – the 'unhelpful campaign' – revealed a different feeling rule: that decision-making should be based on impartial knowledge and information. This picked up on centuries-old beliefs about the need to exclude 'passion' from political deliberation, which had deeply gendered, raced, and classed implications. It can also be located more specifically within the norms and conventions connected to the professionalisation and privatisation of politics in the late twentieth century, which underpinned the rise of the valence model of voter behaviour. This model depoliticised politics in two ways. First, because it presumed voters would make cost–benefit calculations about political actors' competence, rather than voting on the basis of emotional or partisan attachments. And second, because certain issues were removed from the political sphere altogether and placed in the hands of 'independent experts'. Within this context, it is unsurprising that voters wanted to take decisions based on impartial information, and with reliable guidance as to their likely consequences.

The personal testimony of our sources exposes the messy ways in which these two ideas competed and co-existed with one another within the broader emotional context of the referendum. People wanted to make informed decisions based on impartial information about 'what would happen' if Britain left or remained in the EU. But such information was not forthcoming from the campaigns, which left people feeling confused and uncertain. Many doubted their own and the wider public's ability to make this decision. Faced with this unwelcome responsibility, Mass Observers became increasingly conscious of the role of feelings, not just in their own decision-making, but in that of other people too. They turned to their guts as another (albeit diametrically opposed) form of 'apolitical' knowledge.

Chapter 2 showed how the new divisions produced by Brexit were understood through the lens of emotion. Mass Observers drew on a series of cultural resources which imagined feelings as simultaneously dangerous and irrational; authentic and unanswerable; civilised and empathetic. Far from a clash between reason and passion, then, instead we saw contestation over the authority of different types of feelings. Remain supporters frequently represented Leave

Conclusion

voters as irrational, uneducated, and motivated by negative emotions of fear and prejudice. Leave voters were intensely aware of these stereotypes. Although some broadly accepted this interpretation and sought to distance themselves from other Leavers, others asserted their political agency by insisting these characterisations were themselves the result of misinformation and prejudice. It is however notable that stereotypes of Remainers did not present them as rational or calculating, but instead as 'spoilt children' unable to accept the result. Both stereotypes underline the shared cultural assumption that feelings are dangerous, disorderly, and a threat to democratic norms.

We also saw clear evidence of how compassion and expressions of sympathy for the feelings of others were used to establish, maintain, and reinforce racial hierarchies. Some Remain supporters expressed shame about the result and sought connection with European citizens, migrants more generally, and racialised British citizens. We drew on Sara Ahmed's work to show how these expressions of 'bad feeling' worked to reinforce the respondents' views of themselves as 'good', anti-racist, and consequently 'civilised' people.[16] Other Remain supporters expressed compassion for Leave voters, which could be read as attempts to rationalise racist sentiments as a non-elite form of resistance, reflecting 'legitimate concerns' about the socio-cultural impact of (frequently non-white and non-EU) immigration. And yet, these accounts continually reinforced the misleading distinction between race and class. They simultaneously erased the feelings of racialised and migrantised citizens, denied the racism of white *middle*-class voters, and ignored the everyday cosmopolitanism of many working-class communities.[17]

Thinking about the broader implications of these findings for our understanding of Brexit Britain, the feeling rules identified in the first part of the book raise questions about the emergence of a singular, coherent, neoliberal subjectivity or sensibility. Neoliberalism was supposed to produce *homo economicus* – self-interested individuals guided by entrepreneurialism, self-discipline, and market values who 'respond systematically to modifications in the variables of the environment'.[18] But the structural effects of actually existing neoliberalism instead produced new political communities formed not by objective interests, but by shared sentiment.[19] This is the context in which the emergence of nativist identity politics is understood as an emotional backlash against a coldly rational neoliberal polity. And yet, as we saw in chapter 2, this is also a politics which explicitly draws inspiration from the *architects* of British neoliberalism – from Enoch Powell to Margaret Thatcher.[20] In this story, declinist economics, racial anxiety, self-reliance, and national sovereignty are firmly intertwined.

Moreover, we saw that the decision-making processes of Leave and Remain voters did not reflect a binary sentimental/rational model. Instead, both drew distinctions between undesirable and desirable *types* of feelings in politics. If the former was reminiscent of nineteenth-century tirades against the irrational passions of the mob, the latter recalled the eighteenth-century concept of sensibility – whereby passion was seen to guide reason, and to address social, political, and moral engagements.[21] Thus we see multiple sensibilities, which are sometimes understood to have been caused by neoliberalism but might be better understood as forming the conditions for neoliberalism. The contradictions embedded in our sources show how neoliberal common sense – at the level of ideas or ideology – is often messy and multifaceted. But it is at the level of feelings that common sense feels coherent, becomes intuitive, and appears natural.[22]

Conclusion

The second part of the book focused on another public narrative about the feelings of Brexit, which is that they were excessive. The period of the referendum campaign, and its aftermath, was experienced as a peculiarly emotional time, in which feelings carried both greater power and greater danger than usual. It seemed that just as feelings were shaping political decisions and attitudes, so politics were intruding into the most intimate areas of affective life.

Chapter 3 focused on Brexit as a public mood. The 'mood of the country' was a cultural resource that figured in many ways during the Brexit period – from a blunt description of the very marginal vote in favour of leaving the European Union, to dramatic characterisations of a divided and angry national community. Before and after the event, polls attempted to keep track of the nation's mood and shifting attitudes towards the exit negotiations.[23] The idea that Brexit was an excessively emotional event in British politics was pervasive. This emotionality became itself a mood – prickly, tense, febrile. The work of managing this mood, of being constantly on edge, was exhausting. But we also saw that Brexit itself was imagined as a form of 'mood work', something which both required and might inculcate an 'optimistic' public mood. And yet, even amongst Brexit's staunchest supporters, hope soon gave way to frustration, fatalism, and disengagement. The government eventually tried to marshal this collective fatigue in its 2019 election slogan: 'Get Brexit Done'. But even though boredom with the whole affair was perhaps the most pervasive mood of all, it also felt like a deliberate action, a withdrawal from a collective situation.

The final chapter focused on the way that these stresses and strains of the referendum were experienced and managed in daily life and intimate relationships. On the one hand, this was seen to be a problem of politics exceeding its limits and intruding into spaces of private and intimate life, on the other, it was a matter of personal feelings getting in the way of politics and making civic discourse too fraught to sustain. These were not mutually exclusive positions but seemed to reinforce as well as complicate each other. Both popular psychological discourse and democratic theory agree that talking is the way to resolve differences. But as we saw, there are competing views within both spheres about the extent to which such talk should embrace or avoid conflict, and how far speakers should express or suppress their feelings. The evidence from Mass Observation suggests that such concerns also deeply affected people navigating their everyday lives. The idea that Brexit had threatened relationships became a new feeling rule. Observers worried about how – and even whether – to speak to those who had voted differently from themselves, and about the competing obligations to maintain civility, correct misperceptions, and confront differences. Many reported changing their daily routines and re-evaluating long-standing relationships in the wake of the referendum. The public discourse seemed to add to these worries rather than assuage them.

Final thoughts

Throughout the course of writing this book, we have frequently been asked for our thoughts on the role that feelings should play in political life. We have resisted this, for the simple reason that – as we have shown – prescriptions for how people *should* feel are themselves at the heart of many of their political problems. During the referendum, voters were told that feelings had no place in politics, but also that they had been neglected by politicians for too long;

Conclusion

that correct emotional management was a cure for social and political problems, but that emotions were involuntary responses to external reality; that feelings were dangerous and destabilising, and also authentic reflections of their inner selves. As we have argued throughout the book, all of these contradictory stories about feelings had historical trajectories, and they had political consequences.

It is tempting to conclude that the politics of feeling around Brexit were marked more by the intensity of debates about feeling than by the experience of feeling itself. But in truth the two are inextricable. The stories we tell about feelings, shape how we experience them. Accounts that focus on polarised camps of passionate Leavers and rational Remainers not only fail to capture the complexity of Brexit Britain, but themselves feed back into these normative judgements and fuel further polarisation. Instead, our version of an emotionally literate approach to politics would begin by seeking to understand how these stories develop, circulate, and impact on public understandings of feelings and their political (il)legitimacy.

The way that political actors and analysts describe and discuss feelings matters. But they are not the only storytellers we need to consider. As the accounts examined in this book attest, stories are interactive, and inconsistent. They overlap and they contradict one another. Meanings gather as they circulate and mutate, and these in turn can be resisted or internalised (or both). To understand the dynamics of this process, we need to catch these stories in action and see how they are picked up, turned over, held aloft, or cast aside. The Mass Observation Project has allowed us to do that. By looking at the accounts of its writers, we have been able to see the multiple ways people responded to public narratives about feelings and their place in political life. We have seen how these ideas permeated their judgements of other people's feelings, but also how incompletely they seemed to capture their own experiences. The sense of being out of step with an imagined collective was itself a significant part of the politics of feeling in Brexit Britain.

Notes

Introduction

1 Boris Johnson, speech in Downing Street, 24 July 2019: www.gov.uk/government/speeches/boris-johnsons-first-speech-as-prime-minister-24-july-2019 (accessed 4 March 2023).
2 Colin Crouch, 'Balancing Reason and Emotion in Democracy', *British Academy Blog*, 23 February 2017: www.thebritishacademy.ac.uk/blog/balancing-reason-and-emotion-democracy (accessed 4 March 2023); Laura Jenkins, 'Why Do All Our Feelings about Politics Matter?', *British Journal of Politics and International Relations*, 20:1 (2018), pp. 191–205.
3 Fintan O'Toole, *Heroic Failure: Brexit and the Politics of Pain* (New York: Apollo, 2018); Pankaj Mishra, *Age of Anger: A History of the Present* (New York: Farrar, Straus and Giroux, 2017); William Davies, *Nervous States: How Feeling Took Over the World* (London: Jonathan Cape, 2018).
4 Sara Hobolt, Thomas Leeper, and James Tilley, 'Divided by the Vote: Affective Polarization in the Wake of Brexit', *British Journal of Political Science*, 51:4 (2021), pp. 1476–1493; Shanto Iyengar et al., 'The Origins and Consequences of Affective Polarisation in the United States', *American Review of Political Science*, 22 (2019), pp. 129–146.
5 Crouch, 'Balancing Reason and Emotion'.
6 Philippa Perry, 'To mend the Brexit rift, let's respect other people's feelings – and honestly face our own', *Guardian*, 25 June 2016: www.theguardian.com/commentisfree/2016/jun/25/brexit-rift-feelings-honest (accessed 4 March 2023).

Notes

7 BBC, *The Age of Emotion*, BBC Radio 4, 14 February 2018: www.bbc.co.uk/programmes/b09I0svk (accessed 4 March 2023).
8 Thomas Dixon, 'What Is the History of Anger a History Of?', *Emotions: History, Culture, Society*, 4:1 (2020), pp. 1–34 (5).
9 Thomas Dixon, *From Passions to Emotions: The Creation of a Secular Psychological Category* (Oxford: Oxford University Press, 2013).
10 Perry, 'To mend the Brexit rift'.
11 Grayson Perry, 'Acceptance Speech', PSA Annual Awards, Church House, London, 30 November 2016, quoted in Matthew Flinders, 'Why Feelings Trump Facts: Anti-politics, Citizenship and Emotion', *Emotions and Society*, 2:1 (2020), pp. 21–40 (23).
12 *Grayson Perry: Divided Britain* (Channel 4, 2017); *Grayson Perry's Full English* (Channel 4, 2023). These built on work he had already begun – see, for instance, *All in the Best Possible Taste* (Channel 4, 2012).
13 Nick Clarke and Jonathan Moss, 'Popular Imaginative Geographies and Brexit: Evidence from Mass Observation', *Transactions of the British Institute of Geographers*, 46:3 (2021), pp. 732–746.
14 See, for instance, Margrit Pernau et al., *Civilizing Emotions: Concepts in Nineteenth-Century Asia and Europe* (Oxford: Oxford University Press, 2015); Eleanor Jupp, Jessica Pykett, and Fiona M. Smith (eds), *Emotional States: Sites and Spaces of Affective Governance* (Abingdon: Routledge, 2016); J.M. Barbalet, *Emotion, Social Theory, and Social Structure: A Macrosociological Approach* (Cambridge: Cambridge University Press, 2001); Nicole Eustace, 'Emotion and Political Change', in Susan J. Matt and Peter N. Stearns (eds), *Doing Emotions History* (Urbana, IL: University of Illinois Press, 2013), pp. 163–183; William Reddy, *The Navigation of Feeling: A Framework for the History of Emotions* (Cambridge: Cambridge University Press, 2001). For examples of how this distinction has been deployed in modern British politics, see Natalie Hanley-Smith and Sarah Richardson, 'Dangerous or Goodly Passions: The Role of Emotion in Parliament and Politics', *Parliamentary History*, 42 (2023), pp. 1–10; Claire Langhamer, '"The Live Dynamic Whole of Feeling and Behavior": Capital Punishment and the Politics of Emotion, 1945-1957', *Journal of British Studies*, 51:2 (2012), pp. 416–441.
15 Ben Rogaly, *Stories from a Migrant City: Living and Working Together in the Shadow of Brexit* (Manchester: Manchester University Press, 2021); Sarah Marie Hall, 'Waiting for Brexit: Crisis, Conjuncture, Method', *Transactions of the Institute of British Geographers*, 47 (2022), pp. 200–213; Ben Anderson

et al., 'Brexit: Modes of Uncertainty and Futures in an Impasse', *Transactions of the Institute of British Geographers*, 45 (2020), pp. 256–269. One honourable exception is the work of Stephen Coleman, particularly *How People Talk about Politics: Brexit and Beyond* (London: Bloomsbury, 2021) and 'Feeling It/Not Feeling It: Mood Stories as Accounts of Political Intuition', *International Journal of Politics, Culture, and Society*, 35 (2022), pp. 477–495.

16 Ute Frevert and Kerstin Maria Pahl, 'Introducing Political Feelings: Participatory Politics, Institutions, and Emotional Templates', in Ute Frevert et al., *Feeling Political Emotions and Institutions since 1789* (Cham: Palgrave MacMillan, 2022), p. 1–26 (2).

17 Hanley-Smith and Richardson, 'Dangerous or Goodly Passions'; Lisa Berry-Waite, '"A rancour and a passion would be introduced into politics": Perceptions of the Woman MP in Late 19th and Early 20th Century Britain', *Parliamentary History*, 42 (2023), pp. 148–167; Sadiya Akram, 'Dear British Politics – Where is the Race and Racism?', *British Politics* (2023): https://doi.org/10.1057/s41293-023-00224-3.

18 Pavlos Vasilopoulos, 'Affective Intelligence and Emotional Dynamics in Voters' Decision-Making Processes', in David P. Redlawsk (ed.), *Oxford Encyclopedia of Political Decision Making* (Oxford: Oxford University Press, 2021).

19 Examples here stretch back to Aristotle but, for a text produced as Britain became a mass democracy, see Graham Wallas, *Human Nature in Politics*, 3rd edn (London: Constable & Co., 1929 [1920]).

20 Michael Oakeshott, 'Rationalism in Politics' (1947), reprinted in Michael Oakeshott, *Rationalism in Politics and Other Essays* (Indianapolis, IN: Liberty Fund, 1991 [London and New York: Methuen, 1962]), pp. 5–42.

21 Philip Williamson, *Stanley Baldwin: Conservative Leadership and National Values* (Cambridge: Cambridge University Press, 1999); Martin Francis, 'Tears, Tantrums, and Bared Teeth: The Emotional Economy of Three Conservative Prime Ministers, 1951–1963', *Journal of British Studies*, 41:3 (2002), pp. 354–387.

22 Roger Scruton, *The Meaning of Conservatism*, 3rd edn (Basingstoke: Palgrave, 2001 [1980]), p. 28.

23 Mark Bevir, *The Making of British Socialism* (Princeton, NJ: Princeton University Press, 2011), p. 17.

24 Quoted in Martin Francis, 'Economics and Ethics: The Nature of Labour's Socialism, 1945–1951', *Twentieth Century British History*, 6:2 (1995), pp. 220–243 (240). For a discussion of recent iterations of this theme, see Emily Robinson, 'Recapturing Our Traditions? The Rhetorical Shift from New to One Nation Labour

(and Beyond)', in Judi Atkins and John Gaffney (eds), *Voices of the UK Left: Rhetoric, Ideology and the Performance of Politics* (London: Routledge, 2017), pp. 35–59.

25 Richard Hoggart, *The Uses of Literacy* (London: Penguin, 1957); Lawrence Black, *The Political Culture of the Left in Affluent Britain, 1951–64: Old Labour, New Britain?* (Basingstoke: Palgrave, 2003); Geoffrey Foote, *The Republican Transformation of Modern British Politics* (Basingstoke: Palgrave, 2006).

26 Jack Saunders, 'Emotions, Social Practices and the Changing Composition of Class, Race and Gender in the National Health Service, 1970–79: "Lively Discussion Ensued"', *History Workshop Journal*, 88 (2019), pp. 204–228; Diarmaid Kelliher, 'Constructing a Culture of Solidarity: London and the British Coalfields in the Long 1970s', *Antipode*, 49:1 (2017), pp. 106–124; Jon Lawrence, *Me Me Me? The Search for Community in Post-war England* (Oxford: Oxford University Press, 2019).

27 Maurice Glasman, Jonathan Rutherford, Marc Stears, and Stuart White (eds), *The Labour Tradition and the Politics of Paradox: The Oxford-London Seminars 2010–11* (London: Oxford-London Seminars, 2011).

28 Martin Pugh, 'The Rise of Labour and the Political Culture of Conservatism, 1890–1945', *History*, 88:288 (2002), pp. 514–537; George Orwell, *The Road to Wigan Pier* (London: Penguin, 1989 [1937]), chapter 12.

29 Jeremy Nuttall, *Psychological Socialism: The Labour Party and Qualities of Mind and Character, 1931 to the Present* (Manchester: Manchester University Press, 2006).

30 On post-war psychology, see Rhodri Hayward, 'The Pursuit of Serenity: Psychological Knowledge and the Making of the Welfare State', in Sally Alexander and Barbara Taylor (eds), *History and Psyche: Culture, Psychoanalysis and the Past* (Basingstoke: Palgrave, 2012), pp. 283–304; on the New Left see, for instance, Madeleine Davis, 'Reappraising Socialist Humanism', *Journal of Political Ideologies*, 18:1 (2013), pp. 57–81.

31 Michael Freeden, *Liberal Languages: Ideological Imaginations and Twentieth-Century Progressive Thought* (Princeton, NJ: Princeton University Press, 2004).

32 Claire Langhamer, 'An Archive of Feeling? Mass Observation and the Mid-Century Moment', *Insights*, 9 (2016), pp. 1–15 (4). For more on permissivism, see Anna von der Goltz and Britta Waldschmidt-Nelson (eds), *Inventing the Silent Majority in Western Europe and the United States: Conservatism in the 1960s and 1970s* (Cambridge: Cambridge University Press, 2017);

Marcus Collins (ed.), *The Permissive Society and Its Enemies* (London: Rivers Oram, 2008); Emily Robinson, *The Language of Progressive Politics in Modern Britain* (London: Palgrave, 2017), chapter 4.

33 Anthony Giddens, *Modernity and Self-Identity: Self and Society in the Late Modern Age* (Stanford, CA: Stanford University Press, 1991); Mathew Thomson, *Psychological Subjects: Identity, Culture, and Health in Twentieth-Century Britain* (Oxford: Oxford University Press, 2006).

34 Andrea Marie Hyde and James G. LaPrad, 'Mindfulness, Democracy, and Education', *Democracy & Education*, 23:2 (2015), Article 2; Patrick W. Comstock, 'The Politics of Mindfulness', *Democracy & Education*, 23:2 (2015), Article 8; Kyle A. Greenwalt and Cuong H. Nguyen, 'The Mindfulness Practice, Aesthetic Experience, and Creative Democracy', *Education and Culture*, 33:2 (2017), pp. 49–65.

35 George Marcus, 'Emotions in Politics', *Annual Review of Political Science*, 3:1 (2000), pp. 221–250; Michael A. Neblo, 'Philosophical Psychology with Political Intent', in George Marcus et al. (eds), *The Affect Effect: Dynamics of Emotion in Political Thinking and Behaviour* (Chicago, IL: Chicago University Press, 2007), pp. 25–47; Eric Groenendyk, 'Current Emotion Research in Political Science: How Emotions Help Democracy Overcome Its Collective Action Problem', *Emotion Research*, 3:4 (2011), pp. 455–463.

36 For example, Angus Campbell, Philip E. Converse, Warren E. Miller, and Donald E. Stokes, *The American Voter* (Chicago, IL: University of Chicago Press, 1980); Philip E. Converse, 'The Nature of Belief Systems in Mass Publics', in David E. Apter (ed.), *Ideology and Discontent* (New York: Free Press, 1986), pp. 206–261.

37 Pavlos Vasilopoulos, 'Affective Intelligence and Emotional Dynamics in Voters' Decision-Making Processes', in David P. Redlawsk (ed.), *Oxford Encyclopedia of Political Decision Making* (Oxford: Oxford University Press, 2021).

38 George Marcus, Russell Neuman, and Michael MacKuen, *Affective Intelligence and Political Judgment* (Chicago, IL: University of Chicago Press, 2000).

39 See Simon Koschut, 'Emotion, Discourse, and Power in World Politics', in Simon Koschut (ed.) *The Power of Emotion in World Politics* (Abingdon: Routledge, 2020), pp. 1–26 (7).

40 Marcus, 'Emotions in Politics'.

41 Sofia Vasilopoulou and Marcus Wagner, 'Fear, Anger and Enthusiasm about the European Union: Effects of Emotional

Reactions on Public Preferences towards European Integration', *European Union Politics*, 18:3 (2017), pp. 382–405.
42 Monika Verbalyte and Christian von Scheve, 'Feeling Europe: Political Emotion, Knowledge, and Support for the European Union', *Innovation: European Journal of Social Science Research*, 31 (2017), pp. 162–188.
43 George E. Marcus, 'How Affective Intelligence Theory Can Help Us Understand Politics', *Emotion Researcher*, ISRE's Sourcebook for Research on Emotion and Affect, 2017: http://emotionresearcher.com/how-affective-intelligence-theory-can-help-us-understand-politics/ (accessed 3 March 2023).
44 Sara Ahmed, *The Cultural Politics of Emotion* (London: Routledge, 2004); Laura Kounine, 'Emotions, Mind, and Body on Trial: A Cross-Cultural Perspective', *Journal of Social History*, 51:3 (2017), pp. 219–230; Martha Nussbaum, *Political Emotions: Why Love Matters for Justice* (Cambridge, MA: Harvard University Press, 2013); Lisa Feldman Barrett, *How Emotions Are Made: The Secret Life of the Brain* (New York: Houghton Mifflin, 2017); Monique Scheer, 'Are Emotions a Kind of Practice (and Is That What Makes Them Have a History)? A Bourdieuian Approach to Understanding Emotion', *History and Theory*, 51 (2017), pp. 193–220.
45 Dixon, *From Passions to Emotions*; Langhamer, 'An Archive of Feeling?'.
46 See Frevert and Pahl, 'Introducing Political Feelings', pp. 9–10.
47 Tony Kushner, *We Europeans? Mass-Observation, 'Race', and British Identity in the Twentieth Century* (Abingdon: Routledge, 2004); Mike Savage, *Identities and Social Change in Britain since 1940: The Politics of Method* (Oxford: Oxford University Press, 2010); Florence Sutcliffe-Braithwaite, *Class, Politics, and the Decline of Deference in England, 1968–2000* (Oxford: Oxford University Press, 2017); Nick Clarke, Will Jennings, Jonathan Moss, and Gerry Stoker, *The Good Politician: Folk Theories, Political Interaction and the Rise of Anti-politics* (Cambridge: Cambridge University Press, 2017).
48 Alexandre Campsie, 'Mass-Observation, Left Intellectuals and the Politics of Everyday Life', *English Historical Review*, 131:548 (2016), pp. 92–121.
49 Ben Highmore, *Everyday Life and Cultural Theory: An Introduction* (London: Routledge, 2001), chapter 6.
50 Madge to Harrisson, 18 Jan. 1940, cited in James Hinton, '"The 'Class' Complex": Mass-Observation and Cultural Distinction in Pre-War Britain', *Past & Present*, 199:1 (2008), pp. 207–236 (222).
51 Hinton, '"The 'Class' Complex"', p. 221.

Notes

52 Langhamer, 'An Archive of Feeling?'.
53 Francis, 'Tears, Tantrums, and Bared Teeth'; Thomas Dixon, *Weeping Britannia: Portrait of a Nation in Tears* (Oxford: Oxford University Press, 2015).
54 Gabriele Linke, 'The Public, The Private, and the Intimate: Richard Sennett's and Lauren Berlant's Cultural Criticism in Dialogue', *Biography*, 34:1 (2011), pp. 11–24.
55 Alison Pugh, 'What Good Are Interviews for Thinking about Culture? Demystifying Interpretive Analysis', *American Journal of Cultural Sociology*, 1 (2013), pp. 42–68 (51).
56 Coleman, *How People Talk*, p. 39.
57 Pugh, 'What Good Are Interviews?', p. 51, cited in Coleman, *How People Talk*, p. 39.
58 Dixon, 'What Is the History'. See also Barrett, *How Emotions Are Made*.
59 Michael Roper, 'Out of View: Subjectivity and Emotion in Gender History', *History Workshop Journal*, 59:1 (2005), pp. 57–72.
60 Penny Summerfield, *Reconstructing Women's Wartime Lives: Discourse and Subjectivity in Oral History* (Manchester: Manchester University Press, 1998), p. 17.
61 Selina Todd, 'Class, Experience and Britain's Twentieth Century', *Social History*, 56:4 (2014), pp. 489–508 (495).
62 Roper, 'Out of View', pp. 65–66.
63 James Hinton, *Nine Wartime Lives: Mass Observation and the Making of the Modern Self* (Oxford: Oxford University Press, 2010), p. 18.
64 Nick Clarke et al., 'Voter Decision-Making in a Context of Low Political Trust: The 2016 UK EU Membership Referendum', *Political Studies*, 71:1 (2021), pp. 106–124 (108).
65 Coleman, *How People Talk*, p. 20.
66 Ibid., pp. 20–21.
67 Ben Highmore, 'Feeling Our Way: Mood and Cultural Studies', *Communication and Critical/Cultural Studies*, 10:4 (2013), pp. 427–438.
68 Lauren Berlant, *Cruel Optimism* (Durham, NC: Duke University Press, 2010), discussed in Coleman, *How People Talk*, p. 21.
69 Hinton, *Nine Wartime Lives*, p. 18.
70 Clarke et al., *The Good Politician*.
71 Robert Saunders, *Yes to Europe! The 1975 Referendum and Seventies Britain* (Cambridge: Cambridge University Press, 2018).
72 Noah Carl, James Dennison, and Geoffrey Evans, 'European but Not European Enough: An Explanation for Brexit', *European Union Politics*, 20:2 (2018), pp. 282–304; Oliver Daddow, 'The UK

Notes

Media and "Europe": From Permissive Consensus to Destructive Dissent', *International Affairs*, 88:6 (2012), pp. 1219–1236.

73 Carl, Dennison, and Evans, 'European but Not European Enough'; Daddow, 'The UK Media and "Europe"'; Oliver Daddow, 'Interpreting the Outsider Tradition in British European Policy Speeches from Thatcher to Cameron', *Journal of Commonmarket Studies*, 53 (2015), pp. 71–88.

74 James Dennison, Daniel Seddig, and Eldad Davidov, 'The Role of Human Values in Explaining Support for European Union Membership', *Journal of Cross-Cultural Psychology*, 52:4 (2021), pp. 372–387; John Curtice, 'Why Leave Won the UK's EU Referendum', *Journal of Common Market Studies*, 55 (2017), pp. 19–37.

75 Maria Sobolewska and Robert Ford, *Brexitland: Identity, Diversity and the Reshaping of British Politics* (Cambridge: Cambridge University Press, 2020).

76 Sara B. Hobolt, 'The Brexit Vote: A Divided Nation, a Divided Continent', *Journal of European Public Policy*, 23:9 (2016), pp. 1259–1277 (1259).

77 Matthew Goodwin and Oliver Heath, 'The 2016 Referendum, Brexit and the Left Behind: An Aggregate-Level Analysis of the Result', *Political Quarterly*, 87 (2016), pp. 323–332 (331).

78 For a thoughtful critique of the latter, see Robert Saunders, 'Brexit and Empire: "Global Britain" and the Myth of Imperial Nostalgia', *Journal of Imperial and Commonwealth History*, 48:6 (2020), pp. 1140–1174.

79 Franco Zappettini, 'The Tabloidization of the Brexit Campaign: Power to the (British) People?' *Journal of Language and Politics*, 20:2 (2021), pp. 277–303 (277).

80 Andrew Glencross, *Why the UK Voted for Brexit: David Cameron's Great Miscalculation* (London: Palgrave, 2016), p. 35.

81 Adrian Williamson, *Europe and the Decline of Social Democracy in Britain: From Attlee to Brexit* (Woodbridge: Boydell and Brewer, 2019).

82 Hobolt et al., 'Divided by the Vote'.

83 Christopher Achen and Larry Bartels, *Democracy for Realists: Why Elections Do Not Produce Responsive Government* (Princeton, NJ: Princeton University Press, 2016), p. 267.

84 For example, John Curtice, 'Brave New World: Understanding the 2019 General Election', *Political Insight*, 11:1 (2020), pp. 8–12; Robert Ford, 'If Labour can't beat the Tories' polarising game, it should build bridges instead', *Guardian*, 7 November 2021: www.theguardian.com/commentisfree/2021/nov/07/if-labour-cant-beat

-the-tories-polarising-game-it-should-build-bridges-instead (accessed 4 March 2023).
85 Robert Ford, 'Labour wants to move on from Brexit, but English voters just won't let them', *Observer*, 9 May 2021: www.theguardian.com/politics/2021/may/09/labour-wants-to-move-on-from-brexit-but-english-voters-just-wont-let-them (accessed 4 March 2023).
86 Jon Lawrence, 'Labour and the Culture Wars of Modern Politics', *Political Quarterly*, 91 (2020), pp. 31–34 (32).
87 Katherine Davies, 'Sticking Together in "Divided Britain": Talking Brexit in Everyday Family Relationships', *Sociology*, 56:1 (2021), pp. 97–113.

Chapter 1

1 Gavin Hewitt, 'EU Referendum: The people v the elites?', *BBC News*, 8 June 2016: www.bbc.co.uk/news/uk-politics-eu-referendum-36458369 (accessed 4 March 2023); Uta Staiger, 'The heart of the matter: Passion, politics and the EU referendum', *Open Democracy*, 22 June 2016: www.opendemocracy.net/en/brexit-divisions/heart-of-matter-passion-politics-and-eu-referendum/ (accessed 4 March 2023).
2 Graham Robb, 'In my own head versus heart battle on the Brexit debate, the head wins out', *Chronicle Live*, 9 March 2016: www.chroniclelive.co.uk/news/news-opinion/head-versus-heart-battle-brexit-11012641 (accessed 4 March 2023).
3 Karren Brady, 'My heart says Brexit but my head is telling me it's a step that will end in economic catastrophe', *Sun*, 18 June 2016: www.thesun.co.uk/news/opinion/1304491/my-heart-says-brexit-but-my-head-is-telling-me-its-a-step-that-will-end-in-economic-catastrophe (accessed 4 March 2023).
4 Anand Menon, 'Facts and Emotion Matter in the EU Debate', *Times Red Box*, 27 May 2016, now available at *UK in a Changing Europe*: https://ukandeu.ac.uk/facts-and-emotion-matter-in-the-eu-debate/ (accessed 4 March 2023).
5 Hewitt, 'EU Referendum'; Simon Jenkins, 'On Brexit, gender, age and political party are no guide as to how we'll vote', *Guardian*, 31 March 2016: www.theguardian.com/commentisfree/2016/mar/31/brexit-gender-age-political-party-vote (accessed 4 March 2023).
6 Decca Aitkenhead, 'Nigel Farage: "They say I'm toxic. Quite the opposite"', *Guardian*, 20 May 2016: www.theguardian.com/politics/2016/may/20/nigel-farage-ukip-eu-referendum-interview-vote-leave-brief-every-day (accessed 4 March 2023).

Notes

7. 'David Miliband: Brexit not just bad for Britain but also "bad for international order"', *ITV News*, 12 April 2016: www.itv.com/news/2016-04-12/david-miliband-brexit-not-just-bad-for-britain-but-also-bad-for-international-order (accessed 4 March 2023).
8. Hewitt, 'EU Referendum'.
9. John Curtice, 'The Emotional Legacy of Brexit: How Britain Has Become a Country of "Remainers" and "Leavers"', What UK Thinks: EU, 15 October 2018: https://whatukthinks.org/eu/wp-content/uploads/2018/10/WUKT-EU-Briefing-Paper-15-Oct-18-Emotional-legacy-paper-final.pdf (accessed 4 March 2023).
10. William Davies, *Nervous States: How Feeling Took Over the World* (London: Penguin, 2018).
11. Daniel Kahneman, *Thinking, Fast and Slow* (London: Penguin, 2011).
12. Linda Blair, 'Can We Trust Emotion over Reason?', *Daily Telegraph*, 30 May 2016: www.telegraph.co.uk/health-fitness/mind/can-we-trust-emotion-over-reason/ (accessed 4 March 2023); Zaria Gorvet, 'The Reasons Why Politics Feels So Tribal in 2016', *BBC Future*, 24 August 2016: www.bbc.com/future/article/20160823-how-modern-life-is-destroying-democracy (accessed 4 March 2023); R.C., 'The Political Nausea When Feelings Replace Facts', *The Economist*, 21 June 2019: www.economist.com/open-future/2019/06/21/the-political-nausea-when-feelings-replace-facts (accessed 4 March 2023); BBC, *The Age of Emotion*, BBC Radio 4, 14 February 2018: www.bbc.co.uk/programmes/b0910svk (accessed 4 March 2023). It should be noted that the latter programme was far more nuanced than its title suggested, and not only historicised the idea of an 'age of emotion' but also challenged the emotion/reason dichotomy.
13. Alison Flood, '"Post-truth" named word of the year by Oxford Dictionaries', *Guardian*, 15 November 2016: www.theguardian.com/books/2016/nov/15/post-truth-named-word-of-the-year-by-oxford-dictionaries (accessed 4 March 2023).
14. S2083, M, 85, retired shopkeeper, East Sussex, Remain, 2016.
15. B5970, M, 49, unemployed clerk, Cambridge, Leave, 2017.
16. F3409, F, 70, retired civil servant, Nottingham, Leave, 2017.
17. Ibid.
18. C3603, M, 72, retired youth and community officer, Sheffield, didn't vote, 2016.
19. C5782, F, 33, communications officer, Brighton, Remain, 2016.
20. J1890, F, 84, retired shop assistant, Hull, Remain, 2016.
21. J4793, F, 35, writer, Renfrewshire, Remain, 2016.
22. S6115, F, 26, administrative assistant, Nottinghamshire, Leave, 2017; R3546, M, 53, locksmith, North Yorkshire, Leave, 2017.

Notes

23 S5915, M, 56, engineering works manager, Wiltshire, Leave, 2017.
24 S3035, M, 70, retired banker, West Sussex, Leave, 2017.
25 Claire Langhamer, 'An Archive of Feeling? Mass Observation and the Mid-Century Moment', *Insights*, 9 (2016), pp. 1–15 (5).
26 A1706, F, 71, artist, West Sussex, Remain, 2017.
27 Thomas Dixon, *From Passions to Emotions: The Creation of a Secular Psychological Category* (Oxford: Oxford University Press, 2013).
28 Hewitt, 'EU Referendum'.
29 Ambrose Evans-Pritchard, '"Irritation and Anger" May Lead to Brexit, Says Influential Psychologist', *Daily Telegraph*, 6 June 2016: www.telegraph.co.uk/business/2016/06/05/british-voters-succumbing-to-impulse-irritation-and-anger---and/ (accessed 4 March 2023); Jenkins, 'On Brexit'.
30 Lisa Feldman Barrett, *How Emotions Are Made: The Secret Life of the Brain* (New York: Houghton Mifflin, 2017).
31 Lisa Feldman Barrett and Moshe Bar, 'See It with Feeling: Affective Predictions during Object Perception', *Philosophical Transactions of the Royal Society of London: Series B: Biological Sciences*, 364:1521 (2009), pp. 1325–1334.
32 Grant Soosalu, Suzanne Henwood, and Arun Deo, 'Head, Heart, and Gut in Decision Making: Development of a Multiple Brain Preference Questionnaire', *SAGE Open*, 9:1 (2019), pp. 1–17.
33 Gerd Gigerenzer, *Gut Feeling: The Intelligence of the Unconscious* (London: Penguin, 2007).
34 David Dotlich, Peter Cairo, and Stephen Rhinesmith, *Head, Heart and Guts – How the World's Best Companies Develop Complete Leaders* (Hoboken: John Wiley, 2006).
35 Leslie Lytle, 'BRAIN: An Acronym for Informed Decision-Making', *Nurture*, 4 June 2014: https://nurturerva.org/2014/06/04/brain-an-acronym-for-informed-decision-making/ (accessed 4 March 2023).
36 Eric Groenendyk, 'Of Two Minds, but One Heart: A Good "Gut" Feeling Moderates the Effect of Ambivalence on Attitude Formation and Turnout', *American Journal of Political Science*, 63 (2019), pp. 368–384.
37 V3773, F, 53, pharmacist, Solihull, Remain, 2016.
38 B5702, F, 25, waitress and student, Cheshire, Remain, 2016.
39 W3994, F, 43, charity funding development worker, Derbyshire, Remain, 2016.
40 T4715, F, 44, community health worker, Nottingham, Remain, 2016.

Notes

41 D4736, M, 49, air traffic services assistant, Southampton, Remain, 2016.
42 B3227, M, 50, administrator, Birmingham, Remain, 2017.
43 S5866, F, 36, scriptwriter, Bury, Remain, 2016.
44 N5744, M, 38, carer, Sunderland, Leave, 2016.
45 B5342, F, 30, online jewellery retailer, Salisbury, Leave, 2016.
46 M3408, F, 69, retired nursery teacher, Coventry, Leave, 2016.
47 Langhamer, 'An Archive of Feeling?'
48 Sara Ahmed, *The Cultural Politics of Emotion* (London: Routledge, 2004), p. 43. Original emphasis.
49 H1541, M, 71, retired film writer, central Scotland, Remain, 2016.
50 W1382, M, 92, retired technical writer, North Somerset, Remain, 2016.
51 O3436, F, 62, retired civil servant, Dorset, Remain, 2016.
52 D5157, F, 42, NHS worker, Nottingham, vote unknown, 2016.
53 G226, F, 75, retired counsellor, Lancashire, Remain, 2017.
54 N5744, M, 38, carer, Sunderland, Leave, 2016.
55 Claire Langhamer, 'Mass Observing the Atom Bomb: The Emotional Politics of August 1945', *Contemporary British History*, 33:2 (2019), pp. 208–225.
56 Linda Åhäll, 'Affect as Methodology: Feminism and the Politics of Emotion', *International Political Sociology*, 12:1 (2018), pp. 36–52. See also Sara Ahmed, *Living a Feminist Life* (Durham, NC: Duke University Press, 2018), p. 22.
57 Barrett, *How Emotions Are Made*.
58 Quintin Hogg, *Toryism and Tomorrow* (London: Conservative Political Centre, 1957), p. 9.
59 For a more detailed exploration of this argument, see Emily Robinson, 'The Authority of Feeling in Mid-Twentieth-Century English Conservatism', *The Historical Journal*, 63:5 (2020), pp. 1303–1324.
60 Michel Foucault, *The Birth of Biopolitics: Lectures at the Collège de France, 1978–1979* (Basingstoke: Palgrave Macmillan, 2008).
61 Wendy Brown, *In the Ruins of Neoliberalism: The Rise of Antidemocratic Politics in the West* (New York: Columbia University Press, 2019).
62 Martin Francis, 'Tears, Tantrums, and Bared Teeth: The Emotional Economy of Three Conservative Prime Ministers, 1951–1963', *The Journal of British Studies*, 41:3 (2002), pp. 354–387; Thomas Dixon, *Weeping Britannia: Portrait of a Nation in Tears* (Oxford: Oxford University Press, 2015).
63 Francis, 'Tears, Tantrums, and Bared Teeth, p. 359.

Notes

64 Emily Robinson, Camilla Schofield, Florence Sutcliffe-Braithwaite, and Natalie Thomlinson, 'Telling Stories about Post-War Britain: Popular Individualism and the "Crisis" of the 1970s', *Twentieth Century British History*, 28:2 (2017), pp. 268–304.
65 Richard Cockett, 'The New Right and the 1960s: The Dialectics of Liberation', in Geoff Andrews et al. (eds), *New Left, New Right and Beyond: Taking the Sixties Seriously* (Basingstoke: Macmillan, 1999), pp. 85–105 (98).
66 Bill Schwarz, 'The Silent Majority: How the Private Becomes Political', in Anna von der Goltz and Britta Waldschmidt-Nelson (eds), *Inventing the Silent Majority in Western Europe and the United States: Conservatism in the 1960s and 1970s* (Cambridge: Cambridge University Press, 2017), pp. 147–171 (148).
67 Chris Moores, 'Corporeal Conservatism? Bodies, Brains and Moral Movements in England since the 1960s', unpublished paper, delivered at North American Conference on British Studies, Vancouver, 15 November 2019.
68 Claire Langhamer, '"Who the Hell Are Ordinary People?" Ordinariness as a Category of Historical Analysis', *Transactions of the Royal Historical Society*, 28 (2018), pp. 175–195.
69 Jonathan Moss, *Women, Workplace Protest and Political Identity in England, 1968–1985* (Manchester: Manchester University Press, 2019); Florence Sutcliffe-Braithwaite and Natalie Thomlinson, 'Vernacular Discourses of Gender Equality in the Post-war British Working Class', *Past and Present*, 254:1 (2022), pp. 277–313.
70 Nina Eliasoph, *Avoiding Politics: How Americans Produce Apathy in Everyday Life* (Cambridge: Cambridge University Press, 2019), discussed in Stephen Coleman, *How People Talk About Politics: Brexit and Beyond* (London: Bloomsbury, 2021), pp. 13–14; 81–82.
71 For a recent example, see Marc Stears, *Out of the Ordinary: How Everyday Life Inspired a Nation and How It Can Again* (Boston, MA: Harvard University Press 2020).
72 For a more detailed exploration of this argument, see Nick Clarke, Will Jennings, Jonathan Moss, and Gerry Stoker, 'Voter Decision-Making in a Context of Low Political Trust: The 2016 UK EU Membership Referendum', *Political Studies*, 71:3 (2023), pp. 106–124.
73 S5563, F, 38, library manager, Norwich, Remain, 2016.
74 M3190, M, 57, retired civil servant, South Tyneside, Remain, 2016.
75 L5642, M, 43, electronics engineer, Southport, undecided, 2016.

Notes

76 M5578, F, 20, student, East London, Remain, 2016.
77 W729, F, 58, supply teacher, Dundee, Leave, 2016.
78 M5770, M, 21, student, Southampton, Remain, 2016.
79 R5429, F, 40, self-employed, Newcastle-upon-Tyne, Remain, 2016.
80 B3227, M, 49, administrator, Birmingham, Remain, 2016.
81 M4780, F, 32, communication support worker, London, Remain, 2016.
82 M4859, F, 40, software engineer, Devon, Remain, 2016.
83 T4715, F, 44, community health worker, Nottingham, Remain, 2016.
84 S5780, M, 22, student, Lancaster, Remain, 2016.
85 G3187, F, 46, staff nurse, Southport, Remain, 2016.
86 N5744, M, 38, carer, Sunderland, Leave, 2016.
87 M3190, M, 57, retired civil servant, South Tyneside, Remain, 2016.
88 B5702, F, 25, waitress and student, Cheshire, undecided but tending towards Remain, 2016.
89 S5780, M, 22, student, Lancaster, Remain, 2016.
90 E5014, M, 50, civil servant, Bath, Remain, 2016.
91 M5645, F, 42, writer/blogger, North Ayrshire, Remain, 2016.
92 R1227, F, 72, retired primary school teacher, Exeter, Remain, 2016.
93 O4521, M, 42, IT manager, Cambridge, Remain, 2016.
94 W5881, F, 48, self-employed project manager, Brighton, Remain, 2016.
95 J2891, F, 52, caseworker, Clwyd, Remain, 2017.
96 R2144, F, 80, retired teacher, Birmingham, Remain, 2016. Original emphasis.
97 T4715, F, 44, community health worker, Nottingham, Remain, 2016.
98 E5014, M, 50, civil servant, Bath, Remain, 2016.
99 E5551, M, 41, team leader for insurance company, Bristol, Remain, 2016.
100 Matthew D'Ancona, *Post-Truth Politics: The New War on Truth and How to Fight Back* (London: Penguin, 2017); Evan Davis, *Post-Truth: Why We Have Reached Peak Bullshit and What We Can Do About It* (Boston, MA: Little Brown, 2017); James Ball, *Post-Truth: How Bullshit Conquered the World* (London: Biteback Publishing, 2017).
101 Colin Hay and Cyril Benoît, 'Brexit, Positional Populism, and the Declining Appeal of Valence Politics', *Critical Review*, 31:3–4 (2019), pp. 389–404.
102 Ibid.

Notes

103 Ibid.
104 Ronald Inglehart, *The Silent Revolution: Changing Values and Political Styles among Western Publics* (Princeton, NJ: Princeton University Press, 1977); Pippa Norris, *Critical Citizens: Global Support for Democratic Government* (Oxford: Oxford University Press, 1999); Clarke et al., *The Good Politician*.
105 B.R. Berelson, P.F. Lazarsfeld, and W.N. McPhee, *Voting: A Study of Opinion Formation in a Presidential Campaign* (Chicago, IL: University of Chicago Press, 1954), quoted in Jonathan Hopkin and Ben Rosamond, 'Post-Truth Politics, Bullshit and Bad Ideas: "Deficit Fetishism" in the UK', *New Political Economy*, 23:6 (2018), pp. 641–655 (647).
106 Hopkin and Rosamond, 'Post-Truth Politics', pp. 645–646.
107 Clarke et al., *The Good Politician*.

Chapter 2

1 Ann Laura Stoler, 'The Politics of "Gut Feelings": On Sentiment in Governance and the Law', *KNOW: A Journal on the Formation of Knowledge*, 2:2 (2018), pp. 207–228.
2 John Curtice, 'The Emotional Legacy of Brexit: How Britain Has Become a Country of "Remainers" and "Leavers"', What UK Thinks: EU, 15 October 2018: https://whatukthinks.org/eu/wp-content/uploads/2018/10/WUKT-EU-Briefing-Paper-15-Oct-18-Emotional-legacy-paper-final.pdf (accessed 4 March 2023).
3 Sara B. Hobolt, Thomas J. Leeper, and James Tilley, 'Divided by the Vote: Affective Polarization in the Wake of Brexit', *British Journal of Political Science*, 51:4 (2021), pp. 1476–1493.
4 Maria Sobolewska and Robert Ford, *Brexitland: Identity, Diversity and the Reshaping of British Politics* (Cambridge: Cambridge University Press, 2020).
5 See, for instance, Michael Kenny, 'The Return of "Englishness" in British Political Culture – the End of the Unions?', *Journal of Commonmarket Studies*, 53 (2015), pp. 35–51; Oliver Daddow, 'The UK Media and "Europe": From Permissive Consensus to Destructive Dissent', *International Affairs*, 88:6 (2012), pp. 1219–1236.
6 On the rhetoric of 'sensible' politics, see Charlotte Lydia Riley, 'Against "Sensible" Politics', *Prospect*, 25 February 2019: www.prospectmagazine.co.uk/politics/against-sensible-politics-independent-group-centrist-charlotte-riley (accessed 21 June 2023).
7 For a more nuanced take on the complexities of the debate surrounding Britain's entry to the EC, see Robert Saunders, *Yes to*

Europe! The 1975 Referendum and Seventies Britain (Cambridge: Cambridge University Press, 2018).
8. Mark Bevir, Oliver Daddow, and Pauline Schnapper, 'Introduction: Interpreting British European Policy', *Journal of Commonmarket Studies*, 53 (2015), pp. 1–17; Oliver Daddow, 'Interpreting the Outsider Tradition in British European Policy Speeches from Thatcher to Cameron', *Journal of Commonmarket Studies*, 53 (2015), pp. 71–88; Luisa Passerini, *Europe in Love, Love in Europe: Imagination and Politics in Britain between the Wars* (London: I.B. Tauris, 1999).
9. Margrit Pernau et al., *Civilizing Emotions: Concepts in Nineteenth Century Asia and Europe* (Oxford: Oxford University Press, 2015); Lauren Working, *The Making of an Imperial Polity: Civility and America in the Jacobean Metropolis* (Cambridge: Cambridge University Press, 2020).
10. Lynn Hunt, *Inventing Human Rights: A History* (New York: W.W. Norton, 2007).
11. Jane Lydon, *Imperial Emotions: The Politics of Empathy across the British Empire* (Cambridge: Cambridge University Press, 2019).
12. Alison M. Jaggar, 'Love and Knowledge: Emotion in Feminist Epistemology', *Inquiry*, 32:2 (1989), pp. 151–176.
13. Stephen Coleman, *How People Talk About Politics: Brexit and Beyond* (London: Bloomsbury, 2021).
14. Ibid., pp. 126–128.
15. Ernesto Laclau, *On Populist Reason* (London: Verso, 2017); Chantal Mouffe, *For a Left Populism* (London: Verso, 2019).
16. Emmy Eklundh, 'Excluding Emotions: The Performative Function of Populism', *Open Journal of Sociopolitical Studies*, 13:1 (2020), pp. 107–131.
17. Robbie Shilliam, *Race and the Undeserving Poor: From Abolition to Brexit* (Newcastle: Agenda Publishing, 2018).
18. Sadiya Akram, 'Dear British Politics – Where Is the Race and Racism?', *British Politics* (2023): https://doi.org/10.1057/s41293-023-00224-3.
19. B5342, F, 30, online jewellery retailer, Salisbury, Leave, 2016.
20. See Yasmin Serhan, 'Pork Legs Are Shaking up British Politics', *The Atlantic*, 17 May 2018: www.theatlantic.com/international/archive/2018/05/is-gammon-racist/560507/ (accessed 21 June 2023).
21. Roberta Guerrina, Theofanis Exadaktylos, and Simona Guerra, 'Gender, Ownership and Engagement during the European Union Referendum: Gendered Frames and the Reproduction of

Notes

Binaries', *European Journal of Politics & Gender*, 1:3 (2018), pp. 387–404.
22. Camilla Schofield, 'Brexit and the Other Special Relationship', in Stuart Ward and Astrid Rasch (eds), *Embers of Empire in Brexit Britain* (London: Bloomsbury, 2019), pp. 87–99.
23. Gurminder Bhambra, 'Brexit, Trump, and "Methodological Whiteness": On the Misrecognition of Race and Class', *The British Journal of Sociology*, 68:S1 (2017), pp. S214–S232; Shilliam, *Race and the Undeserving Poor*.
24. Aurelien Mondon, 'Populism, Public Opinion, and the Mainstreaming of the Far Right: The "Immigration Issue" and the Construction of a Reactionary "People"', *Politics*, online only (2022): https://doi.org/10.1177/02633957221104726.
25. William Davies, 'Thoughts on the Sociology of Brexit', Political Economy Research Centre, 24 June 2016: www.perc.org.uk/project_posts/thoughts-on-the-sociology-of-brexit/ (accessed 4 March 2023); Colin Hay, 'Brexistential Angst and the Paradoxes of Populism: On the Contingency, Predictability and Intelligibility of Seismic Shifts', *Political Studies*, 68:1 (2020), pp. 187–206.
26. Ellen Boucher, 'Anticipating Armageddon: Nuclear Risk and the Neoliberal Sensibility in Thatcher's Britain', *The American Historical Review*, 124:4 (2019), pp. 1221–1245.
27. Janet Newman, 'Rationality, Responsibility and Rage: The Contested Politics of Emotion Governance', in Eleanor Jupp, Jessica Pykett, and Fiona M. Smith (eds), *Emotional States: Sites and Spaces of Affective Governance* (London: Routledge, 2016), pp. 21–35.
28. Wendy Brown, *In the Ruins of Neoliberalism: The Rise of Antidemocratic Politics in the West* (New York: Columbia University Press, 2019) p. 75.
29. Ben Anderson, 'Neoliberal Affects', *Progress in Human Geography*, 40:6 (2015), pp. 734–753.
30. Alan Finlayson, 'Neoliberalism, the Alt-Right and the Intellectual Dark Web', *Theory, Culture & Society*, 38:6 (2021), pp. 167–190.
31. For more on this, see Anna von der Goltz and Britta Waldschmidt-Nelson (eds), *Inventing the Silent Majority in Western Europe and the United States: Conservatism in the 1960s and 1970s* (Cambridge: Cambridge University Press, 2017) and Emily Robinson, *The Language of Progressive Politics in Modern Britain* (London: Palgrave, 2017), chapter 4.
32. Camilla Schofield, 'Brexit and the Other Special Relationship', in Stuart Ward and Astrid Rasch (eds), *Embers of Empire in Brexit Britain* (London: Bloomsbury, 2019), pp. 87–99 (89).

Notes

33 F3409, F, 72, retired civil servant, Nottingham, Leave, 2019.
34 B4334, F, 78, retired nurse, York, Leave, 2019.
35 B4334, F, 79, retired nurse, York, Leave, 2020. Original emphasis.
36 F3641, F, 80, retired teacher, Leicester, Leave, 2020. Original emphasis.
37 Finlayson, 'Neoliberalism'. For a consideration of the entangled history of neoliberalism and multiculturalism, see Camilla Schofield, Florence Sutcliffe-Braithwaite, and Rob Waters, '"The privatisation of the struggle": Anti-racism in the Age of Enterprise', in Florence Sutcliffe-Braithwaite, Aled Davies, and Ben Jackson (eds), *The Neoliberal Age? Britain since the 1970s* (London: UCL Press, 2021), pp. 119–225.
38 L5604, M, 36, teacher, Newcastle-under-Lyme, Remain, 2017.
39 D4736, M, 49, air traffic services assistant, Southampton, Remain, 2016.
40 B3227, M, 50, administrator, Birmingham, Remain, 2017.
41 E5559, M, 50, creative, Exeter, Remain, 2017.
42 H5845, F, 36, community nurse, Nottingham, Remain, 2017.
43 M5015, M, 60, retired property landlord, Cambridge, Remain, 2016.
44 P5715, M, 32, teacher, Northwich, Remain, 2016.
45 V3773, F, 53, pharmacist, Solihull, Remain, 2016.
46 M3190, M, 57, retired civil servant, South Tyneside, Remain, 2016.
47 E5559, M, 50, creative, Exeter, Remain, 2017.
48 C3210, F, 35, fundraising manager, Watford, Remain, 2016.
49 B1771, F, 80, retired secretary, Mitcham, Remain, 2016.
50 M5645, F, 42, writer, North Ayrshire, Remain, 2016.
51 C5847, F, 39, youth worker, Harborough, Remain, 2016.
52 F5186, M, 38, mature student, North Yorkshire, Remain, 2017.
53 Bhambra, 'Brexit, Trump, and "Methodological Whiteness"'. See also Danny Dorling, 'Brexit: The Decision of a Divided Country', *British Medical Journal*, 354 (2016): https://doi.org/10.1136/bmj.i3697.
54 M4859, F, 40, software engineer manager, Devon, Remain, 2016.
55 G4566, F, 50, PhD student, Huddersfield, Remain, 2017.
56 C5847, F, 39, youth worker, Harborough, Remain, 2016.
57 J4793, F, 35, self-employed writer, Renfrewshire, Remain, 2016.
58 Thomas Dixon, *From Passions to Emotions: The Creation of a Secular Psychological Category* (Cambridge: Cambridge University Press, 2009).
59 N5744, M, 40, carer, Sunderland, Leave, 2017.
60 B5725, F, 55, retired FE lecturer, Chester, Leave, 2016.

Notes

61 Ibid., 2019.
62 Coleman, *How People Talk*.
63 M3408, F, 69, retired nursery teacher, Coventry, Leave, 2016.
64 R4526, M, 55, retired science teacher, Belfast, Leave, 2016.
65 F3641, F, 75, retired school teacher, Leicester, Leave, 2017.
66 B5342, F, 30, online retailer, Sailsbury, Leave, 2016; B5725, F, 58, retired FE lecturer, Chester, Leave, 2019.
67 M3408, F, 69, retired nursery teacher, Coventry, Leave, 2016, and same respondent in 2017.
68 H260, F, 86, retired shop manager, Brentwood, Leave, 2016.
69 Sara Ahmed, *The Cultural Politics of Emotion* (London: Routledge, 2004), p. 3.
70 Todd H. Hall and Andrew A.G. Ross, 'Rethinking Affective Experience and Popular Emotion: World War I and the Construction of Group Emotion in International Relations', *Political Psychology*, 40 (2019), pp. 1357–1372.
71 Ibid., p. 1358.
72 C4131, F, 34, museums and heritage consultant, North Shields, Remain, 2016.
73 J5734, M, 31, charity worker, Newcastle-upon-Tyne, Remain, 2016.
74 R860, F, 68, retired JP, Cheshire, Leave, 2017.
75 B5342, F, 30, online jewellery retailer, Salisbury, Leave, 2016.
76 Ahmed, *The Cultural Politics of Emotion*, pp. 3–4.
77 Ibid., chapter 6.
78 Bhambra, 'Brexit, Trump, and "Methodological Whiteness"'.
79 Ben Rogaly, *Stories from a Migrant City: Living and Working Together in the Shadow of Brexit* (Manchester: Manchester University Press, 2021).
80 Current estimates suggest that fewer than 3 per cent of its respondents identify as anything other than white.
81 Ana Y. Ramos-Zayas, 'Ordinary Whiteness: Affect, Kinship, and the Moral Economy of Privilege', *Journal of Urban History*, 47:2 (2020), pp. 459–464.
82 Marianela Barrios Aquino, 'Affective Citizenship in Brexit Britain: EU Citizens' Responses to Emotional Governance', *Emotions: History, Culture, Society*, 6 (2022), pp. 296–313.
83 S5767, F, 31, academic researcher, Watford, Remain, 2016.
84 H5557, F, 27, PhD student, Manchester, Leave, 2017.
85 Rosa Mas Giralt, 'The Emotional Geographies of Migration and Brexit: Tales of *Unbelonging*', *Central and Eastern European Migration Review*, 9:1 (2020), pp. 29–45 (35); Taulant Guma and Rhys Dafydd Jones, '"Where are we going to go now?" European

Union Migrants' Experiences of Hostility, Anxiety, and (Non-) Belonging during Brexit', *Population, Space and Place*, 25:e2198 (2019); Kate Botterill and Jonathan Hancock, 'Rescaling Belonging in "Brexit Britain": Spatial Identities and Practices of Polish Nationals in Scotland after the U.K. Referendum on European Union Membership', *Population, Space and Place*, 25:e2217 (2019); Marie Godin and Nando Sigona, 'Intergenerational Narratives of Citizenship among EU Citizens in the UK after the Brexit Referendum', *Ethnic and Racial Studies*, 45:6 (2022), pp. 1135–1154; Naomi Tyrrell, Daniela Sime, Claire Kelly, and Christina McMellon, 'Belonging in Brexit Britain: Central and Eastern European 1.5 Generation Young People's Experiences', *Population, Space and Place*, 25:e2205 (2019); Ronald Renta and Nenva Nancheva, 'Unsettled: Brexit and European Union Nationals' Sense of Belonging', *Population, Space and Place*, 25:e2199 (2019); Marianela Barrios Aquino, 'Affective Citizenship in Brexit Britain: EU Citizens' Responses to Emotional Governance', *Emotions: History, Culture, Society*, 6 (2022), pp. 296–313; Elisabetta Zontini and Elena Genova, 'Studying the Emotional Costs of Integration at Times of Change: The Case of EU Migrants in Brexit Britain', *Sociology*, 56:4 (2022), pp. 638–654.
86 B5567, F, 43, freelance reward consultant, East Cheshire, Remain, 2016.
87 Zontini and Genova, 'Studying the Emotional Costs of Integration', p. 650; Mas Giralt, 'The Emotional Geographies of Migration and Brexit'.
88 C5847, F, 39, youth worker, Harborough, Remain, 2016.
89 O3436, F, 63, retired civil servant, Dorset, Remain, 2017; O4521, M, 44, engineering director, Cambridge, Remain, 2017.
90 R5682, M, 43, librarian, South Oxfordshire, Remain, 2016.
91 Sara Ahmed, 'The Politics of Bad Feeling', *Australian Critical Race and Whiteness Studies Association Journal*, 1 (2005), pp. 72–85 (82).
92 Steven Garner, 'A Moral Economy of Whiteness: Behaviours, Belonging and Britishness', *Ethnicities*, 12:4 (2012), pp. 445–464.
93 Alina Rzepnikowska, 'Racism and Xenophobia Experienced by Polish Migrants in the UK before and after Brexit Vote', *Journal of Ethnic and Migration Studies*, 45:1 (2019), pp. 61–77.
94 Ibid.
95 A5854, F, 72, artist, Bath, Remain, 2017; M4859, 40, F, software engineer manager, Devon, Remain, 2016.
96 T4715, F, 44, community health worker, Nottingham, Remain, 2016.

Notes

97 B4334, F, 77, retired nurse, York, Leave, 2017.
98 B5725, F, 57, retired FE lecturer, Chester, Leave, 2017.
99 Eleni Andreouli, Katy Greenland, and Lia Figgou, 'Lay Discourses about Brexit and Prejudice: "Ideological Creativity" and Its Limits in Brexit Debates', *European Journal of Social Psychology*, 50 (2020), pp. 309–322.
100 F3409, F, 70, retired civil servant, Nottingham, Leave, 2017.
101 Garner, 'Moral Economy of Whiteness', citing David Sibley, *Geographies of Exclusion: Society and Difference in the West* (London: Routledge, 1995).
102 H260, F, 88, retired shop manager, Brentwood, Leave, 2016.
103 B4334, F, 77, retired nurse, York, Leave, 2017. Original emphases.
104 H2639, F, 75, retired library assistant, Ipswich, undecided, 2016.
105 M3408, F, 69, retired nursery teacher, Coventry, Leave, 2016.
106 Camilla Schofield, *Enoch Powell and the Making of Postcolonial Britain* (Cambridge: Cambridge University Press, 2013).
107 H260, F, 86, retired shop manager, Brentwood, Leave, 2016. She returned to the sponge metaphor in 2017: 'A sponge can only soak up a certain amount until it's saturated!!'
108 F3641, F, 75, retired school teacher, Leicester, Leave, 2016.
109 P1009, F, 76, retired, occupation unspecified, Worcestershire, Remain, 2016; A1706, F, 69, retired, West Sussex, Remain, 2017.
110 M4859, F, 40, software engineer manager, Devon, Remain, 2016.
111 B3227, M, 52, administrator, Birmingham, Remain, 2019.
112 G4296, M, 40, archive cataloguer, Cardiff, Remain, 2017.
113 P3209, M, 76, artist, Lincolnshire, Remain, 2016.
114 A5854, F, 71, artist, Bath, Remain, 2016.
115 W5881, F, 48, company director, Brighton, Remain, 2017.
116 M5113, F, 38, project manager, West Yorkshire, Remain, 2016.
117 M3190, M, 57, retired civil servant, South Tyneside, Remain, 2016.
118 D5698, M, 73, retired hospital administrator, Gwynedd, Remain, 2016.
119 See Shilliam, *Race and the Undeserving Poor*.
120 T4715, F, 44, community health worker, Nottingham, Remain, 2016.
121 W5881, F, 48, project manager, Brighton, Remain, 2016.
122 Schofield, 'Brexit and the Other Special Relationship'.
123 A6056, M, 67, museum manager, Diss, Remain, 2017.
124 C2579, F, 71, retired factory worker, Suffolk, Leave, 2016.
125 F218, F, 69, retired care worker, Suffolk, Leave, 2017.
126 B4334, F, 77, retired nurse, York, Leave, 2016.
127 A4127, M, 55, theatre usher, Blackpool, Leave, 2017.

Notes

128 Finlayson, 'Neoliberalism'.
129 R4526, M, 55, retired science teacher, Belfast, Leave, 2016.
130 See Richard English and Michael Kenny (eds), *Rethinking British Decline* (Basingstoke: Macmillan, 2000).
131 R4526, M, 55, retired science teacher, Belfast, Leave, 2016.
132 Colin Hay, 'Brexistential Angst and the Paradoxes of Populism: On the Contingency, Predictability and Intelligibility of Seismic Shifts', *Political Studies*, 68:1 (2020), pp. 187–206; R4526, M, 55, retired science teacher, Belfast, Leave 2016.
133 N5744, M, 38, carer, Sunderland, Leave, 2016.
134 R4526, M, 55, retired science teacher, Belfast, Leave, 2016.
135 Newman, 'Rationality', p. 23.
136 Anderson, 'Neoliberal Affects', p. 738.
137 Sobolewska and Ford, *Brexitland*.
138 H6004, M, 63, retired civil servant, West Yorkshire, Remain, 2017; H6109, F, 39, student mental health nurse, London, Remain, 2017.
139 M3190, M, 57, retired civil servant, South Tyneside, Remain, 2016.

Part II

1 Fintan O'Toole, *Heroic Failure: Brexit and the Politics of Pain* (New York: Apollo, 2018); Pankaj Mishra, *Age of Anger: A History of the Present* (New York: Farrar, Straus and Giroux, 2017); William Davies, 'Thoughts on the Sociology of Brexit', Political Economy Research Centre, 24 June 2016: www.perc.org.uk/project_posts/thoughts-on-the-sociology-of-brexit/ (accessed 4 March 2023).
2 Joel Vos, Digby Tantam, and Emmy van Deurzen, 'A Brexistential Crisis?', *The Psychologist*, June 2020: www.bps.org.uk/psychologist/brexistential-crisis (accessed 4 March 2023); Mental Health Foundation, 'Millions have felt "powerless", "angry" or "worried" because of Brexit – results of our new poll', 13 March 2019: www.mentalhealth.org.uk/about-us/news/millions-have-felt-powerless-angry-or-worried-because-brexit-results-our-new-poll (accessed 4 March 2023); British Association for Counselling and Psychotherapy, 'One third of adults say Brexit has affected their mental health, BACP research finds', 11 April 2019: www.bacp.co.uk/news/news-from-bacp/2019/11-april-one-third-of-adults-say-brexit-has-affected-their-mental-health-bacp-research-finds/ (accessed 4 March 2023).
3 Zoe Williams, '"All I hear is anger and frustration": How Brexit is affecting our mental health', *Guardian*, 4 April 2019: www.

Notes

theguardian.com/politics/2019/apr/04/anger-and-frustration-how-brexit-is-affecting-our-mental-health (accessed 4 March 2023); 'How Brexit is affecting mental health', *The Week*, 13 March 2019: www.theweek.co.uk/100186/how-brexit-is-affecting-mental-health (accessed 4 March 2023); Russell Lynch, 'Can Boris Johnson cure the UK's anxiety problem by "getting Brexit done"?', *Daily Telegraph*, 15 November 2019: www.telegraph.co.uk/business/2019/11/15/can-boris-johnson-cure-uks-anxiety-problem-getting-brexit-done/ (accessed 4 March 2023).

Chapter 3

1 Rita Felski and Susan Fraiman, 'Introduction: In the Mood', *New Literary History*, 43:3 (2012), pp. v–xi (v).
2 Sara Ahmed, 'Not in the Mood', *New Formations*, 82 (2014), pp. 13–28 (13).
3 Ibid.
4 Ben Highmore and Jenny Bourne Taylor, 'Introducing Mood Work', *New Formations*, 82 (2014), pp. 5–12.
5 Sarah Marie Hall, 'Waiting for Brexit: Crisis, Conjuncture, Method', *Transactions of the Institute of British Geographers*, 47 (2022), pp. 200–213 (201).
6 Ben Anderson and Helen F. Wilson, 'Everyday Brexits', *Area*, 50 (2018), pp. 291–295 (292).
7 Stephen Coleman, 'Feeling It/Not Feeling It: Mood Stories as Accounts of Political Intuition', *International Journal of Politics, Culture, and Society*, 35 (2022), pp. 477–495 (481).
8 Sibyl Adam, 'Brexit and Literary Mood in Ali Smith's *Autumn*', *Contemporary Women's Writing*, 16:1 (2022), pp. 60–78 (61).
9 Hall, 'Waiting for Brexit', p. 206.
10 For more on the historical development of polling in the UK see Laura Beers, 'Whose Opinion? Changing Attitudes Towards Opinion Polling in British Politics, 1937–1964', *Twentieth Century British History*, 17:2 (2006), pp. 177–205.
11 James A. Stimson, 'On the Meaning and Measurement of Mood', *Daedalus*, 141:4 (2012), pp. 23–34.
12 Matthew Smith, 'An Emotional Year: YouGov's British mood tracker', *YouGov*, 2 July 2020: https://yougov.co.uk/topics/lifestyle/articles-reports/2020/07/02/emotional-year-yougovs-british-mood-tracker (accessed 4 March 2023).
13 Wellbeing datasets are available from the Office of National Statistics: www.ons.gov.uk/peoplepopulationandcommunity/wellbeing (accessed 4 March 2023); David Cameron, speech

on wellbeing, 25 November 2010: www.gov.uk/government/speeches/pm-speech-on-wellbeing (accessed 4 March 2023).

14 See, for example, Rob Boddice, *A History of Feelings* (London: Reaktion Books, 2019), chapter 6: 'The Ministry of Happiness'; William Davies, *The Happiness Industry: How Government and Big Business Sold Us Well-Being* (London: Verso, 2015). For a wider discussion of the politics of happiness, see Sara Ahmed, *The Promise of Happiness* (Durham, NC: Duke University Press, 2010).

15 Robinson Meyer, 'Everything we know about Facebook's secret mood-manipulation experiment', *The Atlantic*, 28 June 2014: www.theatlantic.com/technology/archive/2014/06/everything-we-know-about-facebooks-secret-mood-manipulation-experiment/373648/ (accessed 4 March 2023).

16 John Curtice, 'Brexit Reflections: How the polls got it wrong – again', Centre for Constitutional Change, 28 June 2016: www.centreonconstitutionalchange.ac.uk/opinions/brexit-reflections-how-polls-got-it-wrong-again (accessed 4 March 2023).

17 Bo Pang and Lillian Lee, 'Opinion Mining and Sentiment Analysis, Foundations and Trends', *Information Retrieval*, 2:1–2 (2008), pp. 1–135; Brendan O'Connor et al., 'From Tweets to Polls: Linking Text Sentiment to Public Opinion Time Series', *Proceedings of the Fourth International AAAII Conference on Weblogs and Social Media*, 4:1 (2010), pp. 122–129: https://doi.org/10.1609/icwsm.v4i1.14031; Alexander Pak and Patrick Paroubek, 'Twitter as a Corpus for Sentiment Analysis and Opinion Mining', Proceedings of the International Conference on Language Resources and Evaluation (2010): www.researchgate.net/publication/220746311_Twitter_as_a_Corpus_for_Sentiment_Analysis_and_Opinion_Mining (accessed 4 March 2023).

18 See for instance, Sitarum Asur and Bernardo A. Huberman, 'Predicting the Future with Social Media' (2010), arXiv: https://arxiv.org/abs/1003.5699v1; Johann Bollen, Huina Mao, and Xiaojun Zeng, 'Twitter Mood Predicts the Stock Market', *Journal of Computational Science*, 2:1 (2011), pp. 1–8; Widodo Budiharto and Meiliana Meiliana, 'Prediction and Analysis of Indonesia Presidential Election from Twitter Using Sentiment Analysis', *Journal of Big Data*, 5:1 (2018), pp. 1–10.

19 Miha Grčar et al., 'Stance and Influence of Twitter Users Regarding the Brexit Referendum', *Computational Social Networks*, 4:1 (2017), pp. 6–25; Amit Agarwal, Ritu Singh, and Durga Toshniwal, 'Geospatial Sentiment Analysis Using Twitter Data for UK-EU Referendum', *Journal of Information*

Notes

& *Optimization Sciences*, 39:1 (2018), pp. 303–317; Elena Georgiadou, Spyros Angelopoulos, and Helen Drake, 'Big Data Analytics and International Negotiations: Sentiment Analysis of Brexit Negotiating Outcomes', *International Journal of Information Management*, 51 (2020), pp. 102048.

20 Peter Sheridan Dodds and Christopher M. Danforth, 'Measuring the Happiness of Large-Scale Written Expression: Songs, Blogs, and Presidents, *Journal of Happiness Studies*, 11 (2010), pp. 441–456.
21 Thomas Lansdall-Welfare, Fabon Dzogang, and Nello Cristianini, 'Change-Point Analysis of the Public Mood in UK Twitter during the Brexit Referendum', *IEEE 16th International Conference on Data Mining Workshops* (2016), pp. 434–439.
22 Pierre Bourdieu, 'L'opinion publique n'existe pas', *Temps Moderne*, 318 (1973), pp. 1292–1309 (125). Quoted in Aurelien Mondon, 'Populism, Public Opinion, and the Mainstreaming of the Far Right: The "Immigration Issue" and the Construction of a Reactionary "People"', *Politics*, online only (2022): https://doi.org/10.1177/02633957221104726.
23 Ahmed, 'Not in the Mood', p. 24.
24 Nick Hubble, *Mass Observation and Everyday Life* (Basingstoke: Palgrave Macmillan, 2006), particularly chapter 6.
25 V3773, F, 53, NHS senior pharmacist, Solihull, Remain, 2016; T4715, F, 44, community health worker, Nottingham, Remain, 2016.
26 G4566, 50, other personal details unspecified, Remain, 2016.
27 H1541, M, 71, retired film editor, central Scotland, Remain, 2016.
28 J5734, M, 31, charity worker, Newcastle-upon-Tyne, Remain, 2016.
29 C3210, F, 37, fundraising manager, Watford, Remain, 2017.
30 N5545, M, 23, occupation unknown, Stockport, Remain, 2016.
31 M3408, F, 69, retired nursery teacher, Coventry, Leave, 2016.
32 R4526, M, 55, retired science teacher, Belfast, Leave, 2016.
33 N5744, M, 38, carer, Sunderland, Leave, 2016.
34 P2915, M, 57, teacher, Kingston upon Thames, Remain, 2016.
35 C2677, F, 64, retired teaching assistant, Lacock, Leave, 2016.
36 B5342, F, 30, online jewellery retailer, Salisbury, Leave, 2016.
37 C5782, F, 33, communications officer, Brighton, Remain, 2016.
38 D996, F, 90, retired CAB worker, London, Remain, 2016.
39 M3190, M, 57, retired civil servant, South Tyneside, Leave, 2016.
40 Rosa Mas Giralt, 'The Emotional Geographies of Migration and Brexit: Tales of *Unbelonging*', *Central and Eastern European Migration Review*, 9:1 (2020), pp. 29–45 (35).

Notes

41 C4131, F, 34, museum and heritage consultant, North Shields, Remain, 2016.
42 L1991, F, 79, retired civil servant, Brighton, Remain, 2016.
43 B5541, M, age unknown, customer service administrator, Solihull, Remain, 2016.
44 C3210, F, 35, fundraising manager, Watford, Remain, 2016.
45 B5567, F, 43, freelance reward consultant, East Cheshire, Remain, 2016.
46 R2144, F, 80, retired teacher, Birmingham, Remain, 2016.
47 M5113, F, 38, project manager, West Yorkshire, Remain, 2016.
48 W5881, F, 48, self-employed project manager, Brighton, Remain, 2016.
49 C5847, F, 39, charity worker, Harborough, Remain, 2016.
50 P1009, F, 76, no occupation recorded, Worcestershire, Remain, 2016.
51 N5545, M, 23, occupation unknown, Stockport, Remain, 2016.
52 F218, F, 69, retired care worker, Suffolk, Leave, 2016.
53 B5342, F, 30, online jewellery retailer, Salisbury, Leave, 2016.
54 N5744, M, 38, carer, Sunderland, Leave, 2016.
55 F218, F, 69, retired care worker, Suffolk, Leave, 2016.
56 R1025, F, 73, housewife and former book-keeper, Milton Keynes, Leave, 2016 update.
57 For an overview of these sources, see Dan Degerman, 'Brexit Anxiety: A Case Study in the Medicalization of Dissent', *Critical Review of International Social and Political Philosophy*, 22:7 (2019), pp. 823–840. Some notable examples include: Susie Orbach, 'In therapy, everyone wants to talk about Brexit', *Guardian*, 1 July 2016: www.theguardian.com/global/2016/jul/01/susie-orbach-in-therapy-everyone-wants-to-talk-about-brexit (accessed 4 March 2023); Anon., 'Poor lambs! After trigger warnings and safe spaces students now depressed over Brexit', *Daily Express*, 29 June 2016; Matt Cullen, 'Dealing with BREXIT', YouTube, 5 July 2016: www.youtube.com/watch?v=gXvUBu4UUKI (accessed 4 March 2023).
58 Degerman, 'Brexit Anxiety', p. 831.
59 Nattavudh Powdthavee et al., 'Who Got the Brexit Blues? The Effect of Brexit on Subjective Wellbeing in the UK', *Economica*, 86 (2019), pp. 471–494.
60 G4296, M, 40, archivist, Cardiff, Remain, 2017.
61 M5578, F, 20, student, East London, Remain, 2016.
62 Elisabetta Zontini and Elena Genova, 'Studying the Emotional Costs of Integration at Times of Change: the case of EU migrants in Brexit Britain', *Sociology*, 56:4 (2022), pp. 638–654; Mas Giralt, 'The Emotional Geographies of Migration and Brexit'; Marie Godin

and Nando Sigona, 'Intergenerational Narratives of Citizenship among EU Citizens in the UK after the Brexit Referendum', *Ethnic and Racial Studies*, 45:6 (2022), pp. 1135–1154; Naomi Tyrrell, Daniela Sime, Claire Kelly, and Christina McMellon, 'Belonging in Brexit Britain: Central and Eastern European 1.5 Generation Young People's Experiences', *Population, Space and Place*, 25:e2205 (2019); Kate Botterill and Jonathan Hancock, 'Rescaling Belonging in "Brexit Britain": Spatial Identities and Practices of Polish Nationals in Scotland after the U.K. Referendum on European Union Membership', *Population, Space and Place*, 25:e2217 (2019); Ronald Renta and Nenva Nancheva, 'Unsettled: Brexit and European Union Nationals' Sense of Belonging', *Population, Space and Place*, 25:e2199 (2019); Aija Lulle, Russell King, Veronika Dvorakova, and Aleksandra Szkudlarek, 'Between Disruptions and Connections: "New" European Union Migrants in the United Kingdom before and after the Brexit', *Population, Space and Place*, 25:e2200 (2019); Taulant Guma and Rhys Dafydd Jones, '"Where are we going to go now?" European Union Migrants' Experiences of Hostility, Anxiety, and (Non-)Belonging during Brexit', *Population, Space and Place*, 25:e2198 (2019); Helen N.J. McCarthy, 'Spanish Nationals' Future Plans in the Context of Brexit', *Population, Space and Place*, 25:e2202 (2019); Piotr Teodorowski, Ruth Woods, Magda Czarnecka, and Catriona Kennedy, 'Brexit, Acculturative Stress and Mental Health among EU Citizens in Scotland', *Population, Space and Place*, 27:e2217 (2021).

63 Stephanie Knight, Dean Fido, Henry Lennon, and Craig A. Harper, 'Loss and Assimilation: Lived Experiences of Brexit for British Citizens Living in Luxembourg', *International Journal of Mental Health and Addiction*, 21 (2023), pp. 587–604; Rebekah Grace Miller, '(Un)settling Home during the Brexit Process', *Population, Space and Place*, 27:e2436 (2021).

64 Marianela Barrios Aquino, 'Affective Citizenship in Brexit Britain: EU Citizens' Responses to Emotional Governance', *Emotions: History, Culture, Society*, 6 (2022), pp. 296–313 (301), citing Engin F. Isin, 'The Neurotic Citizen', *Citizenship Studies*, 8:3 (2004), pp. 217–235.

65 C5692, F, 40, sales ledger controller, County Down, Remain, 2016.

66 H6004, M, 63, retired civil servant, West Yorkshire, Remain, 2017 (N.B. he was looking back on the previous year's experience).

67 C4988, M, 62, retired nurse, Nottingham, Remain, 2016.

68 C3210, F, 35, fundraising manager, Watford, Remain, 2016.

Notes

69 Ibid.
70 A3623, M, 58, retired social care manager, Glasgow, Remain, 2016.
71 F4873, M, 50, IT consultant, Exeter, Remain, 2017.
72 J2891, F, 51, administrator, location unspecified, Remain, 2016 update.
73 K5589, genderqueer, 29, NHS library and resources office, Cheshire, Remain, 2016.
74 Degerman, 'Brexit Anxiety'.
75 Verena K. Brändle, Charlotte Galpin, and Hans-Jörg Trenz, 'Marching for Europe? Enacting European Citizenship as Justice during Brexit', *Citizenship Studies*, 22:8 (2018), pp. 810–828.
76 Boris Johnson, speech in Downing Street, 24 July 2019: www.gov.uk/government/speeches/boris-johnsons-first-speech-as-prime-minister-24-july-2019 (accessed 4 March 2023).
77 R4526, M, 55, retired science teacher, Belfast, Leave, 2016 – discussed at length in chapter 3.
78 Ahmed, 'Not in the Mood', p. 26.
79 H2639, F, 75, library assistant, Ipswich, undecided, 2016.
80 J5734, M, 31, charity worker, Newcastle-upon-Tyne, Remain, 2016.
81 P5366, M, 43, teacher, Portsmouth, Remain, 2017.
82 F5629, M, 57, unemployed retail/admin worker, West Lancashire, Leave, 2017.
83 B3227, M, 52, administrator, Birmingham, Remain, 2019.
84 Hall, 'Waiting for Brexit'.
85 For a tongue-in-cheek summary of such pronouncements, see Peter Cole and Peter Chippindale, 'A Euro-binge with all nine remembered', *Guardian*, 6 June 1975, p. 5. For more on this comparison, see Robert Saunders, *Yes to Europe! The 1975 Referendum and Seventies Britain* (Cambridge University Press, 2018), pp. 1–3; Oliver Daddow, 'The UK Media and "Europe": From Permissive Consensus to Destructive Dissent', *International Affairs*, 88:6 (2012), pp. 1219–1236. And on politics as a series of 'historic' moments, see Emily Robinson, *History, Heritage and Tradition in Contemporary British Politics* (Manchester: Manchester University Press, 2012), p. 6.
86 Heather Stewart and Daniel Boffey, 'Theresa May suffers historic defeat in vote as Tories turn against her', *Guardian*, 16 January 2019: www.theguardian.com/politics/2019/jan/15/theresa-may-suffers-historic-defeat-as-tories-turn-against-her (accessed 4 March 2023); BBC, 'Supreme Court giving historic Parliament suspension ruling', *BBC News*, 24 September 2019: www.bbc.

co.uk/news/uk-politics-49805024 (accessed 4 March 2023); George Parker, Peter Foster, and Jim Brunsden, 'UK and EU agree historic Brexit trade deal', *Financial Times*, 24 December 2020: www.ft.com/content/f336aaco-ae6a-4fe5-96e6-673016880922 (accessed 4 March 2023); BBC, 'Brexit: Why is Friday a historic day for the UK?' *Newsround*, 31 January 2020: www.bbc.co.uk/newsround/51296767 (accessed 4 March 2023).

87 F5890, F, 69, retired finance officer, East Lothian, Remain, 2019.
88 F1644, F, 84, retired purchasing manager, Grove, Oxfordshire, Remain, 2019.
89 B1180, F, 82, retired clerk, South Coast, Leave, 2019.
90 D2585, F, 76, retired secretary, Bristol, Remain, 2019; B5725, F, 58, retired FE lecturer, Chester, Leave, 2019.
91 C5847, F, 41, charity worker, Harborough, Remain, 2019.
92 H260, F, 89, retired shop manager, Brentwood, Essex, Leave, 2019.
93 D4736, M, 52, air traffic services assistant, Southampton, Remain, 2019.
94 On the construction of 'ordinariness' as a political category, see Claire Langhamer, '"Who the Hell Are Ordinary People?" Ordinariness as a Category of Historical Analysis', *Transactions of the Royal Historical Society*, 28 (2018), pp. 175–195.
95 F3409, F, 70, retired civil servant, Nottingham, Leave, 2017.
96 John Curtice, 'Political Consequences of Brexit: Has Brexit Damaged Our Politics?' in John Curtice, Nathan Hudson, and Ian Montagu (eds), *British Social Attitudes: The 37th Report* (London: The National Centre for Social Research, 2020).
97 Erik Amnå and Joakim Ekman, 'Standby Citizens: Diverse Faces of Political Passivity', *European Political Science Review*, 6:2 (2014), pp. 261–281.
98 S3779, M, 54, bereavement counsellor, Cheadle, Remain, 2016.
99 A1706, F, 71, artist, West Sussex, Remain, 2017.
100 G2776, F, 43, business analyst, New Zealand, vote unknown, 2016.
101 J5734, M, 31, charity worker, Newcastle-upon-Tyne, Remain, 2016; W5881, F, 48, self-employed project manager, Brighton, Remain, 2016.
102 T4715, F, 44, community health worker, Nottingham, Remain, 2016.
103 W5881, F, 48, self-employed project manager, Brighton, Remain, 2016.
104 O3436, F, 63, retired civil servant, Dorset, Remain, 2017.
105 B5725, F, 57, retired FE lecturer, Chester, Leave, 2017.
106 R1025, F, 74, housewife and former book-keeper, Milton Keynes, Leave, 2017.

Notes

107 B5970, M, 49, unemployed clerk, Cambridge, Leave, 2017.
108 S1399, F, 67, occupation unstated, Tunbridge Wells, Leave, 2016, original emphasis. See also T4715, F, 45, community health worker, Nottinghamshire, Remain, 2017, who commented on the intensification of calls for Scottish independence: 'I could see it leading to civil war'.
109 H5724, F, 62, retired library assistant, Rugby, Leave, 2017.
110 A4127, M, 55, theatre usher, Blackpool, Leave, 2017.
111 B5725, F, 58, retired FE lecturer, Chester, Leave, 2019.
112 H1541, M, 71, retired film editor, central Scotland, Remain, 2016.
113 V5924, F, 30, librarian, Oxford, Remain, 2017.
114 J2891, F, 51, caseworker, Clwyd, Remain, 2016; N5545, M, 23, no occupation noted, Stockport, Remain, 2016.
115 M3190, M, 57, retired civil servant, South Tyneside, Remain, 2016.
116 B5342, F, 30, online jewellery retailer, Salisbury, Leave, 2016.
117 T4715, F, 45, community health worker, Nottinghamshire, Remain, 2017.
118 Ahmed, 'Not in the Mood', p. 15.
119 W5881, F, 48, self-employed project manager, Brighton, Remain, 2016.
120 W5345, M, 20, student, West Midlands, Remain, 2016.
121 P3209, M, 76, artist, Lincolnshire, Remain, 2016.
122 Ahmed, 'Not in the Mood', p. 15.
123 Ibid.
124 E5014, M, 50, civil servant, Bath, Remain, 2016.
125 E5014, M, 51, retired civil servant, Bath, Remain, 2017.
126 Ahmed, 'Not in the Mood', p. 15.
127 C3210, F, 35, fundraising manager, Watford, Remain, 2016.
128 W5881, F, 48, self-employed project manager, Brighton, Remain, 2016.
129 J1890, F, 84, retired shop assistant, Hull, Remain, 2016.
130 B1120, F, age unspecified, mature counsellor and writer, London, Leave, 2016.
131 See, for instance, 'Brexit polls: How the mood has changed in Britain in three charts', *The Week*, 26 March 2019: www.theweek.co.uk/100429/brexit-polls-how-the-mood-has-changed-in-britain-in-three-charts (accessed 4 March 2023).
132 On unfeeling as a political act (albeit in a very different historical and political context), see Xine Yao, *Disaffected: The Cultural Politics of Unfeeling in Nineteenth-Century America* (Durham, NC: Duke University Press, 2021).

Notes

Chapter 4

1 Alina Rzepnikowska, 'Migrant Experiences of Conviviality in the Context of Brexit: Polish Migrant Women in Manchester', *Central and Eastern European Migration Review*, 9:1 (2020), pp. 65–83; Ben Rogaly, *Stories from a Migrant City: Living and Working Together in the Shadow of Brexit* (Manchester: Manchester University Press, 2021).
2 'Brexit breakup: Did it cause a rift between you and your partner?' *Guardian*, 30 December 2016: www.theguardian.com/lifeandstyle/2016/dec/30/brexit-breakup-did-it-cause-a-rift-between-you-and-your-partner (accessed 4 March 2023); 'Has your relationship been affected by Brexit divisions?' *Guardian*, 28 October 2019: www.theguardian.com/lifeandstyle/2019/oct/28/has-your-relationship-been-affected-by-brexit-divisions (accessed 4 March 2023).
3 Sarah Marsh and Guardian readers, 'It's not EU … it's Brexit: The couples in turmoil after the referendum result', *Guardian*, 7 February 2017: www.theguardian.com/commentisfree/2017/feb/07/eu-brexit-couples-turmoil-referendum-relationship (accessed 4 March 2023); Candice Piers and Michael Segalov, 'Love across the divide: Couples on Brexit, politics and religion', *Guardian*, 24 March 2019: www.theguardian.com/lifeandstyle/2019/mar/24/love-across-the-divide-of-brexit-politics-and-religion (accessed 4 March 2023).
4 Charlie Cooper, 'How Brexit ruined Christmas dinner', *Politico*, 22 December 2017: www.politico.eu/article/how-brexit-ruined-christmas-dinner/ (accessed 4 March 2023); Dan Roberts, 'Brexit facts to get you through that awkward Christmas dinner', *Guardian*, 24 December 2016: www.theguardian.com/politics/2016/dec/24/brexit-facts-awkward-christmas-dinner (accessed 4 March 2023); Tom Moseley, 'How to perfect your Brexit chat this Christmas', *BBC News*, 21 December 2017: www.bbc.co.uk/news/uk-politics-42394209 (accessed 4 March 2023); Benedict Spence, 'Don't ruin Christmas by bringing Brexit to the dinner table', *City AM*, 21 December 2018: www.cityam.com/dont-ruin-christmas-bringing-brexit-dinner-table/ (accessed 4 March 2023); Lauren Sharkey, 'How to talk to your family about Brexit over Christmas, because no one likes a mid-dinner argument', *Bustle*, 10 December 2018: www.bustle.com/p/how-to-talk-to-your-family-about-brexit-over-christmas-because-no-one-likes-a-mid-dinner-argument-13606324 (accessed 4 March 2023).

Notes

5 Will Worley, 'Brexit arguments causing rifts between couples, counsellors say', *Independent*, 30 December 2016: www.independent.co.uk/news/uk/home-news/brexit-anxieties-issue-troubled-couples-relationship-counsellors-experts-a7500876.html (accessed 4 March 2023); Anoosh Chakelin, '"He changed – all his nastiness suddenly came out": Meet the people breaking up over Brexit', *New Statesman*, 5 December 2018: www.newstatesman.com/politics/brexit/2018/12/he-changed-all-his-nastiness-suddenly-came-out-meet-people-breaking-over (accessed 4 March 2023).

6 Sarah Niblock, quoted by Zia Haider Rahman, 'Not another Brexit Jeremiad', *New York Review of Books*, 28 March 2019: www.nybooks.com/daily/2019/03/28/not-another-brexit-jeremiad/ (accessed 4 March 2023).

7 B4318, M, 74, retired head teacher, County Durham, Leave, 2017.

8 A1706, F, 71, artist, West Sussex, Remain, 2017.

9 F3641, F, 77, retired teacher, Leicester, Leave, 2017.

10 N5744, M, 40, carer, Sunderland, Leave, 2017.

11 See, for instance, BBC, 'Archive on 4: The Day Brexit Hit Boiling Point', BBC Radio 4, 26 September 2020: www.bbc.co.uk/programmes/m000my3f (accessed 4 March 2023).

12 See, for instance, Philippa Perry, 'To mend the Brexit rift, let's respect other people's feelings – and honestly face our own', *Guardian*, 25 June 2016: www.theguardian.com/commentisfree/2016/jun/25/brexit-rift-feelings-honest (accessed 4 March 2023).

13 Chris Wells et al., 'When We Stop Talking Politics: The Maintenance and Closing of Conversation in Contentious Times', *Journal of Communication*, 67 (2017), pp. 131–157.

14 See, for example, Chris Degeling et al., 'Influencing Health Policy through Public Deliberation: Lessons Learned from Two Decades of Citizens'/Community Juries', *Social Science & Medicine*, 179 (2017), pp. 166–171; Shelley Boulianne, 'Building Faith in Democracy: Deliberative Events, Political Trust and Efficacy', *Political Studies*, 67:1 (2019), pp. 4–30; Ramon van der Does and Vincent Jacquet, 'Small-Scale Deliberation and Mass Democracy: A Systematic Review of the Spillover Effects of Deliberative Minipublics', *Political Studies*, 71:1 (2023), pp. 218–237.

15 Coleman, *How People Talk*, p. 1.

16 F4873, M, 50, IT consultant, Exeter, Remain, 2017.

17 Chantal Mouffe, *Agonistics: Thinking the World Politically* (London: Verso, 2013).

18 Ben Highmore and Jenny Bourne Taylor, 'Introducing Mood Work', *New Formations* 82 (2014), pp. 5–12; Arlie Hochschild,

Notes

The Managed Heart: Commercialization of Human Feeling (Berkeley, CA: University of California Press, 1983).

19 Mariella Frostrup, 'My family is split over Brexit, and now we want to move abroad', *Guardian*, 13 October 2019: www.theguardian.com/lifeandstyle/2019/oct/13/my-family-is-split-over-brexit-now-we-want-to-move-abroad-mariella-frostrup (accessed 4 March 2023).

20 Mariella Frostrup, 'My husband's boasts are worse since Brexit – and I can't stand it', *Guardian*, 12 April 2019: www.theguardian.com/lifeandstyle/2019/apr/07/my-husbands-boasts-are-worse-since-brexit-and-i-cant-stand-it-mariella-frostrup (accessed 4 March 2023). See also Bel Mooney, 'My friend has cut me off because I voted for Brexit', *Daily Mail*, 5 January 2019: www.dailymail.co.uk/femail/article-6558443/BEL-MOONEY-friend-cut-voted-Brexit.html (accessed 4 March 2023); Bel Mooney, 'My furious daughter STILL won't speak to me after I voted for Brexit ', *Daily Mail*, 26 November 2016: www.dailymail.co.uk/femail/article-3972300/BEL-MOONEY-furious-daughter-won-t-speak-voted-Brexit.html (accessed 4 March 2023).

21 Moira Peelo and Keith Soothill, 'Personal Power and Public Control: Sex Crimes and Problem Pages', *The Howard Journal*, 33:1 (1994), pp. 10–24. For a wider discussion of problem pages and their changing characteristics, see Adrian Bingham, 'Problem Pages and British Sexual Culture, c. 1930s to 1970s', *Media History*, 18:1 (2012), pp. 51–63.

22 Frostrup, 'My husband's boasts are worse'.

23 Frostrup, 'My family is split'.

24 Frostrup, 'My husband's boasts are worse'.

25 Susanna Abse, 'Brexit – Trauma, Identity and the Core Complex', *New Associations*, 28 (Summer 2019), pp. 7–11 (7–8).

26 Ibid, p. 10.

27 Ibid, pp. 10; 11.

28 Rhodri Hayward, 'The Pursuit of Serenity: Psychological Knowledge and the Making of the Welfare State', in Sally Alexander and Barbara Taylor (eds), *History and Psyche: Culture, Psychoanalysis and the Past* (Basingstoke: Palgrave, 2012), pp. 283–304; Stephen Brooke, 'Evan Durbin: Reassessing a Labour "Revisionist"', *Twentieth Century British History*, 7 (1996), pp. 27–52 (38–42); Jeremy Nuttall, *Psychological Socialism: The Labour Party and Qualities of Mind and Character, 1931 to the Present* (Manchester: Manchester University Press, 2006).

29 Channel 4 News, 'Psychoanalyst puts Brexit Britain on the couch. Part 3: Lewes', *YouTube*, 8 August 2019: www.youtube.com/watch?v=ONQkgt6VDaQ (accessed 4 March 2023).
30 Channel 4 News, 'Psychoanalyst puts Brexit Britain on the couch. Part 1: Grimsby', *YouTube*, 8 August 2019: www.youtube.com/watch?v=JiMqjWeNOsc (accessed 4 March 2023).
31 For a general overview, see Mathew Thomson, *Psychological Subjects: Identity, Culture, and Health in Twentieth-Century Britain* (Oxford: Oxford University Press, 2006).
32 Sarah Crook, 'The Women's Liberation Movement, Activism and Therapy at the Grassroots, 1968–1985', *Women's History Review*, 27:7 (2018), pp. 1152–1168; Susan L. Miller, *After the Crime: The Power of Restorative Justice Dialogues Between Victims and Violent Offenders* (New York: New York University Press, 2011); Simon Anderson and Julie Brownlie, 'Build It and They Will Come? Understanding Public Views of "Emotions Talk" and the Talking Therapies', *British Journal of Guidance & Counselling*, 39:1 (2011), pp. 53–66.
33 For an account of how the tagline was developed, see Robert Bean, '"It's Good to Talk" – the story behind the campaign', *Campaign*, 16 September 2009: www.campaignlive.co.uk/article/its-good-talk-story-behind-campaign/938629 (accessed 4 March 2023).
34 See for instance, Death Café: https://deathcafe.com/ (accessed 4 March 2023); Alison Pask, 'It's time to talk money', *Financial Times*, 12 November 2018: www.ftadviser.com/your-industry/2018/11/12/it-s-time-to-talk-money/ (accessed 4 March 2023).
35 About StoryCorps: https://storycorps.org/about/ (accessed 4 March 2023).
36 Listening Project, BBC Radio 4: www.bbc.co.uk/programmes/articles/41rDvmTWoT1JWjXkcvZtMqt/about (accessed 4 March 2023).
37 See particularly father and daughter Cath and Frank, Leicester, 10.09.2016; siblings Loui and Chantelle, London, 20.08.2016; and colleagues Matt and Dion, Swansea, 22.08.2016. All available from https://sounds.bl.uk/Oral-history/The-Listening-Project/021M-C1500X1185XX-0001V0 (accessed 4 March 2023).
38 See, for example, Jean Duncombe and Dennis Marsden, 'Love and Intimacy: The Gender Division of Emotion and "Emotion Work": A Neglected Aspect of Sociological Discussion of Heterosexual Relationships', *Sociology*, 27:2 (1993), pp. 221–241.
39 Mairi-Frances and Rory, Leicester, 10.09.2016.
40 Ben and Kenneth, Edinburgh, 23.08.2016.

Notes

41 Denise and Ben, London, 21.09.2016.
42 See anon., 'Bridging the Brexit Divide – Boston comes to Brixton', *Brixton Blog*, 20 June 2018: https://brixtonblog.com/2018/06/bridging-the-brexit-divide-boston-comes-to-brixton/ (accessed 4 March 2023). Programme available here: www.bbc.co.uk/programmes/b05s4fv9 (accessed 4 March 2023).
43 More in Common: www.moreincommon.com/ (accessed 4 March 2023).
44 Lawrence Black, 'The Lost World of Young Conservatism', *Historical Journal*, 51:4 (2008), pp. 991–1024 (1021). See also Helen McCarthy, 'Parties, Voluntary Associations, and Democratic Politics in Interwar Britain', *Historical Journal*, 50:4 (2007), pp. 891–912 (897).
45 Amy Johnson, 'ITV Loose Women's Carol McGiffin erupts over Brexit following "massive" pre-show row', *Daily Express*, 27 September 2019: www.express.co.uk/showbiz/tv-radio/1183516/ITV-Loose-Women-Carol-McGiffin-Brexit-rant-Nadia-Sawalha-row-Boris-Johnson-ITV-watch (accessed 4 March 2023); Lauren Franklin, 'Voting to Remain Silent', *Sun*, 29 March 2017: www.thesun.co.uk/tvandshowbiz/3206955/loose-women-panellists-reveal-theyre-too-scared-to-reveal-how-they-voted-in-brexit-for-fear-of-abuse/ (accessed 4 March 2023).
46 Saira Khan, quoted in Franklin, 'Voting to Remain Silent'.
47 *Loose Women*, 28 June 2016: www.youtube.com/watch?v=tuvlMuuhHIY (accessed 4 March 2023).
48 Saira Khan and Nadia Sawalha, quoted in Johnson, 'ITV Loose Women's Carol McGiffin'.
49 'Are you suffering from Brexit Rage?' *Loose Women*, 10 September 2019: www.youtube.com/watch?v=QZeIaDJV-rA (accessed 4 March 2023).
50 'Archive on 4: The Day Brexit Hit Boiling Point', BBC Radio 4, 26 September 2020: www.bbc.co.uk/programmes/m000my3f (accessed 4 March 2023).
51 Emma Ailes, quoted in Jackie Bischof, 'This Brexit dating show is everything America needs right now', *Quartz*, 2 December 2018: https://qz.com/1478868/this-reality-tv-dating-show-makes-people-talk-about-brexit/ (accessed 4 March 2023).
52 Laurie Ouellette, 'Reality TV Gives Back: On the Civic Functions of Reality Entertainment', *Journal of Popular Film & Television* (2010), pp. 66–71; Todd Graham, 'Beyond "Political" Communicative Spaces: Talking Politics on the Wife Swap Discussion Forum', *Journal of Information Technology & Politics*, 9 (2012), pp. 31–45.

Notes

53 For a summary of the programme see 'Wife Swap: Brexit Special', news release, Channel 4, 31 May 2017: www.channel4.com/press/news/wife-swap-brexit-special-0 (accessed 4 March 2023).
54 Crossing Divides, BBC World Service: www.bbc.co.uk/programmes/p072om3f (accessed 4 March 2023).
55 Francesca Gillett, 'Crossing Divides – I respectfully disagree: How to argue constructively about Brexit', *BBC News*, 13 September 2019: www.bbc.co.uk/news/uk-49648119 (accessed 4 March 2023).
56 Emily Kasriel, 'Crossing Divides on the Move: Conversational Commutes', *BBC Blog*, 12 June 2019: www.bbc.co.uk/blogs/aboutthebbc/entries/e7151eb1-890f-489b-87f3-a1099d56f2c9 (accessed 4 March 2023).
57 BBC Crossing Divides: http://crossingdivides.bbcnewslabs.co.uk/ (accessed 4 March 2023).
58 Gillett, 'Crossing Divides'.
59 Claire Fox, quoted in Gillett, 'Crossing Divides'.
60 Alan Renwick et al., 'The Report on the Citizens' Assembly on Brexit', UCL Constitution Unit, December 2017: https://citizensassembly.co.uk/wp-content/uploads/2017/12/Citizens-Assembly-on-Brexit-Report.pdf (accessed 4 March 2023), p. 79.
61 Wells et al., 'When We Stop Talking Politics'.
62 Renwick et al., 'The Report on the Citizens' Assembly on Brexit'. (accessed 4 March 2023).
63 David M. Farrell, Jane Suiter, and Clodagh Harris, '"Systematizing" Constitutional Deliberation: The 2016–18 Citizens' Assembly in Ireland', *Irish Political Studies*, 34:1 (2019), pp. 113–123.
64 Renwick et al., 'The Report on the Citizens' Assembly on Brexit', p. 77.
65 See, for example Climate Assembly UK (2019): www.climateassembly.uk/ and Citizens' Assembly on Scotland (2019): https://citizensassembly.theapsgroup.scot/doing-politics-differently/ (both accessed 4 March 2023).
66 See James Martin, 'A Feeling for Democracy: Rhetoric, Power and the Emotions', *Journal of Political Power*, 6:3 (2013), pp. 461–476.
67 Mouffe, *Agonistics*, p. 9.
68 Manuel Hensmans and Koen van Bommel, 'Brexit, the NHS and the Double-Edged Sword of Populism: Contributor to Agonistic Democracy or Vehicle of Ressentiment?', *Organization*, 27:3 (2020), pp. 370–384.
69 Ugur Aytac, 'On the Limits of the Political: The Problem of Overly Permissive Pluralism in Mouffe's Agonism', *Constellations*, 28 (2021), pp. 417–431; Bart van Leeuwen, 'Absorbing the Agony of

Notes

Agonism? The Limits of Cultural Questioning and Alternative Variations of Intercultural Civility', *Urban Studies*, 52:4 (2015), pp. 793–808.
70 For more on this, see Charlotte Lydia Riley (ed.), *The Free Speech Wars: How Did We Get Here and Why Does It Matter?* (Manchester: Manchester University Press, 2020).
71 H1543, M, 87, retired local government officer, West Sussex, Leave, 2017; W633, F, 74, retired journalist, County Durham, Leave, 2017.
72 S5866, F, 36, scriptwriter, Bury, Remain, 2016.
73 B5880, F, 24, PhD student, Aberystwyth, Remain, 2017.
74 Katherine Davies, 'Sticking Together in "Divided Britain": Talking Brexit in Everyday Family Relationships', *Sociology*, 56:1 (2021), pp. 97–113.
75 B5342, F, 31, online jewellery retailer, Salisbury, Leave, 2017.
76 Ibid.
77 R2144, F, 81, retired teacher, Birmingham, Remain, 2017.
78 B5342, F, 30, online jewellery retailer, Salisbury, Leave, 2016.
79 G4296, M, 40, archive cataloguer, Cardiff, Remain, 2017.
80 Coleman, *How People Talk*, p. 139.
81 Ibid., p. 166.
82 B5342, F, 30, online jewellery retailer, Salisbury, Leave, 2016.
83 Hochschild, *Managed Heart*.
84 C5706, F, 36, library assistant, Newport, Remain, 2016.
85 Eleni Andreouli, Katy Greenland, and Lia Figgou, 'Lay Discourses about Brexit and Prejudice: "Ideological Creativity" and Its Limits in Brexit Debates', *European Journal of Social Psychology*, 50 (2020), pp. 309–322.
86 T4715, F, 44, community health worker, Nottingham, Remain, 2016.
87 Ibid.
88 T4715, F, 45, community health worker, Nottinghamshire, Remain, 2017.
89 Coleman, *How People Talk*, p. 21.
90 D2585, F, 74, retired secretary, near Bristol, Remain, 2017.
91 E5014, M, 51, retired civil servant, Bath, Remain, 2017.
92 C5991, F, 63, retired office worker, Dagenham, Essex, Leave, 2017.
93 G6158, M, 21, [student?], Brighton, Remain, 2017.
94 D4736, M, 49, air traffic services assistant, Southampton, Remain, 2016.
95 Ibid.

Notes

96 D4736, M, 51, air traffic services assistant, Southampton, Remain, 2017.
97 O4521, M, 44, engineering director, Cambridge, Remain, 2017.
98 W1813, F, 65, retired teacher, Staffordshire, Remain, 2017.
99 G6158, M, 21, [student?], Brighton, Remain, 2017.
100 M5645, F, 43, writer, North Ayrshire, Remain, 2017.
101 G4374, M, 51, freelance researcher, Long Ashton near Bristol, Remain, 2017.
102 H1806, M, 91, retired typesetter, location unknown (Home Counties), Remain, 2017.
103 P6054, M, 19, full-time student, Portsmouth, vote unknown, 2017.
104 B5880, F, 24, PhD student, Aberystwyth, Remain, 2017.
105 H2418, F, 65, retired library worker, London, Remain, 2017.
106 H2637, F, 76, retired librarian, NE Surrey/SW London, Remain, 2016.
107 E5559, M, 50, creative/trainer, Exeter, Remain, 2017.
108 O4521, M, 44, engineering director, Cambridge, Remain, 2017.
109 G6158, M, 21, [student?], Brighton, Remain, 2017.
110 B5638, F, 30, university lecturer, Bangor, Northern Ireland, Remain, 2017.
111 C4988, M, 63, retired nurse, Stapleford, Nottingham, Remain, 2017.
112 Bart van Leeuwen, 'Absorbing the Agony of Agonism? The Limits of Cultural Questioning and Alternative Variations of Intercultural Civility', *Urban Studies*, 52:4 (2015), pp. 793–808 (799).
113 R860, F, 68, retired JP, Cheshire, Leave, 2016.
114 Elisabetta Zontini and Elena Genova, 'Studying the Emotional Costs of Integration at Times of Change: The Case of EU Migrants in Brexit Britain', *Sociology*, 56:4 (2022), pp. 638–654.
115 Rosa Mas Giralt, 'The Emotional Geographies of Migration and Brexit: Tales of *Unbelonging*', *Central and Eastern European Migration Review*, 9:1 (2020), pp. 29-45 (36–37).
116 R860, F, 69, retired JP, Cheshire, Leave, 2017.
117 Coleman, *How People Talk*, p. 1.

Conclusion

1 Bice Maiguashca and Jonathan Dean, 'Lovely People but Utterly Deluded'? *British Politics*, 15 (2020), pp. 48–68 (61).
2 Peter Allen and David Moon, 'Predictions, Pollification, and Pol Profs: The "Corbyn Problem" beyond Corbyn', *Political Quarterly*, 91 (2020), pp. 80–88.

Notes

3 Akram, 'Dear British Politics'.
4 Lise Butler, 'The Social Scientific Turn in Modern British History', *Twentieth Century British History*, 33:3 (2022), pp. 445–450.
5 Alex Mintz, Carly Wayne, and Nicholas Valentino, *Beyond Rationality: Behavioral Political Science in the 21st Century* (Cambridge: Cambridge University Press, 2021).
6 James Tilley and Sara B. Hobolt, 'Losers' Consent and Emotions in the Aftermath of the Brexit Referendum', *West European Politics* (2023): https://doi.org/10.1080/01402382.2023.2168945.
7 Emmy Eklundh, 'Excluding Emotions: The Performative Function of Populism', *Partecipazione e Conflitto; Milan*, 13:1 (2020), pp. 107–131.
8 Robert Ford and Matthew Goodwin, *Revolt on the Right: Explaining Support for the Radical Right in Britain* (London: Routledge, 2014), p. 112; Robert Ford and Matthew Goodwin, 'Understanding UKIP: Identity, Social Change and the Left Behind', *Political Quarterly*, 85:3 (2014), pp. 277–284 (277).
9 A Nexis search shows 227 mentions of 'left behind' and 'voter' in the *Guardian* during 2016, compared with just 12 each in the *Sun* and the *Daily Mail/Mail on Sunday*, 8 in the *Daily Mirror*, and 2 in the *Express*. Searching for 'left behind' and 'Brexit' showed 306 mentions in the *Independent* and 190 in the *Guardian*, compared with 34 in the *Daily Mail/Mail on Sunday*, 29 in the *Sun*, 19 in the *Daily Mirror*, and 9 in the *Express*.
10 John Harris and Jon Domekos, 'We spent 10 years talking to people. Here's what it taught us about Britain', *Guardian*, 3 December 2019: www.theguardian.com/news/2019/dec/03/anywhere-but-westminster-vox-pops-understanding-uk-political-landscape (accessed 4 March 2023).
11 Christina Peter and Kathleen Beckers, 'Vox Pops vs. Poll Results – Effects of Consonant and Dissonant Displays of Public Opinion in News Coverage', *International Journal of Public Opinion Research*, 34:3 (2022).
12 Mondon, 'Populism, Public Opinion'.
13 Jon Lawrence, *Electing Our Masters: The Hustings in British Politics from Hogarth to Blair* (Oxford: Oxford University Press, 2009).
14 Ofcom, *BBC News and Current Affairs Review* (London: PwC Current Affairs, 2019): www.ofcom.org.uk/__data/assets/pdf_file/0024/174066/bbc-news-review-pwc-full-report.pdf (accessed 4 March 2023).
15 Langhamer, '"Who the Hell Are Ordinary People?"'.
16 Ahmed, 'The Politics of Bad Feeling'.

Notes

17 Bhambra, 'Brexit, Trump, and "Methodological Whiteness"'; Rogaly, *Stories from a Migrant City*; Marianela Barrios Aquino, 'Affective Citizenship in Brexit Britain: EU Citizens' Responses to Emotional Governance', *Emotions: History, Culture, Society*, 6 (2022), pp. 296–313.
18 Ben Anderson, 'Neoliberal Affects', *Progress in Human Geography*, 40:6 (2015), pp. 734–753.
19 Alan Finlayson, 'Neoliberalism, the Alt-Right and the Intellectual Dark Web', *Theory, Culture & Society*, 38:6 (November 2021), pp. 167–190.
20 Camilla Schofield, 'Brexit and the Other Special Relationship', in Stuart Ward and Astrid Rasch (eds), *Embers of Empire in Brexit Britain* (London: Bloomsbury, 2019), pp. 87–99.
21 Thomas Dixon, *From Passions to Emotions: The Creation of a Secular Psychological Category* (Cambridge University Press, 2009).
22 Anderson, 'Neoliberal Affects', p. 738.
23 See, for instance, 'Brexit polls: How the mood has changed in Britain in three charts', *The Week*, 26 March 2019: www.theweek.co.uk/100429/brexit-polls-how-the-mood-has-changed-in-britain-in-three-charts (accessed 4 March 2023).

Bibliography

Archival Sources

The Listening Project, British Library Sounds Archive
Mass Observation Project, The Keep

Newspapers and periodicals

City AM
Daily Express
Daily Mail
Daily Telegraph
The Economist
Financial Times
Guardian
Independent
New Statesman
New York Review of Books
Observer
Prospect
The Psychologist
Spectator
Sun
The Week

TV and Radio

The Age of Emotion, BBC Radio 4
All in the Best Possible Taste, Channel 4
Archive on 4, BBC Radio 4

Bibliography

Channel 4 News
Gogglebox, Channel 4
Grayson Perry's Divided Britain, Channel 4
Grayson Perry's Full English, Channel 4
How Europe Stole My Mum, Channel 4
Loose Women, ITV
Two Rooms, BBC Radio 4
Victoria Derbyshire, BBC2
Wife Swap: Brexit Special, Channel 4

Blogs and websites

The Atlantic
BBC Blog
BBC Future
BBC News online
BBC Newsround
BBC World Service
British Academy blog
British Association for Counselling and Psychotherapy
Brixton Blog
Bustle
Centre for Constitutional Change
Citizens' Assembly on Scotland
Chronicle Live
Climate Assembly UK
Death Café
ITV News online
Mental Health Foundation
More in Common
Nurture: The OmMama Resource Center
Office of National Statistics
Open Democracy
Political Economy Research Centre blog
Politico
Quartz
StoryCorps
UK in a Changing Europe
YouGov
YouTube

Bibliography

Speeches

Cameron, David, speech on wellbeing, 25 November 2010: www.gov.uk/government/speeches/pm-speech-on-wellbeing.

Johnson, Boris, speech in Downing Street, 24 July 2019: www.gov.uk/government/speeches/boris-johnsons-first-speech-as-prime-minister-24-july-2019.

Reports

Curtice, John, 'The Emotional Legacy of Brexit: How Britain Has Become a Country of "Remainers" and "Leavers"', What UK Thinks: EU, 15 October 2018: https://whatukthinks.org/eu/wp-content/uploads/2018/10/WUKT-EU-Briefing-Paper-15-Oct-18-Emotional-legacy-paper-final.pdf.

Curtice, John and Montagu, Ian (eds), *British Social Attitudes: 37th Report* (London: National Centre for Social Research, 2020).

Marcus, George E., 'How Affective Intelligence Theory Can Help Us Understand Politics', *Emotion Research*, ISRE's Sourcebook for Research on Emotion and Affect (2017): http://emotionresearcher.com/how-affectiveintelligence-theory-can-help-us-understand-politics/.

Ofcom, *BBC News and Current Affairs Review* (London: PwC Current Affairs, 2019): www.ofcom.org.uk/__data/assets/pdf_file/0024/174066/bbc-news-review-pwc-full-report.pdf.

Renwick, Alan, et al., 'The Report on the Citizens' Assembly on Brexit', UCL Constitution Unit, December 2017: www.ucl.ac.uk/constitution-unit/sites/constitution-unit/files/The_Report_of_the_Citizens__Assembly_on_Brexit.pdf.

Published sources

Abse, Susanna, 'Brexit – Trauma, Identity and the Core Complex', *New Associations*, 28 (2019), 7–11.

Achen, Christopher and Bartels, Larry, *Democracy for Realists: Why Elections Do Not Produce Responsive Government* (Princeton, NJ: Princeton University Press, 2016).

Adam, Sibyl, 'Brexit and Literary Mood in Ali Smith's *Autumn*', *Contemporary Women's Writing*, 16:1 (2022), 60–78.

Agarwal, Amit, Singh, Ritu, and Toshniwal, Durga, 'Geospatial Sentiment Analysis Using Twitter Data for UK-EU Referendum', *Journal of Information & Optimization Sciences*, 39:1 (2018), 303–317.

Bibliography

Åhäll, Linda, 'Affect as Methodology: Feminism and the Politics of Emotion', *International Political Sociology*, 12:1 (2018), 36–52.

Ahmed, Sara, *The Cultural Politics of Emotion* (London: Routledge, 2004).

Ahmed, Sara, 'The Politics of Bad Feeling', *Australian Critical Race and Whiteness Studies Association Journal*, 1 (2005), 72–85.

Ahmed, Sara, *The Promise of Happiness* (Durham, NC: Duke University Press, 2010).

Ahmed, Sara, 'Not in the Mood', *New Formations*, 82 (2014), 13–28.

Akram, Sadiya, 'Dear British Politics – Where Is the Race and Racism?' *British Politics* (2023): https://doi.org/10.1057/s41293-023-00224-3.

Allen, Peter and Moon, David, 'Predictions, Pollification, and Pol Profs: The "Corbyn Problem" beyond Corbyn', *Political Quarterly*, 91 (2020), 80–88.

Amnå, Erik and Ekman, Joakim, 'Standby Citizens: Diverse Faces of Political Passivity', *European Political Science Review*, 6:2 (2014), 261–281.

Anderson, Ben, 'Neoliberal Affects', *Progress in Human Geography*, 40:6 (2015), 734–753.

Anderson, Ben and Wilson, Helen F., 'Everyday Brexits', *Area*, 50 (2018), 291–295.

Anderson, Ben, Wilson, Helen, F., Forman, Peter J., Heslop, Julia, Ormerod, Emma, and Maestri, Gaja, 'Brexit: Modes of Uncertainty and Futures in an Impasse', *Transactions of the Institute of British Geographers*, 45 (2020), 256–269.

Anderson, Simon and Brownlie, Julie, 'Build It and They Will Come? Understanding Public Views of "Emotions Talk" and the Talking Therapies', *British Journal of Guidance & Counselling*, 39:1 (2011), 53–66.

Andreouli, Eleni, Greenland, Katy, and Figgou, Lia, 'Lay Discourses about Brexit and Prejudice: "Ideological Creativity" and Its Limits in Brexit Debates', *European Journal of Social Psychology*, 50 (2020), 309–322.

Asur, Sitarum and Huberman, Bernardo A., 'Predicting the Future with Social Media' (2010), arXiv: https://arxiv.org/abs/1003.5699v1.

Aytac, Ugur, 'On the Limits of the Political: The Problem of Overly Permissive Pluralism in Mouffe's Agonism', *Constellations*, 28 (2021), 417–431.

Ball, James, *Post-Truth: How Bullshit Conquered the World* (London: Biteback Publishing, 2017).

Barrett, Lisa Feldman, *How Emotions Are Made: The Secret Life of the Brain* (New York: Houghton Mifflin, 2017).

Bibliography

Barrett, Lisa Feldman and Bar, Moshe, 'See It with Feeling: Affective Predictions during Object Perception', *Philosophical Transactions of the Royal Society of London: Series B: Biological Sciences*, 364:1521 (2009), 1325–1334.

Barrios Aquino, Marianela, 'Affective Citizenship in Brexit Britain: EU Citizens' Responses to Emotional Governance', *Emotions: History, Culture, Society*, 6 (2022), 296–313.

Beers, Laura, 'Whose Opinion? Changing Attitudes Towards Opinion Polling in British Politics, 1937–1964', *Twentieth Century British History*, 17:2 (2006), 177–205.

Berlant, Lauren, *Cruel Optimism* (Durham, NC: Duke University Press, 2010).

Berry-Waite, Lisa, '"A rancour and a passion would be introduced into politics": Perceptions of the Woman MP in Late 19th and Early 20th Century Britain', *Parliamentary History*, 42 (2023), 148–167.

Bevir, Mark, *The Making of British Socialism* (Princeton, NJ: Princeton University Press, 2011).

Bevir, Mark, Daddow, Oliver, and Schnapper, Pauline, 'Introduction: Interpreting British European Policy', *Journal of Common Market Studies*, 53 (2015), 1–17.

Bhambra, Gurminder, 'Brexit, Trump, and "Methodological Whiteness": On the Misrecognition of Race and Class', *British Journal of Sociology*, 68:S1 (2017), S214–S232.

Bingham, Adrian, 'Problem Pages and British Sexual Culture, c. 1930s to 1970s', *Media History*, 18:1 (2012), 51–63.

Black, Lawrence, *The Political Culture of the Left in Affluent Britain, 1951–64: Old Labour, New Britain?* (Basingstoke: Palgrave, 2003).

Black, Lawrence, 'The Lost World of Young Conservatism', *Historical Journal*, 51:4 (2008), 991–1024.

Boddice, Rob, *A History of Feelings* (London: Reaktion Books, 2019).

Bollen, Johann, Mao, Huina, and Zeng, Xiaojun, 'Twitter Mood Predicts the Stock Market', *Journal of Computational Science*, 2:1 (2011), 1–8.

Botterill, Kate and Hancock, Jonathan, 'Rescaling Belonging in "Brexit Britain": Spatial Identities and Practices of Polish Nationals in Scotland after the U.K. Referendum on European Union Membership', *Population, Space and Place*, 25:e2217 (2019).

Boucher, Ellen, 'Anticipating Armageddon: Nuclear Risk and the Neoliberal Sensibility in Thatcher's Britain', *The American Historical Review*, 124:4 (2019), 1221–1245.

Boulianne, Shelley, 'Building Faith in Democracy: Deliberative Events, Political Trust and Efficacy', *Political Studies*, 67:1 (2019), 4–30.

Bibliography

Brändle, Verena K, Galpin, Charlotte, and Trenz, Hans-Jörg, 'Marching for Europe? Enacting European Citizenship as Justice during Brexit', *Citizenship Studies*, 22:8 (2018), 810–828.

Brooke, Stephen, 'Evan Durbin: Reassessing a Labour "Revisionist"', *Twentieth Century British History*, 7 (1996), 27–52.

Brown, Wendy, *In the Ruins of Neoliberalism: The Rise of Antidemocratic Politics in the West* (New York: Columbia University Press, 2019).

Budiharto, Widodo and Meiliana, Meiliana, 'Prediction and Analysis of Indonesia Presidential Election from Twitter Using Sentiment Analysis', *Journal of Big Data*, 5:1 (2018), 1–10.

Butler, Lise, 'The Social Scientific Turn in Modern British History', *Twentieth Century British History*, 33:3 (2022), 445–450.

Campbell, Angus, Converse, Philip E., Miller, Warren E., and Stokes, Donald E., *The American Voter* (Chicago, IL: University of Chicago Press, 1980).

Campsie, Alexandre, 'Mass-Observation, Left Intellectuals and the Politics of Everyday Life', *The English Historical Review*, 131:548 (2016), 92–121.

Carl, Noah, Dennison, James, and Evans, Geoffrey, 'European but Not European Enough: An Explanation for Brexit', *European Union Politics*, 20:2 (2018), 282–304.

Clarke, Nick, Jennings, Will, Moss, Jonathan, and Stoker, Gerry, *The Good Politician: Folk Theories, Political Interaction and the Rise of Anti-politics* (Cambridge: Cambridge University Press, 2017).

Clarke, Nick, Jennings, Will, Moss, Jonathan, and Stoker, Gerry, 'Voter Decision-Making in a Context of Low Political Trust: The 2016 UK EU Membership Referendum', *Political Studies*, 71:1 (2021), 106–124.

Clarke, Nick and Moss, Jonathan, 'Popular Imaginative Geographies and Brexit: Evidence from Mass Observation', *Transactions of the British Institute of Geographers*, 46 (2021), 732–746.

Cockett, Richard, 'The New Right and the 1960s: The Dialectics of Liberation', in Geoff Andrews et al. (eds), *New Left, New Right and Beyond: Taking the Sixties Seriously* (Basingstoke: Macmillan, 1999), 85–105.

Coleman, Stephen, *How People Talk About Politics: Brexit and Beyond* (London: Bloomsbury, 2021).

Coleman, Stephen, 'Feeling It/Not Feeling It: Mood Stories as Accounts of Political Intuition', *International Journal of Politics, Culture, and Society*, 35 (2022), 477–495.

Collins, Marcus (ed.), *The Permissive Society and Its Enemies* (London: Rivers Oram, 2008).

Bibliography

Comstock, Patrick W., 'The Politics of Mindfulness', *Democracy & Education*, 23:2 (2015), Article 8.
Converse, Philip. E., 'The Nature of Belief Systems in Mass Publics' in David E. Apter (ed.), *Ideology and Discontent* (New York: Free Press, 1986), 206–261.
Crook, Sarah, 'The Women's Liberation Movement, Activism and Therapy at the Grassroots, 1968–1985', *Women's History Review*, 27:7 (2018), 1152–1168.
Curtice, John, 'Why Leave Won the UK's EU Referendum', *Journal of Common Market Studies*, 55 (2017), 19–37.
Curtice, John, 'Brave New World: Understanding the 2019 General Election', *Political Insight*, 11:1 (2020), 8–12.
Curtice, John and Montagu, Ian, 'Political Consequences of Brexit: Has Brexit Damaged Our Politics?' in John Curtice, Nathan Hudson, and Ian Montagu (eds), *British Social Attitudes: The 37th Report* (London: The National Centre for Social Research, 2020).
Daddow, Oliver, 'The UK Media and "Europe": From Permissive Consensus to Destructive Dissent', *International Affairs*, 88:6 (2012), 1219–1236.
Daddow, Oliver, 'Interpreting the Outsider Tradition in British European Policy Speeches from Thatcher to Cameron', *Journal of Common Market Studies*, 53 (2015), 71–88.
D'Ancona, Matthew, *Post-Truth Politics: The New War on Truth and How to Fight Back* (London: Penguin, 2017).
Davies, Katherine, 'Sticking Together in "Divided Britain": Talking Brexit in Everyday Family Relationships', *Sociology*, 56:1 (2021), 97–113.
Davies, William, *The Happiness Industry: How Government and Big Business Sold Us Well-Being* (London: Verso, 2015).
Davies, William, *Nervous States: How Feeling Took Over the World* (London: Penguin, 2018).
Davis, Evan, *Post-Truth: Why We Have Reached Peak Bullshit and What We Can Do About It* (Boston, MA: Little Brown, 2017).
Davis, Madeleine, 'Reappraising Socialist Humanism', *Journal of Political Ideologies*, 18:1 (2013), 57–81.
Degeling, Chris et al., 'Influencing Health Policy through Public Deliberation: Lessons Learned from Two Decades of Citizens'/Community Juries', *Social Science & Medicine*, 179 (2017), 166–171.
Degerman, Dan, 'Brexit Anxiety: A Case Study in the Medicalization of Dissent', *Critical Review of International Social and Political Philosophy*, 22:7 (2018), 823–840.
Dennison, James, Seddig, Daniel, and Davidov, Eldad, 'The Role of Human Values in Explaining Support for European Union

Membership', *Journal of Cross-Cultural Psychology*, 52:4 (2021), 372–387.

Dixon, Thomas, *From Passions to Emotions: The Creation of a Secular Psychological Category* (Cambridge: Cambridge University Press, 2009).

Dixon, Thomas, *Weeping Britannia: Portrait of a Nation in Tears* (Oxford: Oxford University Press, 2015).

Dixon, Thomas, 'What Is the History of Anger a History Of?', *Emotions: History, Culture, Society*, 4:1 (2020), 1–34.

Dorling, Danny, 'Brexit: The Decision of a Divided Country', *British Medical Journal*, 354 (2016): https://doi.org/10.1136/bmj.i3697.

Dotlich, David, Cairo, Peter, and Rhinesmith, Stephen, *Head, Heart and Guts – How the World's Best Companies Develop Complete Leaders* (Hoboken: John Wiley, 2006).

Eklundh, Emmy, 'Excluding Emotions: The Performative Function of Populism', *Open Journal of Sociopolitical Studies*, 13:1 (2020), 107–131.

Eliasoph, Nina, *Avoiding Politics: How Americans Produce Apathy in Everyday Life* (Cambridge: Cambridge University Press, 2019).

English, Richard and Kenny, Michael (eds), *Rethinking British Decline* (Basingstoke: Macmillan, 2000).

Eustace, Nicole, 'Emotion and Political Change', in Susan J. Matt and Peter N. Stearns (eds), *Doing Emotions History* (Urbana, IL: University of Illinois Press, 2013), 163–183.

Farrell, David M, Suiter, Jane, and Harris, Clodagh, '"Systematizing" Constitutional Deliberation: The 2016–18 Citizens' Assembly in Ireland', *Irish Political Studies*, 34:1 (2019), 113–123.

Felski, Rita and Fraiman, Susan, 'Introduction: In the Mood', *New Literary History*, 43:3 (2012), v–xi.

Finlayson, Alan, 'Neoliberalism, the Alt-Right and the Intellectual Dark Web', *Theory, Culture & Society*, 38:6 (2021), 167–190.

Flinders, Matthew, 'Why Feelings Trump Facts: Anti-politics, Citizenship and Emotion', *Emotions and Society*, 2:1 (2020), 21–40.

Foote, Geoffrey, *The Republican Transformation of Modern British Politics* (Basingstoke: Palgrave, 2006).

Ford, Robert and Goodwin, Matthew, *Revolt on the Right: Explaining Support for the Radical Right in Britain* (London: Routledge, 2014).

Ford, Robert and Goodwin, Matthew, 'Understanding UKIP: Identity, Social Change and the Left Behind', *Political Quarterly*, 85:3 (2014), 277–284.

Foucault, Michel, *The Birth of Biopolitics: Lectures at the Collège de France, 1978–1979* (Basingstoke: Palgrave Macmillan, 2008).

Bibliography

Francis, Martin, 'Economics and Ethics: The Nature of Labour's Socialism, 1945–1951', *Twentieth Century British History*, 6:2 (1995), 220–243.

Francis, Martin, 'Tears, Tantrums, and Bared Teeth: The Emotional Economy of Three Conservative Prime Ministers, 1951–1963', *Journal of British Studies*, 41:3 (2002), 354–387.

Freeden, Michael, *Liberal Languages: Ideological Imaginations and Twentieth-Century Progressive Thought* (Princeton, NJ: Princeton University Press, 2004).

Frevert, Ute and Pahl, Kerstin Maria, 'Introducing Political Feelings: Participatory Politics, Institutions,and Emotional Templates', in Ute Frevert et al., *Feeling Political: Emotions and Institutions since 1789* (Cham: Palgrave Macmillan, 2022), 1–26.

Garner, Stephen, 'A Moral Economy of Whiteness: Behaviours, Belonging and Britishness', *Ethnicities*, 12:4 (2012), 445–464.

Georgiadou, Elena, Angelopoulos, Spyros, and Drake, Helen, 'Big Data Analytics and International Negotiations: Sentiment Analysis of Brexit Negotiating Outcomes', *International Journal of Information Management*, 51 (2020), 102048.

Giddens, Anthony, *Modernity and Self-Identity: Self and Society in the Late Modern Age* (Stanford, CA: Stanford University Press, 1991).

Gigerenzer, Gerd, *Gut Feeling: The Intelligence of the Unconscious* (London: Penguin, 2007).

Glasman, Maurice, Rutherford, Jonathan, Stears, Marc, and White, Stuart (eds), *The Labour Tradition and the Politics of Paradox: The Oxford-London Seminars 2010–11* (London: Oxford-London Seminars, 2011).

Glencross, Andrew, *Why the UK Voted for Brexit: David Cameron's Great Miscalculation* (London: Palgrave, 2016).

Godin, Marie and Sigona, Nando, 'Intergenerational Narratives of Citizenship among EU Citizens in the UK after the Brexit Referendum', *Ethnic and Racial Studies*, 45:6 (2022), 1135–1154.

Goodwin, Matthew and Heath, Oliver, 'The 2016 Referendum, Brexit and the Left Behind: An Aggregate-Level Analysis of the Result', *Political Quarterly*, 87 (2016), 323–332.

Graham, Todd, 'Beyond "Political" Communicative Spaces: Talking Politics on the Wife Swap Discussion Forum', *Journal of Information Technology & Politics*, 9 (2012), 31–45.

Grčar, Miha et al., 'Stance and Influence of Twitter Users Regarding the Brexit Referendum,' *Computational Social Networks*, 4:1 (2017), 6–25.

Bibliography

Greenwalt, Kyle A. and Nguyen, Cuong H., 'The Mindfulness Practice, Aesthetic Experience, and Creative Democracy', *Education and Culture*, 33:2 (2017), 49–65.

Groenendyk, Eric, 'Current Emotion Research in Political Science: How Emotions Help Democracy Overcome Its Collective Action Problem', *Emotion Research*, 3:4 (2011), 455–463.

Groenendyk, Eric, 'Of Two Minds, but One Heart: A Good "Gut" Feeling Moderates the Effect of Ambivalence on Attitude Formation and Turnout', *American Journal of Political Science*, 63 (2019), 368–384.

Guerrina, Roberta, Exadaktylos, Theofanis, and Guerra, Simona, 'Gender, Ownership and Engagement during the European Union Referendum: Gendered Frames and the Reproduction of Binaries', *European Journal of Politics & Gender*, 1:3 (2018), 387–404.

Guma, Taulant and Dafydd Jones, Rhys, '"Where are we going to go now?" European Union Migrants' Experiences of Hostility, Anxiety, and (Non-)Belonging during Brexit', *Population, Space and Place*, 25:e2198 (2019).

Hall, Sarah Marie, 'Waiting for Brexit: Crisis, Conjuncture, Method', *Transactions of the Institute of British Geographers*, 47 (2022), 200–213.

Hall, Todd H. and Ross, Andrew A.G., 'Rethinking Affective Experience and Popular Emotion: World War I and the Construction of Group Emotion in International Relations', *Political Psychology*, 40 (2019), 1357–1372.

Hay, Colin, 'Brexistential Angst and the Paradoxes of Populism: On the Contingency, Predictability and Intelligibility of Seismic Shifts', *Political Studies*, 68:1 (2020), 187–206.

Hay, Colin and Benoît, Cyril, 'Brexit, Positional Populism, and the Declining Appeal of Valence Politics', *Critical Review*, 31:3–4 (2019), 389–404.

Hayward, Rhodri, 'The Pursuit of Serenity: Psychological Knowledge and the Making of the Welfare State', in Sally Alexander and Barbara Taylor (eds), *History and Psyche: Culture, Psychoanalysis and the Past* (Basingstoke: Palgrave, 2012), 283–304.

Hensmans, Manuel and van Bommel, Koen, 'Brexit, the NHS and the Double-Edged Sword of Populism: Contributor to Agonistic Democracy or Vehicle of Ressentiment?', *Organization*, 27:3 (2020), 370–384.

Highmore, Ben, *Everyday Life and Cultural Theory: An Introduction* (London: Routledge, 2001).

Highmore, Ben, 'Feeling Our Way: Mood and Cultural Studies', *Communication and Critical/Cultural Studies*, 10:4 (2013), 427–438.

Bibliography

Highmore, Ben and Bourne Taylor, Jenny, 'Introducing Mood Work', *New Formations*, 82 (2014), 5–12.

Hinton, James, '"The 'Class' Complex": Mass-Observation and Cultural Distinction in Pre-War Britain', *Past & Present*, 199:1 (2008), 207–236.

Hinton, James, *Nine Wartime Lives: Mass Observation and the Making of the Modern Self* (Oxford: Oxford University Press, 2010).

Hobolt, Sara B., 'The Brexit Vote: A Divided Nation, a Divided Continent', *Journal of European Public Policy*, 23:9 (2016), 1259–1277.

Hobolt, Sara B., Leeper, Thomas J., and Tilley, James T., 'Divided by the Vote: Affective Polarization in the Wake of Brexit', *British Journal of Political Science*, 51:4 (2021), 1476–1493.

Hochschild, Arlie Russell, *The Managed Heart: Commercialization of Human Feeling* (Berkeley, CA: University of California Press, 1983).

Hogg, Quintin, *Toryism and Tomorrow* (London: Conservative Political Centre, 1957).

Hoggart, Richard, *The Uses of Literacy* (London: Penguin, 1957).

Hopkin, Jonathan and Rosamond, Ben, 'Post-Truth Politics, Bullshit and Bad Ideas: "Deficit Fetishism" in the UK', *New Political Economy*, 23:6 (2018), 641–655.

Hubble, Nick, *Mass Observation and Everyday Life* (Basingstoke: Palgrave Macmillan, 2005).

Hunt, Lynn, *Inventing Human Rights: A History* (New York: W.W. Norton, 2007).

Hyde, Andrea Marie and LaPrad, James G., 'Mindfulness, Democracy, and Education', *Democracy & Education*, 23:2 (2015), Article 2.

Inglehart, Ronald, *The Silent Revolution: Changing Values and Political Styles among Western Publics* (Princeton, NJ: Princeton University Press, 1977).

Iyengar, Shanto et al., 'The Origins and Consequences of Affective Polarisation in the United States', *American Review of Political Science*, 22 (2019), 129–146.

Jaggar, Alison M., 'Love and Knowledge: Emotion in Feminist Epistemology', *Inquiry*, 32:2 (1989), 151–176.

Jenkins, Laura, 'Why Do All Our Feelings about Politics Matter?', *British Journal of Politics and International Relations*, 20:1 (2018), 191–205.

Kahneman, Daniel, *Thinking, Fast and Slow* (London: Penguin, 2011).

Kelliher, Diarmaid, 'Constructing a Culture of Solidarity: London and the British Coalfields in the Long 1970s', *Antipode*, 49:1 (2017), 106–124.

Bibliography

Kenny, Michael, 'The Return of "Englishness" in British Political Culture – the End of the Unions?', *Journal of Commonmarket Studies*, 53 (2015), 35–51.

Knight, Stephanie, Fido, Dean, Lennon, Henry, and Harper, Craig A., 'Loss and Assimilation: Lived Experiences of Brexit for British Citizens Living in Luxembourg', *International Journal of Mental Health and Addiction*, 21 (2023), 587–604.

Koschut, Simon, 'Emotion, Discourse, and Power in World Politics', in Simon Koschut (ed.), *The Power of Emotion in World Politics* (Abingdon: Routledge, 2020), 1–26.

Kounine, Laura, 'Emotions, Mind, and Body on Trial: A Cross-Cultural Perspective', *Journal of Social History*, 51:3 (2017), 219–230.

Kushner, Tony, *We Europeans? Mass-Observation, 'Race', and British Identity in the Twentieth Century* (Abingdon: Routledge, 2004).

Laclau, Ernesto, *On Populist Reason* (London: Verso, 2017).

Langhamer, Claire, '"The Live Dynamic Whole of Feeling and Behavior": Capital Punishment and the Politics of Emotion, 1945-1957', *Journal of British Studies*, 51:2 (2012), 416–441.

Langhamer, Claire, 'An Archive of Feeling? Mass Observation and the Mid-Century Moment', *Insights*, 9 (2016), 1–15.

Langhamer, Claire, '"Who the Hell Are Ordinary People?" Ordinariness as a Category of Historical Analysis', *Transactions of the Royal Historical Society*, 28 (2018), 175–195.

Langhamer, Claire, 'Mass Observing the Atom Bomb: The Emotional Politics of August 1945', *Contemporary British History*, 33:2 (2019), 208–225.

Lansdall-Welfare, Thomas, Dzogang, Fabon, and Cristianini, Nello, 'Change-Point Analysis of the Public Mood in UK Twitter during the Brexit Referendum', *IEEE 16th International Conference on Data Mining Workshops (ICDMW)* (2016), 434–439.

Lawrence, Jon, *Electing Our Masters: The Hustings in British Politics from Hogarth to Blair* (Oxford: Oxford University Press, 2009).

Lawrence, Jon, *Me Me Me? The Search for Community in Post-War England* (Oxford: Oxford University Press, 2019).

Lawrence, Jon, 'Labour and the Culture Wars of Modern Politics', *The Political Quarterly*, 91 (2020), 31–34.

Linke, Gabriele, 'The Public, the Private, and the Intimate: Richard Sennett's and Lauren Berlant's Cultural Criticism in Dialogue', *Biography*, 34:1 (2011), 11–24.

Lulle, Aija, King, Russell, Dvorakova, Veronika, and Szkudlarek, Aleksandra, 'Between Disruptions and Connections: "New" European Union Migrants in the United Kingdom before and after the Brexit', *Population, Space and Place*, 25:e2200 (2019).

Bibliography

Lydon, Jane, *Imperial Emotions: The Politics of Empathy across the British Empire* (Cambridge: Cambridge University Press, 2019).
Maiguashca, Bice and Dean, Jonathan, 'Lovely People but Utterly Deluded'? *British Politics*, 15 (2020), 48–68.
Marcus, George, 'Emotions in Politics', *Annual Review of Political Science*, 3:1 (2000), 221–250.
Marcus, George, Neuman, Russell, and MacKuen, Michael, *Affective Intelligence and Political Judgment* (Chicago, IL: University of Chicago Press, 2000).
Martin, James, 'A Feeling for Democracy: Rhetoric, Power and the Emotions', *Journal of Political Power*, 6:3 (2013), 461–476.
Mas Giralt, Rosa, 'The Emotional Geographies of Migration and Brexit: Tales of *Unbelonging*', *Central and Eastern European Migration Review*, 9:1 (2020), 29–45.
McCarthy, Helen, 'Parties, Voluntary Associations, and Democratic Politics in Interwar Britain', *Historical Journal*, 50:4 (2007), 891–912.
McCarthy, Helen N.J., 'Spanish Nationals' Future Plans in the Context of Brexit', *Population, Space and Place*, 25:e2202 (2019).
Miller, Rebekah Grace, '(Un)settling Home during the Brexit Process', *Population, Space and Place*, 25:e2203 (2019).
Miller, Susan L., *After the Crime: The Power of Restorative Justice Dialogues Between Victims and Violent Offenders* (New York: New York University Press, 2011).
Mintz, Alex, Wayne, Carly, and Valentino, Nicholas, *Beyond Rationality: Behavioral Political Science in the 21st Century* (Cambridge: Cambridge University Press, 2021).
Mishra, Pankaj, *Age of Anger: A History of the Present* (New York: Farrar, Straus and Giroux, 2017).
Mondon, Aurelien, 'Populism, Public Opinion, and the Mainstreaming of the Far Right: The "Immigration Issue" and the Construction of a Reactionary "People"', *Politics*, online only (2022): https://doi.org/10.1177/02633957221104726.
Moores, Chris, 'Corporeal Conservatism? Bodies, Brains and Moral Movements in England since the 1960s', unpublished paper, delivered at North American Conference on British Studies, Vancouver, November 2019.
Moss, Jonathan, *Women, Workplace Protest and Political Identity in England, 1968–1985* (Manchester: Manchester University Press, 2019).
Mouffe, Chantal, *Agonistics: Thinking the World Politically* (London: Verso, 2013).
Mouffe, Chantal, *For a Left Populism* (London: Verso, 2019).

Bibliography

Neblo, Michael A., 'Philosophical Psychology with Political Intent', in George Marcus et al. (eds), *The Affect Effect: Dynamics of Emotion in Political Thinking and Behaviour* (Chicago, IL: Chicago University Press, 2007), 25–47.

Newman, Janet, 'Rationality, Responsibility and Rage: The Contested Politics of Emotion Governance', in Eleanor Jupp, Jessica Pykett, and Fiona M. Smith (eds), *Emotional States: Sites and Spaces of Affective Governance* (London: Routledge, 2016), 21–35.

Norris, Pippa, *Critical Citizens: Global Support for Democratic Government* (Oxford: Oxford University Press, 1999).

Nussbaum, Martha, *Political Emotions: Why Love Matters for Justice* (Cambridge, MA: Harvard University Press, 2013).

Nuttall, Jeremy, *Psychological Socialism: The Labour Party and Qualities of Mind and Character, 1931 to the Present* (Manchester: Manchester University Press, 2006).

Oakeshott, Michael, 'Rationalism in Politics' (1947), reprinted in Michael Oakeshott, *Rationalism in Politics and Other Essays* (Indianapolis, IN: Liberty Fund, 1991 [London and New York: Methuen, 1962]), 5–42.

O'Connor, Brendan et al., 'From Tweets to Polls: Linking Text Sentiment to Public Opinion Time Series', *Proceedings of the Fourth International AAAII Conference on Weblogs and Social Media*, 4:1 (2010), 122–129: https://doi.org/10.1609/icwsm.v4i1.14031.

Orwell, George, *The Road to Wigan Pier* (London: Penguin, 1989 [1937]).

O'Toole, Fintan, *Heroic Failure: Brexit and the Politics of Pain* (New York: Apollo, 2018).

Ouellette, Laurie, 'Reality TV Gives Back: On the Civic Functions of Reality Entertainment', *Journal of Popular Film & Television* (2010), 66–71.

Pang, Bo and Lee, Lillian, 'Opinion Mining and Sentiment Analysis, Foundations and Trends', *Information Retrieval*, 2:1–2 (2008), 1–135.

Passerini, Luisa, *Europe in Love, Love in Europe: Imagination and Politics in Britain between the Wars* (London: I.B. Tauris, 1999).

Peelo, Moira and Soothill, Keith, 'Personal Power and Public Control: Sex Crimes and Problem Pages', *The Howard Journal*, 33:1 (1994), 10–24.

Pernau, Margrit et al., *Civilizing Emotions: Concepts in Nineteenth Century Asia and Europe* (Oxford: Oxford University Press, 2015).

Pugh, Alison, 'What Good Are Interviews for Thinking about Culture? Demystifying Interpretive Analysis', *American Journal of Cultural Sociology*, 1 (2013), 42–68.

Bibliography

Pugh, Martin, 'The Rise of Labour and the Political Culture of Conservatism, 1890–1945', *History*, 88:288 (2002), 514–537.

Ramos-Zayas, Ana Y., 'Ordinary Whiteness: Affect, Kinship, and the Moral Economy of Privilege', *Journal of Urban History*, 47:2 (2020), 459–464.

Reddy, William, *The Navigation of Feeling: A Framework for the History of Emotions* (Cambridge: Cambridge University Press, 2001).

Renta, Ronald and Nancheva, Nenva, 'Unsettled: Brexit and European Union Nationals' Sense of Belonging', *Population, Space and Place*, 25:e2199 (2019).

Riley, Charlotte Lydia (ed.), *The Free Speech Wars: How Did We Get Here and Why Does It Matter?* (Manchester: Manchester University Press, 2020).

Robinson, Emily, *History, Heritage and Tradition in Contemporary British Politics: Past Politics and Present Histories* (Manchester: Manchester University Press, 2012).

Robinson, Emily, 'Recapturing Our Traditions? The Rhetorical Shift from New to One Nation Labour (and Beyond)', in Judi Atkins and John Gaffney (eds), *Voices of the UK Left: Rhetoric, Ideology and the Performance of Politics* (London: Routledge, 2017), 35–59.

Robinson, Emily, *The Language of Progressive Politics in Modern Britain* (London: Palgrave, 2017).

Robinson, Emily, 'The Authority of Feeling in Mid-Twentieth-Century English Conservatism', *The Historical Journal*, 63:5 (2020), 1303–1324.

Robinson, Emily, Schofield, Camilla, Sutcliffe-Braithwaite, Florence, and Thomlinson, Natalie, 'Telling Stories about Post-War Britain: Popular Individualism and the "Crisis" of the 1970s', *Twentieth-Century British History*, 28:2 (2017), 268–304.

Rogaly, Ben, *Stories from a Migrant City: Living and Working Together in the Shadow of Brexit* (Manchester: Manchester University Press, 2021).

Roper, Michael, 'Out of View: Subjectivity and Emotion in Gender History', *History Workshop Journal*, 59:1 (2005), 57–72.

Rzepnikowska, Alina, 'Racism and Xenophobia Experienced by Polish Migrants in the UK before and after Brexit Vote', *Journal of Ethnic and Migration Studies*, 45:1 (2019), 61–77.

Rzepnikowska, Alina, 'Migrant Experiences of Conviviality in the Context of Brexit: Polish Migrant Women in Manchester', *Central and Eastern European Migration Review*, 9:1 (2020), 65–83.

Saunders, Jack, 'Emotions, Social Practices and the Changing Composition of Class, Race and Gender in the National Health

Service, 1970–79: "Lively Discussion Ensued"', *History Workshop Journal*, 88 (2019), 204–228.

Saunders, Robert, *Yes to Europe! The 1975 Referendum and Seventies Britain* (Cambridge: Cambridge University Press, 2018).

Saunders, Robert, 'Brexit and Empire: "Global Britain" and the Myth of Imperial Nostalgia', *The Journal of Imperial and Commonwealth History*, 48:6 (2020), 1140–1174.

Savage, Mike, *Identities and Social Change in Britain since 1940: The Politics of Method* (Oxford: Oxford University Press, 2010).

Scheer, Monique, 'Are Emotions a Kind of Practice (and Is That What Makes Them Have a History)? A Bourdieuian Approach to Understanding Emotion', *History and Theory*, 51 (2017), 193–220.

Schofield, Camilla, *Enoch Powell and the Making of Postcolonial Britain* (Cambridge: Cambridge University Press, 2013).

Schofield, Camilla, 'Brexit and the Other Special Relationship', in Stuart Ward and Astrid Rasch (eds), *Embers of Empire in Brexit Britain* (London: Bloomsbury, 2019), pp. 87–99.

Schofield, Camilla, Sutcliffe-Braithwaite, Florence, and Waters, Rob, '"The privatisation of the struggle": Anti-racism in the Age of Enterprise', in Florence Sutcliffe-Braithwaite, Aled Davies, and Ben Jackson (eds), *The Neoliberal Age? Britain since the 1970s* (London: UCL Press, 2021), 119–225.

Schwarz, Bill, 'The Silent Majority: How the Private Becomes Political', in Anna von der Goltz and Britta Waldschmidt-Nelson (eds), *Inventing the Silent Majority in Western Europe and the United States: Conservatism in the 1960s and 1970s* (Cambridge: Cambridge University Press, 2017), 147–171.

Scruton, Roger, *The Meaning of Conservatism*, 3rd edn (Basingstoke: Palgrave, 2001 [1980]).

Sheridan Dodds, Peter and. Danforth, Christopher M., 'Measuring the Happiness of Large-Scale Written Expression: Songs, Blogs, and Presidents', *Journal of Happiness Studies*, 11 (2010), 441–456.

Shilliam, Robbie, *Race and the Undeserving Poor: From Abolition to Brexit* (Newcastle: Agenda Publishing, 2018).

Sobolewska, Maria and Ford, Robert, *Brexitland: Identity, Diversity and the Reshaping of British Politics* (Cambridge: Cambridge University Press, 2020).

Soosalu, Grant, Henwood, Suzanne, and Deo, Arun, 'Head, Heart, and Gut in Decision Making: Development of a Multiple Brain Preference Questionnaire', *SAGE Open*, 9:1 (2019), 1–17.

Stears, Marc, *Out of the Ordinary: How Everyday Life Inspired a Nation and How It Can Again* (Cambridge, MA: Harvard University Press, 2020).

Bibliography

Stimson, James A., 'On the Meaning and Measurement of Mood', *Daedalus*, 141:4 (2012), 23–34.

Stoler, Ann Laura, 'The Politics of "Gut Feelings": On Sentiment in Governance and the Law', *KNOW: A Journal on the Formation of Knowledge*, 2:2 (2018), 207–228.

Summerfield, Penny, *Reconstructing Women's Wartime Lives: Discourse and Subjectivity in Oral History* (Manchester: Manchester University Press, 1998).

Sutcliffe-Braithwaite, Florence, *Class, Politics, and the Decline of Deference in England, 1968-2000* (Oxford: Oxford University Press, 2017).

Sutcliffe-Braithwaite, Florence and Thomlinson, Natalie, 'Vernacular Discourses of Gender Equality in the Post-war British Working Class', *Past and Present*, 254:1 (2022), 277–313.

Teodorowski, Piotr, Woods, Ruth, Czarnecka, Magda, and Kennedy, Catriona, 'Brexit, Acculturative Stress and Mental Health among EU Citizens in Scotland', *Population, Space and Place*, 27:e2217 (2021).

Thomson, Matthew, *Psychological Subjects: Identity, Culture, and Health in Twentieth-Century Britain* (Oxford: Oxford University Press, 2006).

Tilley, James and Hobolt, Sara B., 'Losers' Consent and Emotions in the Aftermath of the Brexit Referendum', *West European Politics* (2023): https://doi.org/10.1080/01402382.2023.2168945.

Todd, Selina, 'Class, Experience and Britain's Twentieth Century', *Social History*, 56:4 (2014), 489–508.

Tyrrell, Naomi, Sime, Daniela, Kelly, Claire, and McMellon, Christina, 'Belonging in Brexit Britain: Central and Eastern European 1.5 Generation Young People's Experiences', *Population, Space and Place*, 25:e2205 (2019).

van der Does, Ramon and Jacquet, Vincent, 'Small-Scale Deliberation and Mass Democracy: A Systematic Review of the Spillover Effects of Deliberative Minipublics', *Political Studies*, 71:1 (2023), 218–237.

van Leeuwen, Bart, 'Absorbing the Agony of Agonism? The Limits of Cultural Questioning and Alternative Variations of Intercultural Civility', *Urban Studies*, 52:4 (2015), 793–808.

Vasilopoulou, Sofia, and Wagner, Marcus, 'Fear, Anger and Enthusiasm about the European Union: Effects of Emotional Reactions on Public Preferences towards European Integration', *European Union Politics*, 18:3 (2017), 382–405.

Vasilopoulos, Pavlos, 'Affective Intelligence and Emotional Dynamics in Voters' Decision-Making Processes', in David P.

Bibliography

Redlawsk (ed.), *Oxford Encyclopedia of Political Decision Making* (Oxford: Oxford University Press, 2021): https://doi.org/10.1093/acrefore/9780190228637.013.767.

Verbalyte, Monika and von Scheve, Christian, 'Feeling Europe: Political Emotion, Knowledge, and Support for the European Union', *Innovation: European Journal of Social Science Research*, 31 (2017): 162–188.

von der Goltz, Anna and Waldschmidt-Nelson, Britta (eds), *Inventing the Silent Majority in Western Europe and the United States: Conservatism in the 1960s and 1970s* (Cambridge: Cambridge University Press, 2017).

Wells, Chris et al., 'When We Stop Talking Politics: The Maintenance and Closing of Conversation in Contentious Times', *Journal of Communication*, 67 (2017), 131–157.

Williamson, Adrian, *Europe and the Decline of Social Democracy in Britain: From Attlee to Brexit* (Woodbridge: Boydell and Brewer, 2019).

Williamson, Philip, *Stanley Baldwin: Conservative Leadership and National Values* (Cambridge: Cambridge University Press, 1999).

Working, Lauren, *The Making of an Imperial Polity: Civility and America in the Jacobean Metropolis* (Cambridge: Cambridge University Press, 2020).

Yao, Xine, *Disaffected: The Cultural Politics of Unfeeling in Nineteenth-Century America* (Durham, NC: Duke University Press, 2021).

Zappettini, Franco, 'The Tabloidization of the Brexit Campaign: Power to the (British) People?' *Journal of Language and Politics*, 20:2 (2021), 277–303.

Zontini, Elisabetta and Genova, Elena, 'Studying the Emotional Costs of Integration at Times of Change: The Case of EU Migrants in Brexit Britain', *Sociology*, 56:4 (2022), 638–654.

Index

1975 referendum 126
9/11 attacks 120

Abdication Crisis 15, 114
Abse, Susanna 144–146
Achen, Christopher 25
activism 54
Adam, Sibyl 110–111
affective intelligence theory 11–13
ageism 79–80
'age of anger' 2–3
agonism 154–155
agony aunts/uncles 143–144
Åhäll, Linda 52
Ahmed, Sara 49–50, 86, 89, 96, 183
  mood analysis 114, 125, 132
Akram, Sadiya 72, 176
alienation 9, 123
Allen, Peter 176
alt-right 77, 99
America *see* United States of America (USA)
Anderson, Ben 110
Andreouli, Eleni 90
anger 2–3, 5–6, 7, 18, 129–130
  campaign management 56, 59–61
  voters 12, 38

antagonism 154–155
anti-establishment sentiment 24, 54
antiracism 88–89
anxiety 7, 12, 29, 70, 112, 113, 122–125, 139, 156, 180
apathy 126–127
atmosphere *see* mood
attachment 68
attunement 132, 133–135
authenticity 8, 9, 16, 18–19, 31, 34, 40, 46, 51, 52, 158, 159
authority 7, 8, 34, 35, 40, 46, 52, 54, 55, 60, 62, 65, 70, 181, 182

Barnett, Corelli 100
Barrett, Lisa Feldman 18
Barrios Aquino, Marianela 87, 123
Bartels, Larry 25
Benoît, Cyril 61
Berlant, Lauren 16, 21
Bhambra, Gurminder 80–81, 86
Black Lives Matter (BLM) 76
Boles, Nick 145
Boucher, Ellen 75
Bourdieu, Pierre 114
Brady, Karren 37
Brändle, Verena K. 124

Index

Brexit
  anxiety 122–125
  campaign 55–61, 65, 181–182
  Citizens' Assembly 153–154
  decision-making 27–28
  feelings 1–2, 3–6, 7, 13, 30–31
  heads vs hearts narrative
    33–34
  intensity of 29–30
  mood of 105–107, 109–111,
    113, 115–116, 119–121,
    128–137
  MO reflections 17–18, 21–22
  onslaught 125–128
  personal relationships 138–146,
    172–174
  political science 176–178
  politics of feeling 23–26
  valence politics 61–62
  see also Leave voters; Remain
    voters
Brexit Britain on the Couch (TV
  segment) 140, 145–146
BritainThinks 112
British Empire 23
Brown, Wendy 75

Cambridge Analytica 112–113
Cameron, David 24–25, 56,
  59–60, 112, 127, 132
Christmas 139
citizens' assemblies 153–154
citizenship 122–123, 128
civility 34, 70, 71, 103, 106, 138,
  158–159, 173, 186
civil war trope 130
Clarke, John 54
class 8, 26, 34, 79–81, 151
  see also working classes
Coleman, Stephen 17, 19–20, 71,
  82–83, 158
  debate opportunities 141
  mood stories 110

collectivism 21
common sense 7, 49, 53–54, 65,
  99, 102, 184
communal emotion 84–86
community 8, 85, 87, 102, 120,
  127, 149, 170, 171, 178, 185
composure 18–19
concerns 92–94
Conservative Party 24, 59
  see also Conservative politics
Conservative politics 7–8, 26,
  52–54, 68
  see also Cameron, David
Constitution Unit 153–154
control 24, 62
Corbyn, Jeremy 25, 176
COVID-19 pandemic 26
Cox, Jo 113, 130–131, 149
crime 26
Crosland, Tony 8
culture 8, 9, 21
Curtice, John 39

Daily Mail (newspaper) 79
Darwin, Charles 11
Davies, Katherine 26, 156
Dean, Jonathan 176
debate 141, 155
decision-making 11–12, 27–28,
  37–44, 69–70, 180–182
  gut feelings 44–48
declinism 99–100, 101–102
Degerman, Dan 122, 124
deindustrialisation 23
democracy 2, 7, 10–11, 152–156
Derbyshire, Victoria 150–151
'Diana moment' 16
directives 5, 14–15, 180
discursive exclusion 71–72
dispositional system 11
distrust 31, 55
divisions 68–70
Dixon, Thomas 2–3, 4, 18

248

Index

Domekos, Jon 178
dual process model 11, 44–45

Eastern Europeans 88
economics 16, 24, 93
education 23, 26, 78–79, 82
Eklundh, Emmy 177
Ekman, Paul 18
elections 25–26, 137
  see also voters
Eliasoph, Nina 54
emotion see feelings
emotional labour 16, 88, 142, 159, 171
empathy 24, 30, 70, 75, 94–97, 103–104
EU referendum see Brexit
Eurobarometer 12, 23
European Coal and Steel Community 23
European Economic Community (EEC) 23, 99
European Union (EU) 12, 17, 69, 87–88, 99, 122–123
  see also Brexit
Euroscepticism 12, 23, 24, 69
evidence 42–44, 46–50
evolution 11
exceptionalism 69
excessive emotions narrative 177, 179, 185
exclusion 71–72
expertise 7, 10, 11, 34, 35, 40, 46, 49, 50–52, 60, 62, 65, 68, 139, 141, 146

Fabianism 8
Facebook 79, 112–113, 157, 164
fake news 61
Farage, Nigel 38–39, 47, 80, 100, 102
far-right politics 7, 121
  see also alt-right

fatigue 29, 137, 138, 150, 160, 185
fear 1, 2, 7, 13, 24, 54, 78, 79, 92, 97, 106, 112, 123, 124, 130, 133, 158, 163, 170, 183
feelings 1–6, 69
  bad 87–89, 90–91, 94–97
  clash of 30–31
  communal 84–86
  decision-making 180–181
  intensity of 29
  (il)legitimacy of 70–73
  meta 17–20
  personal relationships 156–159
  politics of 6–14, 16, 23–26, 179–180, 186–188
  suppression of 154–155
  voting decisions 27–28
  see also anxiety; gut feelings; heads vs hearts narrative; mood
feelings-evidence 43–44, 46–50
feeling rules 20, 22, 31, 34, 40, 41, 53, 55, 67, 70, 77, 85, 88, 90, 94, 138, 139, 146, 150, 155, 156, 158, 169, 173, 180–181, 183, 186
Figgou, Lia 90
financial crisis 63–64
Finlayson, Alan 77, 99
First World War 18, 84–85
focus groups 19
Ford, Robert 26, 68, 102
Fox, Claire 152
Freedland, Jonathan 105–106, 109
Frevert, Ute 6
Frostrup, Mariella 143–144

Garner, Steve 89, 97
gender 71, 72–73
  see also women

Index

'Get Brexit Done' slogan 137, 185
Gigerenzer, Gerd 45
Giralt, Rosa Mas 171
globalisation 23, 24
Glover, Fi 149
Greenland, Katy 90
grief 5–6, 124
Groenendyk, Eric 45
group identity 2
gut feelings 27, 34, 65, 181
   decision-making 38, 40, 44–48
   discriminatory aspects 67–68
   historicising 52–55
   knowledge, lack of 50–52

Hall, Sarah Marie 111
Hall, Stuart 100
Hall, Todd H. 84–85
Hannan, Daniel 100, 102
happiness 112, 125
Harris, John 178
hate crime 9
Hay, Colin 61–62
heads vs hearts narrative 27–28, 33–34, 37–44, 179
healthcare systems 45
Heidegger, Martin 132
Hewitt, Gavin 38
hierarchies 8, 68, 71–72, 183
Highmore, Ben 21, 142
Hinton, James 15, 19
historical narratives 120–121
Hobolt, Sara 24, 25
Hochschild, Arlie 142
hope 12
Hopkin, Jonathan 62–63, 64
housing crisis 93–94
humanitarianism 8
human rights 70

identity 7–8, 68–69, 76, 84–86
ignorance 78–79, 82

immigration 24, 26, 38, 81
   anxiety 122–123
   bad feelings 87–88, 90–91
   Leave voters 100–102
   'legitimate concerns' 92–94
   Remain voters 96, 97–98
   welfare state 98–99
imperialism 24, 70–71
individualism 8, 18–20, 53
insecurity 24
integration 12, 24
intimacy 16–17, 29–30
intolerance 2
irrationalism 7, 77–78

Jamelia 150
James, William 11
Jenkins, Simon 38
Johnson, Boris 47, 124
judgements 68

Khan, Saira 149–150
knowledge *see* expertise

Labour Party 25, 99, 145
   see also Labour politics; New Labour
Labour politics 8, 25
Laclau, Ernesto 71
Langhamer, Claire 9, 15–16, 43, 54
Lawrence, Jon 26
Leave voters 3, 21–22
   anger trope 5–6
   apathy 126–127
   clashes 129–130
   communal emotion 85–86
   decision-making 27–28, 37–44
   gut feelings 46, 48–52
   identity 68–69
   immigration 98, 100–102
   mood 116–117, 121, 136

Index

neoliberalism 74
polarisation of 25–26
pride 104
race 90, 165–169
relationships 144–146, 156–162
socio-political changes 23–24
stereotypes 34, 72, 77–84, 182–183
tolerance 162–165
'left behind' feelings 24, 94, 177–179
left politics 8–9
'legitimate concerns' 92–94
LGBT rights 26
liberalism 2, 68
 see also neoliberalism
liberal politics 9
Linke, Gabriele 16
Listening Project, The (radio show) 140, 147–149
Loose Women (TV show) 140, 149–150

MacKuen, Michael 11
Maiguashca, Bice 176
Major, Sir John 39
Marcus, George 11
marginalisation 24
Marxism 8, 9
Mass Observation (MO) 5, 14–22, 180
 decision-making 41–43
 ethnicity 87
 feelings 27, 28, 44–46
 mood 114–115
mass parties 62–63
May, Theresa 126
media 16, 23, 24
 'left behind' feelings 178–179
 onslaught 126, 127–128
 problem pages 143–144
 see also radio; television

Menon, Anand 38
mental health 106
meta-feelings 17–20, 22
migrants, experiences of 87–88, 117–118, 169–171
 see also immigration
Miliband, David 39
mindfulness 10
misinformation 24, 47, 61, 65, 80, 82, 155, 183
mob, the 30, 184
Mondon, Aurelien 73, 114, 178
mood 105–107, 109–111, 119–121, 128–137, 185
 national 114–119
 public 111–114
 work 142
Moon, David 176
More in Common 149
MO see Mass Observation (MO)
Mosley, Oswald 120
Mouffe, Chantal 71, 154
Murdoch, Rupert 80
Muslims 49–50, 76, 93

narratives 18–19, 179
 heads vs hearts 27–28, 33–34
 historical 120–121
national decline 99–100, 124
National Front 120
National Health Service (NHS) 93–94
national identity 7–8
nationalism 2, 42, 73, 97, 131, 155
national mood 114–119
nativism 2, 9
neoliberalism 53, 73–77, 81, 97–102, 184
Neuman, Russell 11
neuroscience 11, 45
Neveu, Catherine 54
New Labour 9

Index

Newman, Janet 75, 102
Northern Ireland 123

Observers *see* Mass Observation (MO)
oral history 18–19
ordinary people 4–5, 9, 15, 17, 30, 181
   political engagement of 54–55
Osborne, George 56
otherness 87
Pahl, Kerstin Maria 6
Parliament suspension 126
passion 10, 35, 38–39, 41 42, 82, 150, 154, 159, 175, 177, 181, 184
   association with Leave 1, 28, 30, 38–39, 72, 187
   see also reason–passion dichotomy

patriotism 37, 38
Peelo, Moira 143
permissiveness 9
Perry, Grayson 3–4, 95, 177
Perry, Philippa 2, 3
personal relationships 8, 26, 29–30, 106, 172–174, 185–186
   breakdowns 138–143
   preservation of 156–159
   psychotherapy approach 142–146
   racism tropes 165–169
   reconciliation 169–172
   talking therapy 146–153
   tolerance 162–165
   uncertainty of 159–162
pessimism 24
phenomenology 11
physical responses 132
polarisation 25, 58, 70, 95, 111, 187
political agency 82–83

political science 175–178
politics 19–21, 54–55
   of feeling 5–14, 16, 23–26
   hierarchies 71–72
   valence 61–64
polls 112, 114, 178, 185
populism 2, 7, 61, 71, 154–155, 177–178
post-truth 34, 40, 61–64
Powellism 77, 93, 99–100, 101–102, 184
prejudice 77–80, 82, 86, 89–90, 129
psychology 3, 11, 45, 146–152
   relationships 139, 140–141, 142–146
public mood 111–114
Pugh, Alison 17

Question Time (TV show) 178–179

race 8, 34, 70–71, 72–73, 89–92
   attacks 129
   hierarchies 183
   Leave voters 79
   personal relationships 165–169
   political science approach 176
   Remain voters 80–81
   TV commentary 149–150
   see also immigration; Muslims; white supremacy
radio 140, 147–149, 150–151
Ramos-Zayas, Ana Y. 87
rationalism 7, 28
   association with Remain 28, 30, 187; *see also* reason, association with Remain
   see also heads vs hearts narrative; irrationalism; reason
reason 1, 2, 4, 6, 7, 10, 27, 41, 42, 61, 78

Index

association with Remain 177
and emotion/feeling 11-2, 25, 31, 35, 41, 44–46, 52–53, 82, 179, 181, 184
neoliberal 75, 184
politics of 72
reason–passion dichotomy 6, 35, 67, 70, 71, 84, 86, 180, 182
reconciliation 146–147, 169–172
refugees 97–98
relationships *see* personal relationships
Remain voters 3, 21–22
anxiety 123–124
apathy 126–127
campaign of 24
communal emotion 85–86
decision-making 27–28, 37–44
empathy 94–96, 103–104
grieving trope 5–6
gut feelings 46–52
identity 68–69
immigration 97–98
mood 117–119, 132–135
neoliberalism 74–75
polarisation of 25–26
race 89–90, 165–169
relationships 144–146, 156–162
stereotypes 34, 77–84, 182–183
tolerance 162–165
resentment 38, 41
'right to feel' 15–16
Rogaly, Ben 86
Roper, Michael 18
Rosamond, Ben 62–63, 64
Ross, Andrew A. G. 84–85

sadness 18
Sandbrook, Dominic 99, 101
Scheve, Christian von 12
Schofield, Camilla 76, 77, 93
Scotland 24

Scruton, Roger 7–8
Second World War 19, 114
self-expression 16
self-improvement 9–10
Sennett, Richard 16
sensibility 70, 82, 184
Sleight, Nelson 146
Smith, Ali: *Autumn* 110–111
Sobolewska, Maria 68, 102
socialism 8–9
social media *see* Facebook; Twitter
Soothill, Keith 143
sovereignty 43–44
space 90–91
stereotypes 28, 34, 67, 68–69, 77–84, 182–183
class 151
Stoler, Ann Laura 67–68
StoryCorps 147
Summerfield, Penny 19
surveillance system 11

talking 146–156
see also debate
Taylor, Jenny Bourne 142
television 140, 145–146, 149–150, 151–152
Thatcherism 53–54, 100, 102, 184
tolerance 162–165
Tories *see* Conservative politics
trade unions 63
traditions 7–10, 69
Trump, Donald 2, 7
trust 24, 62–64, 128, 144, 181
Turkey 79
Twitter 84, 113, 127, 158
Two Rooms (radio show) 149

UKIP *see* United Kingdom Independence Party
UK Office of National Statistics 112

Index

unhelpful campaign 34, 40, 55–61, 65, 174, 181–182
United Kingdom Independence Party (UKIP) 26, 59, 76
  see also Farage, Nigel
United States of America (USA) 2, 7, 17, 147
  activisim 54
  partisanship 25
  public mood 111–112

valence politics 61–64, 181–182
Vasilopoulou, Sofia 12
Verbalyte, Monika 12
victimhood 73, 129
voters 10–11, 12, 62–64
  see also Leave voters; Remain voters
vox pops 178–179

Wagner, Marcus 12
welfare state 9, 16, 98–99
white supremacy 73, 76–77, 86–87, 89
Wife Swap (TV series) 140, 151
Williams, Raymond 15
Wilson, Helen 110
women 54
working classes 54, 71, 72–73
workplace solidarity 8
writing 22

xenophobia 80, 89–90, 131, 155

YouGov 112

EU authorised representative for GPSR:
Easy Access System Europe, Mustamäe tee 50,
10621 Tallinn, Estonia
gpsr.requests@easproject.com